PRENTICE-HALL
FOUNDATIONS OF MODERN SOCIOLOGY SERIES
Alex Inkeles, Editor

DEVIANCE AND CONTROL
Albert K. Cohen

MODERN ORGANIZATIONS
Amitai Etzioni

SOCIAL PROBLEMS
Amitai Etzioni

LAW AND SOCIETY: An Introduction
Lawrence M. Friedman

THE FAMILY
William J. Goode

SOCIETY AND POPULATION, Second Edition
David M. Heer

WHAT IS SOCIOLOGY? An Introduction to the Discipline and Profession
Alex Inkeles

THE SOCIOLOGY OF SMALL GROUPS
Theodore M. Mills

SOCIAL CHANGE, Second Edition
Wilbert E. Moore

THE SOCIOLOGY OF RELIGION
Thomas F. O'Dea

THE EVOLUTION OF SOCIETIES
Talcott Parsons

RURAL SOCIETY
Irwin T. Sanders

THE AMERICAN SCHOOL: A Sociological Analysis
Patricia C. Sexton

THE SOCIOLOGY OF ECONOMIC LIFE, Second Edition
Neil J. Smelser

FOUNDATIONS OF MODERN SOCIOLOGY
Metta Spencer / Alex Inkeles

SOCIAL STRATIFICATION: The Forms and Functions of Inequality
Melvin M. Tumin

INDUSTRIAL SOCIOLOGY

IVAR BERG
Vanderbilt University

Prentice-Hall, Inc., Englewood Cliffs, New Jersey 07632

Library of Congress Cataloging in Publication Data

Berg, Ivar E. (date)
   Industrial sociology.

   (Prentice-Hall foundations of modern sociology series)
   Bibliography: p.
   Includes index.
   1. Industrial sociology. 2. Industry—Social aspects—United States. I. Title.
HD6955.B43   301.18'32   78-23593
ISBN 0-13-463240-0
ISBN 0-13-463232-X pbk.

For Geoffrey Berg

© 1979 by Prentice-Hall, Inc., Englewood Cliffs, N.J. 07632

All rights reserved. No part of this book may be reproduced in any form or by any means without permission in writing from the publisher.

Printed in the United States of America

10 9 8 7 6 5 4 3 2 1

Prentice-Hall International, Inc., London
Prentice-Hall of Australia Pty. Limited, Sydney
Prentice-Hall of Canada, Ltd., Toronto
Prentice-Hall of Japan, Inc., Tokyo
Prentice-Hall of Southeast Asia Pte. Ltd., Singapore
Whitehall Books Limited, Wellington, New Zealand

CONTENTS

PREFACE, ix

INTRODUCTION, 1

CHAPTER 1

INDUSTRIALIZATION AND MODERNIZATION, 6

    Industrialism and Modernity, 6
    Industrialization and the Industrial Revolution, 9
    Industrialization, Modernization, and Social Integration, 14
    Modern Industrial Man, 16
    Varieties in Industrial Systems, 20
    Conclusion, 30

CHAPTER 2

INDUSTRIALISM AND THE MOBILIZATION OF RESOURCES, 32

    Capital Formation: "Market" and "Planning" Approaches, 33
    Social Technology, 41
    "Human Capital" Formation, 48
    Conclusion, 55

vi   CONTENTS

CHAPTER 3

OCCUPATIONS AND INDUSTRIAL STRUCTURE, 57

The Work Force, 58
Technological Change, 68
Occupations, Industry, and Community, 73
The Service Sector, 77
The "Web of Rules", 82
Conclusion, 86

CHAPTER 4

CORPORATIONS AND MANAGERS, 87

Introduction, 87
Corporate Political and Economic Power, 88
Corporations, Managers, and the Economy, 98
Managers, 106
Conclusion, 119

CHAPTER 5

UNIONS AND UNION LEADERS, 120

Introduction, 120
Unions and Society, 122
Unions and the Social System, 127
Unions, Communities, and Members, 143
Unions and Members, 146
Conclusion, 150

CHAPTER 6

MANAGERS, WORKERS, AND ORGANIZATIONS, 152

Introduction, 152
Industrial Relations, 154
Human Relations, 155
Industrial Relations, 174
Conclusions, 182

CHAPTER 7

PASTS, PROLOGUES, AND PROSPECTS, 183

    Introduction, **183**
    Macroscopic Issues: International and
    National Developments, **183**
    Mezzoscopic Issues: Labor Force Developments, **186**
    Microscopic Issues, **189**
    Conclusion, **189**

INDEXES, 191

PREFACE

In this book I have sought to identify a number of linkages between three layer-like universes of discourse and to join a number of issues that emerge in this identification process. Specifically, I have sought to reintroduce materials from political sociology, economics, history, and other fields, on industrial societies as systems, and related materials on the critical institutions in these social systems, into the study of industrial sociology. During the period 1965-1975 a great many of these materials, which I term macroscopic and mezzoscopic in character, were neglected in favor of emphases in industrial sociology on the more microscopic level of analyses, on complex organizations, "leadership," production processes, work flows, and work groups. One senses, in 1979, a growing interest, even an urge, among industrial sociologists in the repossession of a number of the more macroscopic and mezzoscopic materials, an interest born of the recognition that intraorganizational phenomena are influenced in signficant ways by historical developments and by forces operating in their political and social-economic environments. It is my fond hope that the volume will serve that interest.

Next, I have endeavored to be faithful to the belief that sociological discussions be rooted in the traditions of liberal arts studies and the humanities as well as in the emerging traditions of the younger social sciences. Finally, I have stressed the proximal relationships between a number of theoretically problematical issues in the field of industrial sociology, on one side, and the lively, "real life" issues facing men and women in industrial societies and their leaders in public and private sectors of society, on the other side.

Classroom experiences and discussions with colleagues lead me to suggest that the volume may prove useful to readers in several different contexts: (1) for those who do "Industrial Sociology;" (2) for those interested in "Economy and

Society" especially in those strands in this field that focus upon developed economies; (3) for those concerned with "Industrial and Labor Relations;" (4) for relevant segments of studies of "Human Behavior in Organizations" and related studies about "Complex Organizations." (5) The book may also be useful in important portions of studies of the sociology of work, the sociology of occupations, and in "Business and Society." (6) Finally, the book may prove useful in studies in general education in which efforts are made to link social science perspectives to philosophical and other perspectives useful in identifying and specifying the character of social forces, and of man's circumstances in the modern world.

I have enjoyed the benefits of innumerable conversations with many more colleagues, in the preparation of segments of this book, than I can possibly acknowledge in this space; I can only offer a general statement of appreciation for valuable advice. I am particularly indebted to two anonymous reviewers and to Richard Peterson, Peter Cattan, and John Ehnes, all of Vanderbilt, whose comments on an earlier draft I attended with alacrity, gratitude, and with as much detailed care as my capabilities allowed. At each stage of the book's preparation I was the grateful beneficiary of the pointed criticisms, detailed suggestions, and great patience of Alex Inkeles of Stanford, general editor of the Foundations of Modern Sociology Series; beyond his specifically substantive comments, his comments on matters of exposition have added considerably to whatever qualities of clarity the book may claim. I owe thanks too, to Mayer Zald of the University of Michigan for his collaboration in efforts, published elsewhere, that have been distilled in portions of chapter 4.

I am also grateful to Ms. Amy Midgley of Prentice-Hall for her valuable editorial counsel, to Winifred M. Berg for her encouragement and her expert manuscript preparation, and to Ms. Cindy Miller for her cheerful assistance with typing chores. Finally, I am indebted to Darci and Renee De Young who shared the joys of the summer and the Christmas season of their third and fifth years, respectively, with a delighted author.

INTRODUCTION

The ways in which people in different societies and in different times have organized themselves for economically productive activities, and the impact these activities and their organization have on their lives, have long been the subjects of commentary and study. Indeed, one is struck by the volume of the body of available materials bearing on these subjects, by the highly diversified character of the credentials of those who have contributed to it, and by the number of debatable issues that are joined in treatments that stretch back to the beginnings of recorded history. Thus, questions about interest rates, about the "just price," and about work and exchange relationships, for example, were debated almost as often in the earliest major historical religions as they are in currently heated arguments over inflation and unemployment.

In recent times a great deal of attention has been focused specifically on the character of "industrial society," upon isolating the prerequisites for "industrial development," upon delineating the consequences—or at least the correlates—of "modernization" and of "industrialization" or "industrialism," and upon the relations among differentially "developed" nations. We need only open our daily newspapers or watch a televised newscast to be reminded that the issues attending "modernization" and "development" are urgently pressing ones to millions of the world's ordinary citizens, not just the stuff of social science studies or of the programs of political leaders. Consider, in this context, the hue and cry over the gaps in the material circumstances between the so-called developed and underdeveloped nations, over multinational corporations, over environmental dispoilation, over frightening food production and energy problems, over blue-collar blues and white collar woes.

Roughly equivalent issues having to do with economic growth and social development emerged as early as the eighteenth century, especially in detailed analyses of labor conditions and of the quests of producers, in some nations, after resources and customers in other nations. There were also studies, early on, of the roles of employers and producers in the events that led to colonization, to wars, to revolutions, to labor strife, on one side, and to peace treaties, to the formation of commonwealths, to emergent systems of relatively peaceful trade, and to stable "industrial" relations systems, on the other.

THREE CONTEMPORARY VIEWS OF "INDUSTRIALISM"

As these observations will suggest, "industrialization's" causes and correlates have been the continuing subjects of great controversies: some yearn for its frivolous no less than its significant benefits—its Coca-Cola bottling plants not less than its life-saving artificial kidneys; its wind-up toys and underarm deodorants not less than its mammoth earth-moving tractors and mining devices; and its hair blowers, whiskey distilling equipment, and vending machines no less than its knitting, weaving, and sewing machines, its cobalt rays, and its building insulation materials.

Others are appalled by pollution, by consumerism, by the waste that attends market imperfections, business cycles and product obsolescence, by actions attributable to faceless transnational enterprises, and by the oppressive quality of machine-paced labor. Especially vexing to many has been the "eclipse of community," the displacement of social, communal, and human welfare considerations, and the suppression of traditional codes by the more calculating economic-rationalistic logics in the ordering of relationships among groups and among persons—logics that appear to be the governing ones in the course of industrialization. A few would set limits to growth out of fears that tyranny will accompany growing struggles over resources that are increasingly in limited supply.

Between industrialism's admirers and its critics are those who, while they admire the industrial cornucopia, are quite prepared to admit to many of the painful, costly, or disruptive consequences of "industrialism." These observers see decent prospects, however, for identifying a given public's interests, and for the introduction of compensatory measures and webs of rules that can meliorate the worst violations of these interests. A few optimists even envision that a "post-industrial" age will follow upon the long-term growing pains of extensive "industrialization" and its frequent twin, urbanization. These observers are fairly confident that the benefits of income-generating growth, of leisure, and of improved working conditions, could well accrue to ever-larger numbers of society's members. This new society, they argue, will be one in which fewer and fewer people work tediously to produce goods, a society in which growing numbers of people will provide services and engage otherwise in cleaner, more cerebral, more "civilized" activities.

The enduring quality of the debates over industrialism, the liveliness of the questions in the newer versions of the debate, and the highly diversified character of the backgrounds of the antagonists in public policy making and intellectual circles constitutes formidable evidence that any attempt to synthesize all the relevant material would involve a lifetime's collaborative work for each of several analysts from several of the social, historical, psychological, and political sciences. In a world in which there are growing concerns about human rights and the rights of legitimate interest groups, there might also be useful ideas to be elicited from the ranks of investors, workers, and managers or from their informed representatives. It is regrettably not possible, at present, to draw upon works that even begin to approach such syntheses.

It is possible, however, to conduct a survey of some samples of evidence relevant to joining several of the critical issues bearing upon the prerequisites, correlates and consequences of "industrialization," evidence that is of particular interest to us as citizens, in the last quarter of the present century, of what the late legal theorist and statesman, A. A. Berle, called the American Economic Republic. It is precisely such a survey we undertake in this volume. Since this book is written from a sociological perspective we will be especially concerned with values bearing upon production and distribution; with the institutions, organizations and roles which collectively become the units and components of the social structures that may most clearly be identified with life in "industrial societies;" and with the norms that affect many of the relationships whose contents are influenced, in goodly measure, by "industrial" social experience.

We may add in this brief introduction that we will hereafter drop the quotation marks around the words industrial, industrialized, industrialism, and industrialization. These terms will simply be treated as variations on what lawyers are wont to call a compendius term or "a term of art." They will severally and separately be used to refer (1) to the continuously unfolding processes in social systems that parallel the process of modernization, in which (2) more and more of the activities associated with production and distribution take place outside the boundaries of home and family systems; (3) in which labor is divided and subdivided again, essentially in accordance with the principle (4) that productive and distributive activities (whether connected with machine-technological means or more abstract technologies, like accounting) are economically rational in proportion (a) to the degree to which they are more and more "specialized," and (b) to the degree to which these activities are amenable to analyses in quantitative terms.

THE AIMS OF THIS BOOK

It is one of our central aims in this book to identify some of the linkages between a few of the main industrial developments in societies and their modernization, more generally. As we will see, industrial developments take place in societies whose histories, cultures and social structures both shape and are shaped by their industrial ways. It is accordingly a corollary of this first aim to identify some of the sociological variations among the ways and means of different modern, industrial peoples that are reflective of differences in their national histories and cultures.

It is a second aim to impose some intellectual ordering on representative materials that bear upon the developments attending the use of "nontraditional" social groupings, of newer tools, of newer machines, of intellectual systems and social technologies related to production and distribution processes, and of specialized divisions of labor in social systems. Some of these developments cut across entire social systems in their impacts and consequences; some primarily affect particular clusters of workers, managers, and property owners in an industry, an occupation, a region, or a larger or smaller political jurisdiction; some, finally, are immediately palpable to and often even substantially influenced by industrial citizens, themselves, in their workplaces and in their lives, day to day.

Our third aim is to identify and explore relevant materials bearing upon a few of the major theoretical controversies that have appeared in assessments of industrial systems. As we will see, the resolutions of these issues involve questions of both an evidentiary and political-evaluative nature; to consider them in the present context will serve to illustrate the point, among others, that abstract social science efforts are really not very distant from lively public, political questions. The particular choices among illustrative examples and of issues selected for treatment, meantime, have been made with eyes to timeliness, to public and private policy salience, to the availability of evidence, and to social-scientific theoretical importance. The pursuit of this fourth aim thus enables us to examine a number of developments that help one to relate the often too-widely separated worlds of ideas and of action. While an exposition that strives to be realistic forces us to be selective in the choices of problematic issues to be joined, it reduces the hazards inherent in more abstract, or purely academic-theoretical modes of discourse. Thus we will be concerned, in several different contexts, with the controversial implications of technology and of changing property relations but we will seek to tie these implications to fairly concrete questions.

PROGRAM OF THE BOOK

The second of our aims, of imposing some order on industrial sociological materials that are not only highly diverse in character but which come to the fore at different analytical levels, has encouraged the adoption of a tripartite scheme of presentation: In chapters 1 and 2 we consider a number of macroscopic issues, issues having to do with the overall character of industrialization, its imperatives and a number of its most general consequences. In these chapters we are concerned with a few critically important central or molar traits of industrial systems and their structures.

In chapter 3, at what we may regard as a middle or mezzoscopic level, we focus somewhat more specifically on a number of institutional arrangements that make up the analytically distinguishable subsets of the larger structures of industrial societies.

In chapters 4, 5, and 6 we move to consider some of a number of proximal and organizational elements, to what we may think of as the molecular structure of industrial life. In these three chapters we move ever closer to the actual settings in which the larger realities facing men and women in industry are converted into palpable realities, in which the more vaguely discernible forces are transferred into daily and weekly events, pressures, challenges, and opportunities in the world of work.

In following this sequential plan we may liken ourselves to mountaineers who have been dropped off on the highest of many peaks in a tolerably large mountain range; from these Olympian heights the lowest peaks, beyond our immediate ken and scope, look almost flat, while we see the higher peaks in starker terms. As we descend, figuratively speaking, in successive chapters, the features of the lowest peaks are more readily apprehended, and we discover that they are indeed not as small as they appeared to be when surveyed from the vantage points at the higher altitudes. In our descent to different intellectual base camps we must inevitably leave room periodically, to take stock and, especially, to drop and add conceptual baggage.

CHAPTER 1
INDUSTRIALIZATION AND MODERNIZATION

It is one of the basic premises of this volume that the industrialization process with its familiar factories, corporations, and unions, its machines and time-and-motion engineers, its open hearth furnaces, its powerhouses, its mines, its computers, its vocational education systems, its strikes, and its bank vaults, is an expression of a complex of forces that are really rooted in more general processes, in what are most aptly characterized as the processes of modernization. We do not in short conceive of industrialization as an "uncaused cause." It is accordingly our purpose in this initial chapter to identify a few of the critical dimensions of the industrialization process but to link them to some of the historical, social, and cultural developments that are connoted by the term "modernization." In the process we will identify the advantages to our understanding of industrialization that derive from the widened perspective, one that evokes recollections of materials from studies in humanistic learning about western civilization.

INDUSTRIALISM AND MODERNITY

We do not, of course, mean to suggest that industrialization as we have broadly defined it in the Introduction, does not by itself, so to speak, have manifestly important consequences. Thus certain typical characteristics of industrial production methods—the widespread application of power conversion and power transfer devices especially—are often usefully seen as independent elements whose effects on the occupational roles in social structures and on workplace relationships are subject to systematic study; indeed we will have cause to consider some of these effects in later chapters.

But the demonstrably specific correlates of industrial production techniques should not obscure the fact that strategic historical changes in these techniques and methods generally occurred in fairly close associations with shifts in peoples' political, religious, and others values, and of their societies' institutional arrangements. These developments tend, in the language of science, to be covariant in character. Although industrial progress imposes logical imperatives on what leading theorists regard as a society's subsystems,[1] it is generally the case that industrial processes in different nations are affected reciprocally by the imperatives of the others of their social and cultural structures and traditions.[2]

To put it another way, even in those societies in which small groups of elites have dominated the shift from traditional to industrial ways and fairly well controlled the range of their fellow citizens' responses, there are signs of the interactions of changes in the value systems and the normative arrangements associated with the political, religious, and other complexes of a nation's institutional structures.[3] The varying operational effects of the interactions among their institutional structures, including the stable elements of their economic structures, may be conceived collectively as modernizing national adaptations, adaptations in which economic growth, development and industrialization are highly implicated. In this context, "growth" pertains to increase in income per capita;[4] the term "development" we reserve for cases in which the fruits of growth are relatively widely distributed; by "modern" we mean the increasing secularization of belief systems, the growing role of the scientific mode of thought, and the imputation of a good deal of formal freedom to members of a society's labor force.[5] Note that these distinctions leave much room for particulars; thus we do not assume that "modern" necessarily means "western" or "American," nor that it always means "urban," or "democratic."[6] Our form-

---

1. See Talcott Parsons and Neil J. Smelser, *Economy and Society* (New York: Free Press, 1956).

2. See Neil J. Smelser, *The Sociology of Economic Life,* 2nd ed. (Englewood Cliffs, N.J.: Prentice-Hall, 1976), pp. 45-94.

3. In one of the earliest statements of a society's legacies by the social theorist Wilfredo Pareto, they were described as "residues," "derivations" and "persistent aggregates." For a brief and illuminating discussion of social and cultural change, see Metta Spencer, *Foundations of Modern Sociology* (Englewood Cliffs, N.J.: Prentice-Hall, 1976), pp. 543-68.

4. This definition is typically employed by economists. See, e.g., R. Nurkse, *Problems of Capital Formation in Underdeveloped Countries and Patterns of Trade and Development* (New York: Oxford University Press, 1968); and Arthur Lewis, *Theory of Economic Growth* (New York: Harper & Row, 1970).

5. For a discussion of "growth," "development," and "modernity," see James Kocher, *Rural Development, Income Distribution, and Fertility Decline* (New York: Population Council, 1973).

6. For a critique of the inclination to see "modern" and "traditional" in strictly dichotomous terms, see J. Gusfield, "Tradition and Modernity: Misplaced Polarities

ulation is specifically conceived, furthermore, to help us avoid the simplistic assignment of sociological primacy to industrialization, given the numerous historical instances in which multiplicities of "causes" and "effects" are effectively more cobweb-like than linear in character.

We may recall that New York's Con Edison, a company that has been both admired and maligned by those who see it as a mighty independent force in the lives of millions of people, owes a great deal to Ben Franklin's kite-flying experiments. Ben Franklin, meanwhile, was much more a stateman, philosopher, and founding father of the Republic than a key person in the evolution of the heavy electrical equipment industry or of the modern utility company.

The case is not a unique one: Industry has often been as beholden to artists and philosophers—whose liberated imaginations led them to identify mechanical laws, fulcrums, levers, navigational techniques, hydromechanical processes, and mathematics—as to more recent generations of entrepreneurs, organizational innovators, and production engineers serving on corporate payrolls. Thus many cultural, religious, artistic, educational, and scientific developments, occurring over very long stretches of time, have served as either fuel or lubricants to the more apparently routinized, mechanical qualities that come to mind with the term industrialization. To the more subtle sources of industrialization—the liberating, secularizing, and rationalizing elements in the settings in which industrialization took (and is taking) place—we give the name modernization.

The modernization process, furthermore, has evoked some of the same reactions that the industrialization process has evoked in more recent days. Thus the aggravated relations between the engineer in modern times, a virtual symbol of industry who helps managers to establish optimal factory machine speeds, and workers' representatives, who speak angrily of "stretch outs" and "speed ups,"[7] would not shock earlier churchmen, philosophers, and national leaders who dreaded the effects of profane rationalism upon the sacredness of society, as Nisbet has pointed out.[8]

These older themes, in which the imperatives of science and community, respectively, are regularly juxtaposed, are clearly discernible as well in recent and contemporary misgivings about industry's effects on society. Concerns have thus been expressed especially about the differences between production requirements and human needs, differences that are seen to inhere, especially, in

---

in the Study of Social Change" *American Journal of Sociology,* 72, 3 (1967), 351-62, and Anthony Oberschall, "Social Change: A Resource Management Model," paper presented to the American Sociological Association, 67th Annual Meeting, San Francisco, 1972.

7. One such case, involving members of the United Automobile Workers and the workers at General Motors assembly plant in Lordstown, Ohio in 1972, was a major subject for nearly two years in the daily press.

8. Robert Nisbet, *The Sociological Tradition* (New York: Basic Books, 1967).

conflicts between specialized work roles and community or family ties. It follows from these observations that industrial structures, industrial organizations, and industrial-technical processes are vulnerable to assessments rooted in other values than those obviously linked to standards of mechanical efficiency. As a corollary, industrialization processes in different national settings, for all the many common features we can identify, will take on a variety of distinctive and important colorations reflective of differences in the conditions and in the particular modes of individual nations' modernization experiences.

INDUSTRIALIZATION AND THE INDUSTRIAL REVOLUTION

"The more *some* things change, the more other things change with them." This formulation would serve well as a handy revision in the pithy old French aphorism to make it applicable to what Polanyi called the "great transformation"[9] from the medieval to the modern age. Eisenstadt had probably succeeded best in the effort to describe the transformation by singling out, as a critical dimension of this change, "social mobilization . . . the process in which major clusters of old social, economic and psychological commitments are eroded and broken and people become available for new patterns of socialization and behavior (through various exposures). . . ." He adds that "modern societies are also highly differentiated and specialized with respect to individual activities and institutional structures."[10]

Several important virtues attach to the view that the modernization process involves a number of deep changes in the "spheres"[11] of societies evolving out of the medieval period. Accordingly, to identify the independent effects of industrialization is to conceive of this process as one that builds upon many of a society's older ways. One may thereby discover what, in the old, is essentially adapted and what is radically changed.

The assignment of conceptual priority to modernization over industrialization usefully distracts us, for example, from the industrial revolution as the initial cause of the industrialization process. The more revealing view provides

---

9. Karl Polanyi, *The Great Transformation* (New York: Holt, Rinehart and Winston, 1977). For Polanyi the emergence of markets for the purchase and sale of land and labor was the hallmark of the transformation. Such markets, he emphasized, were "man-made," and were neither natural nor inevitable social mechanisms.

10. S. N. Eisenstadt, *Modernization: Protest and Change* (Englewood Cliffs, N.J.: Prentice-Hall, 1966), p. 2.

11. Eisenstadt, *Modernization*, p. 3. We may remind ourselves that, at its core, industrialization involves the relocation of production processes beyond the family household unit, the application of power transmission techniques and mechanical devices to production, and a division of labor based on the principles of specialization and simplification.

an evolutionary picture of the development of industrial systems that are ". . . based on high levels of technology, on growing specialization of economic roles and of units of economic activity—production, consumption, and marketing—and on the growth of the scope and complexity of the major markets, the markets for goods, labor, and money."[12]

The fact is that the factory system did not spring, full blown, from the heads of England's utilitarian philosophers, as is commonly supposed, though Jeremy Bentham and others gave industrial capitalism a legitimating ideology or belief system in which behavior that is economically useful was very nearly equated with moral behavior. Nor did it spring from England's much heralded inventors, or from countinghouse scribes in London who improved upon but did not invent the logic of "double-entry" bookkeeping, an important social-technological invention of the fifteenth century.

It is not an accident of calendars and convenient history, furthermore, that the England of 1750 "was a richer country than most of today's underdeveloped economies."[13] As Dean implies, England was well primed for what, in the parlance of some modern students of growth and development is called economic "take-off."[14] Even after acknowledging England's readiness for "take-off," however, Dean avoids the next nagging historical question of whether the industrial revolution should actually be dated from the middle of the sixteenth century or, much later, from the 1780s, by the simple expedient of begging it. In her mind, and in the minds of others, the debate over this question is not an important one because "fundamentally, the differences between the protagonists in the debate are differences of emphasis rather than substance."[15] It would be something of a distraction to review all the major and minor aspects of the differences referred to, and to haggle over what is really substance rather than simply a matter of emphasis.

The issues are not trivial ones, however, because they bear upon the prospects for industrial development in our own times. Thus we may note that hospitable attitudes toward scientific discovery, attitudes that are critical to the industrialization process, were conceived in the period of the Renaissance, not in the eighteenth century. These attitudes or postures regarding rationalism were born in long agonized struggles over the legitimacy of secular knowledge and

---

12. Ibid., p. 4. See also W. Moore, "The Social Framework of Economic Development," in R. Braibanti and J. Spengler (eds.), *Tradition, Values and Socio-Economic Development* (Durham, N.C.: Duke University Press, 1961), pp. 57-82.

13. Phyllis Dean, *The First Industrial Revolution* (New York: Cambridge University Press, 1965).

14. The term is taken from a controversial analysis of the historical prerequisites to economic development. Walt W. Rostow, *The Stages of Economic Growth: A Non-Communist Manifests* (Cambridge, England: Cambridge University Press, 1971).

15. For a brief discussion see S. J. Hurwitz's review of Professor Dove's volume in *Industrial and Labor Relations Review*, 20 (April 1967), 510-11.

over its social role—struggles that helped to shape the later applications of science to man's productive efforts. The struggles persist in modern times as lively arguments have continued over the socially corrosive effects of secularization and rationalism on traditional virtues and values.

It is similarly an oversimplification, in emphases on the industrial revolution, to divorce commerce involving finished goods from the earlier commercialization of agriculture and from what has been termed the commercial revolution. The earliest modern, i.e. "free," workers were thus poor agricultural peasants who were driven from common lands, not workers who entered freely—and much later—into factory jobs. The enclosures of common lands used by peasants, in the sixteenth century and after, by sheep-raising English landlords, moreover, triggered a series of social and economic changes, involving population movements, especially, that helped in very substantial ways to pave the way for the commercialization (and capitalization) of nonagricultural economic activities and for the emergence of an economic middle class. These social and economic changes occurred in less dramatic ways, however, than an identification of industrialization with the industrial revolution allows.

The guild system, which constrained the growth of overly wealthy masters by restrictions on technological changes in all branches of thirteenth-century goods-producing industries, for example, continued to exist, "side by side with the other systems of production for many centuries."[16] This "preindustrial" system only gradually lost its primary significance under the force of a series of developments that are of great substantive importance to the development of *modern* (i.e. eighteenth-century) industrial ways. As Schneider points out, "Merchant capitalism" in the form of the cottage industry or "putting-out system," in which "the formal relations of production departed sharply from those of the guild in favor of *contractual* arrangements between entrepreneur-merchants and *formally free* workers," was itself rooted in earlier changes. These critical changes were associated with the weakening, much earlier, of the guild system.[17]

More specifically, the "inner harmony" of the guild system, in which, significantly, everyone had a prescribed place in the economy, was disrupted by growing misgivings among journeymen workers who needed very little encouragement to enlist the aid of *town* authorities in their opposition to the closed ranks of their guild masters. The socioeconomic strength of the guilds, meantime, "aroused the hostility of other groups . . . (who) were able to use the *state* to strike at the guilds. The state forced the reduction of initiation fees, curbed the power of the guild wardens, and placed the guilds under the

---

16. For a brief and lucid review of the nature of the guild system see Eugene V. Schneider, *Industrial Sociology*, 2nd ed. (New York: McGraw-Hill, 1969), p. 40. For a discussion of what Marxists call the "commodification" of labor, see K. Polanyi, *The Great Transformation*, passim.

17. Schneider, *Industrial Sociology*, pp. 39ff (emphases added).

courts."[18] Our emphases here upon the competing uses, by antagonists, of town and state, which is to say of political units, is intended to dramatize the interplay of "economic" and "noneconomic" forces. If one neglects developments prior to the industrial revolution one thus loses sight of the interesting quality of social forces that contribute to social change as one's vision is blocked by the factories and machines that are the hallmarks of that revolution.

There were, of course, other important factors at work in the guild system contributing to its weakness. Thus, capital was accumulated in the hands of both masters and guild outsiders. This accumulation contributed to new and significant controls over the production process in guilds given to production even as it facilitated the growth of merchant guilds. It contributed, as well, to the expansion of "foreign" markets, and to trade, in the conventional sense of the term. Each of these developments contributed, in turn, to increases in the mobility of goods, funds, and people, and to the formation of cosmopolitan attitudes that endorsed these developments.[19]

The point is that England's social and economic experiences in the industrial revolution of the 1750s and beyond were continuous with a large number of earlier developments. These earlier developments contributed, on one side, to the end of the medieval system with its other-worldly emphases, its antiscientific biases and its constrainingly stable role relationships. On the other side, these experiences were organic to a modernization process of which there were manifestations in science, in the arts, in philosophy, in religion, and, not least, in politics.

Modernization, Industrialization, and "Technological Imperatives"

A second virtue of assigning a kind of historical and conceptual priority to modernization over the industrialization process per se is that it helps us avoid a tempting, analytically deficient, and misleading reductionism in which explanatory powers are attributed almost solely to *machine* technology, to factory methods of production, and to large economic enterprises in shaping social relations in industrial societies.

To think (as many do) in terms of "technological determinism," however, is to obscure a number of issues concerning the nature and sources of similarities and differences among industrial societies. The belief that the use of machines and factory production methods simply forces a very limited number of particular and predictable social relationships on a population to the exclusion of alternative relationships—which is what is meant by "technological determinism"—distracts attention (1) from the "man-made" quality of the social institutions in which industry is embedded; (2) from the crucial roles of slower

18. Ibid., p. 39.

19. Ibid., pp. 39–40.

changing values; and (3) from the preferences, in more normative terms, informing the strategic political and other choices made by industrial citizens, preferences that are significantly influenced by their particular cultures and histories.

It is also important to note that while machine technology does make some inescapable demands on social systems and their members, these demands apply directly to smaller population segments even in the most highly industrial systems in present times. This is so because growing numbers of persons in these systems are employed in providing services, not manufactured goods. Although we will often be obliged to return to this point, we may consider in this context that the contemporary United States, government—federal, state, and local—employs well over one-third of the persons in the professional and technical manpower pool (we look at these growing demographic shifts more closely in chapter 3). The large size of this service category, meantime, is often taken nowadays to be one of the *key* characteristics of advanced, industrial social systems: The more industrialized a society, the more rapid the growth of its service-producing sectors.

It is accordingly judicious to keep a weather eye on the larger social system despite the strategically important role played by large organizational-industrial concentrations of human and especially of machine-technical resources. Thus, although 27 percent of U.S. wage and salary workers do belong to machine-paced industrial organizations, and although many of these workers belong to the labor unions concentrated therein, the large percentage of persons who are employed by the 1,250 largest employers and their managers are not able, as a bloc to enter into international "detentes," to start or stop inflation, to shape birth rates, to set tuition rates for nine million college students or to create all of the $2.5 trillion in credit "money" that has become such an important factor in running America's bureaucratic-industrial machine. Those who manage and work in large industrial apparatuses are simply not sovereign in their powers in the American economic republic.[20]

The fact of the matter is that technology is an important—but by no means the only—factor influencing the society shaped by those in and out of the system's heavily capitalized and technologically sophisticated core units. The men and women in small dry goods stores, auto assembly plants, provincial banks, large steel mills, and medium-sized construction companies, after all, are members of political groupings, are of diverse ages, have backgrounds rich in ethnic traditions, differ in their religious and other beliefs. And these men and women can, themselves, become sufficiently "modern" to institute some limits on the demands made by the sterotypical machines, time clocks, and production

20. We will be obliged to return to the economic and political powers of corporations and unions in a later chapter. We may mention, in passing, that even the observable connections between corporate and military leaders do not add up to a picture of a unilaterally potent "military-industrial complex" in the determination of defense expenditure policies. See Stanley Lieberson, "An Empirical Study of Military-Industrial Linkages" *American Journal of Sociology*, 76, 4 (January 1971), 562–84.

schedules through collective bargaining, through regulation, and through occasional exploitation of labor market opportunities and other acts suggestive of personal autonomy.

INDUSTRIALIZATION, MODERNIZATION, AND SOCIAL INTEGRATION

An awareness of the conceptual priority of modernization over industrialism can help quicken our perceptions and apperceptions, furthermore, of the "loose" qualities of most social systems. The fact that a society is industrialized does not necessarily mean that it will be more "tightly" or "coherently" structured. Systems they may well be, in that there are relatively consistent, stable, and enduring patterns and structures in industrial, no less than in preindustrial societies, "such that some [patterns and structures] more regularly 'go with' others;"[21] The issue is an important one in debates over the degrees of choices available to citizens of developed and developing societies about their institutions. Although he recognizes utility in the search for uniformities, Moore cautions against what he calls the *sociologistic error* and its twin, the *functional equilibrium error*. These errors follow from the tendency of some, on the one hand, to ignore "the intrinsic sources of change in all societies," as well as the interdependence of the parts of social systems with each other. The errors follow, on the other hand, from the temptation to exaggerate the inherent functional interdependence of the parts of social systems.[22] An awareness that social systems' component parts are imperfectly integrated, meanwhile, helps sharpen our sensibilities concerning the nature of interpenetrations—what two leading sociological theorists refer to as "boundary exchanges"—among the economic, the narrowly technical, the broadly political, and the other "spheres" or subsets of social systems.[23] Dissatisfactions with the character of these interpenetrations, among the members of groups with different specialized interests, are among the major sources of conflict in society. These conflicts, in turn, are among the clearest stimuli to the invention of social technology designed to reduce the socially disruptive effects of conflict both within and surrounding industrial-economic structures.

21. Alex Inkeles, "Continuity and Change in the Interaction of the Personal and the Socio-cultural Systems" in Bernard Barber and Alex Inkeles (eds.), *Stability and Social Change* (Boston: Little, Brown, 1971), p. 266.

22. For an extended discussion, see Wilbert E. Moore, "Social Aspects of Economic Development," in Robert E. L. Faris (ed.), *Handbook of Modern Sociology* (Chicago: Rand McNally, 1964), ch. 23. For a briefer but most helpful discussion see Wilbert E. Moore, *The Impact of Industry* (Englewood Cliffs, N.J.: Prentice-Hall, 1965), esp. 2.

23. Talcott Parsons and Neil J. Smelser, *Economy and Society* (London: Routledge and Kegan Paul, 1957).

Industrialization, Modernization, and Adaptation

Mindful as we must be of the disciplining effects of industrial ways on our lives in industrial society, we thus cannot be oblivious to political and social innovations (including broader modernizing trends) that alter long-established patterns of industrial recruitment, job assignments, contract interpretations and, in general, of manpower utilization, in very fundamental ways. Once again, the structuring of jobs and occupations and their allocations among industrial citizens is not machine-wrought; the structuring process results from a series of social decisions that are influenced by both industrial and nonindustrial developments in society. An occupational structure's contours are thus shaped by values, for example, like those informing equal opportunity and affirmative action regulations, values governing policies that regularly impinge upon the economy's own structure.

A comparative case will serve to correct an alternatively extreme view, however, that the industrialization process is nothing more than a very modest "one-among-more-potent-ones." Thus, it was a popular view in the 1950s that France's economy, then still a victim of war and of an economic depression beginning in 1929, was significantly different from other western economies in its almost backward ways. It was argued that France's slow growth could be linked to the fact that the typical French firm, family owned, was fated to remain small by a pervasive value system that emphasized family proprietorship, privacy, and other noneconomic "utilities" that blocked expansion and diversification.[24] The advents, however, of the European Economic Community (within which the markets for a number of products were virtually allocated among the participating nations, and within which tariffs were coordinated) and, soon thereafter, of General deGaulle's system of "indicative planning,"[25] a system that reduced the force of competition upon otherwise vulnerable enter-

---

24. See David Landes, "French Business and the Businessman: A Social and Cultural Analysis," in E. M. Earle (ed.), *Modern France* (Princeton, N.J.: Princeton University Press, 1951), pp. 334–53.

25. "Indicative planning" involves a broad concensus among major groups about economic means and ends. "While the term . . . is meant to stress . . . only the framework and guidelines for future economic activities [it] does not preclude the use of rather strong instruments by the government to carry out the plan. . . ." Gregory Grossman, *Economic Systems*, 2nd ed. (Englewood Cliffs, N.J.: Prentice-Hall, 1967), p. 87. In Lebanon, dependence on family ties apparently facilitated economic progress, as it did in Japan and in early New England. See Samir Khalaf and Emilo Shwayri, "Family Firms and Industrial Development: The Lebanese Case," *Economic Development and Cultural Change*, 15, 1 (October 1966), 59–96; Ezra F. Vogel, "Kinship Structure, Migration to the City and Modernization," in R. P. Dore (ed.), *Aspects of Social Change in Modern Japan*, (Princeton, N.J.: Princeton University Press, 1967), pp. 91–111; Bernard Bailyn, "Kinship and Trade in Seventeenth Century New England," *Explorations in Entrepreneurial History*, 6, 4 (May 1954), 197–206. For a general discussion, see Smelser, *The Sociology of Economic Life*, pp. 78–87.

prises blew sizable holes through these constraining values! It would appear that entrepreneurship and other economically important characteristics were dormant in many French enterprises. Among the revivifying or awakening agents were predictable markets; a somewhat less unpredictable (or more permissive) system of tax collections requiring less secretiveness (and therefore less family-bound personnel recruiting practices); and a relatively well developed national policy of depreciation allowances in tax laws that provided incentives to invest and diversify by permitting investors to "write off," quickly, the costs of plant and equipment against corporate earnings.

France's economic experiences, beginning in the late 1960s, were of course far more complicated than the treatment accorded them in these few lines reveals, but two points are evident: First, the motives associated with industrial development sometimes require only an institutional assist; these motives are not *necessarily* outside of a population's ken and scope because "traditional" values or traditional institutional forms have prevented them, entirely, from developing. (The issue of "motives" in respect of investment and labor force commitments to work and the public's role in assisting these motives, meantime, will concern us again in chapter 3.) Second, an industrial economy can be highly fragmented, highly disintegrated, and then, in accordance with newer economic theories, can be made *more* integrated by political means.[26]

MODERN INDUSTRIAL MAN

The preceding discussion had emphasized the somewhat disjunctive character of the interplay of social values and of actions in a society's "spheres" or "subsystems." The process of modernization itself, however, has been only slightly more linear in character. Ironically, after what has already been said about giving priority, in conceptual terms, to modernization over industrialization, we are obliged to call attention now to the extraordinary discontinuities that were the hallmarks of the French and the industrial revolutions. The origins of *both* these revolutions were clearly rooted in earlier developments—including the Renaissance; the Protestant reformation; and the Age of Discoveries. But the French and industrial revolutions did in fact have considerably forceful *independent* effects of their own. These revolutions, as Nesbit has put it, broke up the older order:

> The breakup of the old order in Europe—an order that had rested on kinship, land, social class, religion, local community, and monarchy—set free, as it were, the varied elements of power, wealth, and status that had been consolidated . . . ever since the Middle Ages. Dislocated by

---

26. Reinhard Bendix "Tradition and Modernity Reconsidered," *Comparative Studies in Society and History,* 9 (April 1967), 292-346. See also Bert Hoselitz, *Sociological Aspects of Economic Growth* (New York: Free Press, 1960).

revolution, scrambled by industrialism and the forces of democracy, these elements can be seen fumbling across the political landscape of Europe throughout the nineteenth century in search of new and more viable contexts.[27]

The five critical aspects of the industrial revolution that Nesbit identifies are of interest to industrial sociologists because these were crucial aspects of the modernization process itself. Nisbet's key terms are the basic coin of the industrial sociological realm:

> ". . . the *condition of labor*, the *transformation of property*, the *industrial city*, technology and the *factory system*. . . . Beyond question, the most striking and widely treated of these aspects was the condition of the working class."[28]

To these aspects of the industrial revolution, Nisbet adds: "All that industrialism is to English letters, social movements, and legislation in the 19th century, the democratic revolution in France at the end of the 18th century is to French."[29] In countless ways, then, "the [French] revolution must be seen in fact for what it was in image to generations of intellectuals afterward: the *combined* work of *liberation*, of *equality*, and of rationalism."[30] And the French and industrial revolutions ". . . embodied in *common* . . . , three . . . especially striking . . . processes . . . : *Industrialization, abstraction* and *generalization*."[31]

Nisbet's formulations help heighten our sensitivity to the interpenetrations of industrialization and modernization: The latter had pervasive impacts on traditions, on communities, on status systems, on roles, and, on many more of the strands woven into societies' warp and weft. Indeed, modernization may be understood as having three basic facets—economic modernization, political modernization, and ideational modernization—each of which may be conveniently regarded as syndromes. The last of these syndromes is deserving here of specific consideration.

Modernity as a State of Mind

A number of social scientists have recently sought to explore the traits and attitudes of "the modern man" subsumed in these syndromes and to conceptualize "modernity," in Inkeles' words, as the embodiment of a "certain

---

27. Nisbet, *The Sociological Tradition*, p. 21.

28. Ibid., p. 24 (emphases in the original).

29. Ibid., p. 31.

30. Ibid., p. 39 (emphases added).

31. Ibid., p. 43 (emphases added).

way of doing things, as in patterns of education, urbanization, industrialization, bureaucratization, rapid communications, and transportation." After reviewing the defining characteristics others have attributed to economic and political modernization, in which stress is placed on *ways of doing and on organizing*, Inkeles had emphasized modern *ways of thinking and feeling*, thereby adding a sociological-psychological perspective that parallels a more institutional, which is to say a more sociological-political-economic perspective, in which emphases are placed on patterns of roles and the structures thus elaborated:

> The modern is defined as a mode of individual responding, a set of dispositions to act in certain ways. It is, in other words, an "ethos," or a "spirit," in the sense in which Max Weber spoke of "the spirit of capitalism." As Robert Bellah expressed it, the modern may be seen not "as a form of political system, but as a spiritual phenomenon or a kind of mentality." As such, it is much less tied to a particular time and place than is the definition of modernity in terms of institutional arrangements."[32]

Inkeles goes on to characterize "the modern" in analytical, topical, and behavioral terms: The modern man's personality is shaped *in part* by experiences in employment in the industrial order,[33] but it is also shaped by changes "in the social and physical environment which men experience as they shift from the more traditional settings of village, farm, and tribe to city residence ... and national citizenship."[34] The modern man (1) in a modern nation thus takes an active interest in public affairs, exercises his rights, and performs duties as a member of a larger community. Involved (2) in modern institutions, modern man attends to schedules, to abstract rules, and to objective evidence, and he follows those whose authority is made legitimate by their technical competence rather than by their appeal to traditional or religious sanctions. As a member (3) of an industrial order, specifically, modern man increasingly accepts an elaborate division of labor and the need for coodination, and he increasingly values rewards based on objective standards of technical competence. He is also responsive to the need for strict hierarchies of authority, for machine pro-

---

32. Alex Inkeles, "A Model of the Modern Man: Theoretical and Methodological Issues," in Nancy Hammond (ed.), *Social Science and the New Societies: Problems in Cross Cultural Research and Theory Building* (East Lansing: Michigan State University Social Science Research Bureau, 1973), p. 61. For outlines of the structural differentiations paralleling these social-psychological changes, see William H. Friedland, "A Sociological Approach to Modernization," in Chandler Morse et al., *Modernization by Design: Social Change in the Twentieth Century* (Ithaca, N.Y.: Cornell University Press, 1969), pp. 61–84; and Smelser, *The Sociology of Economic Life*, pp. 148–55.

33. Alex Inkeles and David H. Smith, *Becoming Modern: Individual Change in Six Developing Countries* (Cambridge, Mass.: Harvard University Press, 1974), p. 4.

34. Alex Inkeles, "The Role of Occupational Experience," C. S. Brembeck and T. J. Thompson (eds.), *New Strategies for Educational Development* (Lexington, Mass.: D.C. Heath, 1973), p. 21.

duction's imperatives, and for the separation of product and producer. Political and social no less than industrial-economic institutions, meanwhile, also demand that modern man accept geographic and occupational mobility, that he be tolerant of impersonal relationships, that he be disposed to be innovative, to be impartial toward others' attributes, and that he have a tolerance for and ability to adapt to changes in his circumstances. "Modern man's" traits are thus inclusive of but they are by no means exhausted by a narrower notion of industrial man.[35]

Inkeles' and Smith's analysis argues tellingly for the conclusion that *factory experiences* have large statistical effects on a number of measurable characteristics of modern man, but these investigators' findings are entirely consistent with Nisbet's conceptions, noted earlier, of the *cultural-characterological residues* of the French and industrial revolutions! Inkeles, like Eisenstadt accordingly stresses the simultaneous effects of historical forces that facilitated and paralleled those centrally linked to the industrialization process, but which are analytically and empirically distinguishable from them. The fact of the matter is that contemporary notions about rational administration, about "meritocracy," about career advancement and career systems, and about education can be found in the texts of authors long before the steam engine drove the first piston, before 12-year old children worked nearly "round the clock" in "satanic" English mills, and before spinning jennies and frames were smashed in the early nineteenth century by cottage workers (the so-called Luddites, in the English midlands).

Nominal familiarity with two of the most significant of contemporary issues, those bearing upon the world's food and energy supplies, will persuade one of the validity of the discussion so far as it applied to today's developments. It is indeed simply nonsensical to think about these contemporary issues as though they could be extracted from a larger social-political context.

Fuel and food, it is no exaggeration to state, have become international political tools—some would say weapons—in the efforts of nations to affect what Henry Kissinger was fond of calling the "structure of international relations." The age in which earlier industrialized nations benefited from the low price cash crops from "underdeveloped nations"—whose lands might well have been advantageously turned to subsistence crops, in other days—and in return sold finished goods to "lesser developed" or to other specialized developed nations, appears to be ending.[36] As these phases have given way, one to another, they reveal a host of interests that may be called "economic" only by one who is

---

35. The list of traits is from Inkeles and Smith, *Becoming Modern,* p. 4. For a brief defense of the concept of modernity, see Alex Inkeles "Understanding and Misunderstanding Individual Modernity," in Lewis A. Coser and Otto N. Larsen (eds.), *The Uses of Controversy in Sociology* (New York: Free Press, 1976), pp. 103-30.

36. For a discussion of the advantages inhering in the evolutionary development of internal markets built upon domestic agricultural exchange in lesser developed countries (instead of rapid industrialization) see Gunnar Myrdal, *The Asian Dream* (New York: Pantheon, 1968).

blind to the other urges and demiurges embodied in the foreign, the trade, and the domestic policies of nations. These interests have run the gamut from naked and crude mercantilists' concerns with tangible wealth[37] as a means to build strong military forces in the sixteenth, seventeenth, and eighteenth centuries, to "lofty" concerns with the "white man's burden" and with stops in between for admixtures of vengeful national pride and messianic national-ideological utopianism.

To fail to recognize the highly interactive character of industrial with other social processes is to fail to appreciate relevant complexities and automatically, therefore, to misread the nature of choices—policy and otherwise—both past and present, facing the members of industrial societies and their leaders. A more parochial view which focuses on industrialism as an independent force, we have argued, leads to confusions of causes with effects and encourages us, too often, to entertain analytical perspectives about industry that are deterministic and reductionistic. With this construction of modernity and industrialization clearly before us we are in a position to examine a parallel distinction, that between industrialism conceived abstractly, and a few of the key variations in specific cases of industrialization that have materialized around the globe as a result of the inclinations of nations to develop along essentially different political-economic lines.

VARIETIES IN INDUSTRIAL SYSTEMS

The logic of the position we have taken may most fruitfully be expanded, first, by a brief examination of the propositions that there are gross and significant differences among industrial societies, depending in part upon whether an industrial society has developed along "capitalist" or along alternative lines. A second examination shows that there are significant if somewhat more subtle differences in the structures and operational arrangements among industrial societies *within* the so-called capitalist camp. The question before us is, most assuredly, not an idle one! To attempt to join the issues having to do with interindustrial society differences is to attempt to come to grips with some of the important questions of the degrees to which the nations now on the "road to Huddersfield"[38] have choices in respect of the institutions, mechanisms, and devices that

---

37. It was one of Adam Smith's valuable contributions in *The Wealth of Nations* (published in 1786) that, in contrast to mercantilists, he saw not gold, silver, jewelry, spices, and other such tangible goods, but a nation's people—with their skills, discipline, and energey—as its wealth.

38. For a popular, thoughtful, and critical discussion of some of those issues in developing countries, commissioned by the World Bank but executed quite independently of the Bank's control, see James Morris, *The Road to Huddersfield: A Journey to Five Continents* (New York: Pantheon Books, 1963). Huddersfield, in England, is seen symbolically by many as the eighteenth-century home of the industrial revolution.

will help facilitate, augment, regulate, and control the results of the processes involved. To attend only nominally to these larger forces is to misinterpret, by simplifications, many of the events in the workaday world of managers, foremen, and workers in their communities, shops, and offices that will occupy us in later chapters.

Growth and Development

The first of the important sources of differences among the already industrialized nations inheres in the different ideas about "growth" and "development," in the economic sense, that informed (and continues to inform) their individual transformations into industrial societies.

These ideas or theories have been distilled, for all their philosophical complexities and subtleties, by Berger into two types, as follows: Those that emphasize capitalistic market conditions and the policies ". . . intended to create, maintain, or improve this 'engine' of development; and those, deriving mainly from Marxism, which commonly reject not only the market as a key allocative mechanism by the 'specific forms of ownership and social organization' that are associated with 'market capitalism,' as well."[39] Berger relates the differences between these two modes of industrial-economic development directly to the differences

> between an economic principle of competition and an alternative principle of allocation. . . . The difference, though, is not only between economic principles. Indeed, it may be expressed as a sort of trade-off between economics and politics. . . . It is not an accident that the critique of capitalism usually starts with the miseries of economics, the critique of socialism with those of politics.[40]

Berger does not deny that there are admixtures of competitive and planned elements to be observed in the already industrialized developed societies in the passages cited. Nor would he deny important similarities between the modal types. Thus, one observes the glorification of productivity and a specific creed of rationality adding up to

---

39. For a discussion of the main "critiques" of "capitalism" and "socialism," and of the distinctions outlined here, see Peter L. Berger, *Pyramids of Sacrifice: Political Ethics and Social Change* (New York: Basic Books, 1974), chs. 1-3. For a carefully executed review of the sets of institutions that characterize the main economic forms see Grossman, *Economic Systems*. For a view, not unlike Berger's, according to which "development" unlike "per capita growth," is defined in terms of the degree to which income distribution is moving in egalitarian directions, in which general health, nutrition, and education is improving, see Kocher, *Modern Economic Growth*. These improvements can lead to declining fertility rates, a factor in increasing per capita income, rising gross national product and, thus, to growth in the narrower sense.

40. Berger, *Pyramids of Sacrifice*, p. 33.

a materialism of practice, which manages to coexist with various idealisms lurking in the background as mythic inspirations or theoretical justifications...."[41]

One also observes criticisms and challenges directed at the "repressions" inherent in growth and in the ethics of productivity and rationality coming from observers who regard *both* modalities—Market or Marxist— as "pathological deformations of human nature." Some critics of growth are accordingly more impressed by the "shared universe of discourse of the technocrats," in all industrial societies, than by national-ideological differences in the "mythic inspiration" behind which industrial leaders hide.[42] For growth critics the differences between Market and Marxist systems are less important than their—to them—intolerable similarities.

Berger and many others, however, are less critical of growth per se and emphasize crucial differences in the thrusts of capitalism and socialism, crucial in that the differences are related to the very different roles of the state, the individual, and the economic enterprise in the two systems; capitalism and socialism are best conceived as thrusts, rather than clean clear delineations, meantime, because there are variations and even very notable exceptions around the central tendencies in both east and west:

> Capitalism posits individual achievement and competition as against collective ascription and allocation. . . .
> Similarly, capitalism posits an 'agnostic' ideal of society, in which individuals and groups struggle with each other for economic success and social status. . . . By contrast, both socialism and most premodern traditions posit an ideal of society in which harmony prevails, a harmony pre-established by the political order . . . the empirical consequence of this is that capitalism has a strong pluralistic thrust, while socialism (even in its most anti-totalitarian versions) has a built-in tendency to contain plurality and especially to "harmonize" conflicts. . . . The ultimate questions are those of value.[43]

These value-laden questions have to do with the viability of productivity as an end; with the costs and sacrifices that attend the pursuit of production; with the relative importance of the sum of goods and services and the means by which they are produced as opposed to the manner of their distribution; with relative equality; and with questions of the priorities to be assigned among individual freedoms and collective security, between "pluralism" and community, and between individualistic competitive enterprise and social harmony.

41. Ibid., p. 41.

42. Ibid., p. 41.

43. Ibid., pp. 62–63.

Pluralism in the Industrial World

Some analysts urge us to go beyond the essentially "moral" and political differences among industrial societies delineated by Berger and suggested to him from a reading of industrialization processes as processes of secular and material redemption, complete with their "pyramids of sacrifice." Thus, Moore writes of divergences in industrialization processes that

> the world may be viewed as a single system for some purposes, particularly in view of the common pool of knowledge, ideas and techniques. But that system retains strong elements of persistent pluralism. . . .[44]

Among the differentially significant elements of change that command attention are the ways by which barriers to modernization are overcome in a specific system. These barriers may affect the course of social change not only for a transitional period but may leave their stamps on the ideas and social structures, the social, intellectual, and psychological endowments of a society. After pointing out that the major variable affecting the trajectory of change is the "era or stage at which a political unit enters on a course of rapid economic change," Moore writes that

> latecomers have available several models of historical transformation and of forms of political regime. They are bound neither by the rate nor by the sequence established by their predecessors in adding products and processes, forms of social organization, strategies of communication or scientific knowledge.[45]

One of the conspicuous differences among industrial nations, implied earlier, relates to the ways in which power and authority are exercised within the structures of political states. Thus social systems persist

> not only through orderly continuity of establishment patterns but also through tension management and change. . . . If societies differ in their characteristic tensions, because of varying historic legacies and the ways these intersect with current problems of achieving social goals, then it is readily understandable that the principal agency functionally responsible for tension management for the system as a whole, the state, will differ in its structure and forms of action.[46]

A principal tension will be that which arises over the failure, for whatever rea-

---

44. Moore, *The Impact of Industry,* p. 18. See also Kocher, *Modern Economic Growth.*

45. Moore, *The Impact of Industry,* p. 17.

46. Ibid., pp. 17-18.

son, of a society to fulfill its ideals, whether these involve "reliable conformity with norms"[47] or behavior that is "appropriate" to new standards and aspirations that enjoy social and political sanction. In dealing with tensions about order, meantime, societies may scrap or adapt older customs and techniques. Developing areas and nations will accommodate their different histories and traditions and they will both borrow and invent social techniques some of which may even be joined with archaic ways. As Moore points out "Some of the new customs may be as exotic as the old despite their novelty."[48]

Capitalism in Comparative Perspective

The patient reader might still wonder whether subscription to the more differentiated perspectives about industrial societies endorsed here does not essentially gainsay a number of central tendencies in industrial societies, whether it does not define these tendencies out of the way by its relativistic position. Specifically, does not emphasis on the complexities in the interplay of "economic" with "noneconomic," and of moral and political with social and economic forces, leave us with an overly fragmented picture of what *are,* after all, several fairly well integrated industrialized social systems as economists, especially, would be quick to point out?

It is not in the least disrespectful of economists, whose works bear so directly and significantly on our subject, to answer the question at least partly in the negative.

> The economic point of view is rooted in three fundamental observations about the world. The first is that resources are scarce in relation to human wants. . . . The second observation is that resources have alternative uses. . . . Finally, economists note that people do indeed have different wants, and that there is significant variation in the relative importance that people attach to them.[49]

Many economists will accordingly acknowledge that the "propensities," the "tastes," the "preferences" and the other psychological states they impute to the populations whose transactions are reported in their carefully aggregated data, are highly nominal ones, based on inferences from curves that describe *data,* not people or institutions. The problem of resource scarcity and the prospect of

---

47. Ibid., p. 18.

48. Ibid., p. 18.

49. Victor R. Fuchs, *Who Shall Live? Health, Economics and Social Choice* (New York: Basic Books, Inc., 1974). For an assessment of the deficiencies in this fairly commonplace conception of "the economic point of view" from a Marxist or "radical economics" perspective, see Raymond S. Franklin, *American Capitalism: Two Visions* (New York: Random House, 1977) especially pp. 1-112 and 277-304.

resource substitutability creates obstacles and opportunities to a population and its leaders: The responses to these may be selected from a fairly wide margin of social choices, even within one of the two modal systems mentioned earlier.

It is of course possible to gainsay the significance of these choices in favor of more sweeping historical analyses in which the world economy, of which particular national economies are subsystems, is taken to be the relevant subject of study. In this view, some nations are at the core and others are at the periphery of an international system; the differences among nations are thus understood (1) partly as manifestations of their respective cultural legacies, and (2), nonessentially, as reflections of their disadvantaged positions as nations that are differentially dependent upon the "core," the more developed and thus more powerful nations who shape many of the ways of "satellites," "colonies," or "peripheral" states.[50]

The issues involved in the divergence question must be argued at an almost rhetorical level because the assessment of evidence is vulnerable to well developed prejudices on all sides about the history of capitalism and about the international ways of east, west, and their respective "military-industrial" characters in modern times. A few of these issues may be joined in somewhat more concrete but only slightly less charged fashion when discussion is confined to industrialized nations that are, in political-ideological terms, more like each other than any one of them is like nations more or less readily identified with the nonmarket camp. A brief, selective discussion of some of the most relevant differences among a few particular arrangements in the United States, the United Kingdom, and Japan will illustrate the point. Of particular illustrative interest are differences in the nature of employment, the recruitment of workers, the roles of unions and collective bargaining, and the political roles of organized labor. (The highly schematic quality of the comparisons needs to be stressed. Space limitations force us to bypass most of the very cultural, political, social— and historical—differences to which this chapter has alluded.)

At a strategically important level, the United Kingdom, Japan, and the United States have a great deal in common. Consider that in each of these countries there are large economic segments that, though regulated by sundry public bodies, are owned by private investors. They may be managed by their owners or by professional personnel some of who may own claims against the equity repre-

---

50. For various versions of this perspective, see V. I. Lenin, *Imperialism as the Highest Stage of Capitalism* (Peking: Foriegn Policy Press, 1916); Paul Baran, *The Political Economy of Growth* (New York: Monthly Review Press, 1957); Andre Gunder Frank, *Capitalism and Under-development in Latin America* (New York: Monthly Review Press, 1969); Emmanuel Wallerstein, *The Modern World System: Capitalism, Agriculture and the Origin of European Economy in the 16th Century* (New York: Academic Press, 1974); C. Furtado, "The Concept of External Dependence in the Study of Underdevelopment" in Charles K. Wilbur (ed.), *The Political Economy of Development and Underdevelopment* (New York: Random House, 1973); and F. Cardoso (trans. by Joseph Alan Kahl), *Modernization, Exploitation and Dependency in Latin America* (New Brunswick, N.J.: Transaction Books, 1976).

26 INDUSTRIALIZATION AND MODERNIZATION

sented by these "publicly" held enterprises. They are not managed by the *officially* designated appointees of the state or those acting for the state,[51] though patterns of mutual influence among industry and government leaders are not totally unknown.[52]

Beyond similarities in ownership patterns in the three nations, are gross but significant similarities in public regulatory arrangements, in corporate charters, and in the legal rights, privileges, and immunities of owners, managers, and employees. Indeed, these areas of similarities are growing almost daily under pressures generated by the operational requirements of "multinational" corporations, upon whose activities, like those of the old British Empire, the sun literally never sets. It is evident, at this writing, however, that these large, diversified organizations, with management teams whose members are often drawn from each of the nations in which the firms have going concerns, can operate comfortably within a framework that makes room for considerable international variations in economic structures and their endemic "webs of rules" (discussed in detail in chapter 3). As a matter of fact, these variations often prove useful to multinational corporation executives who pick and choose among prospective locations for manufacturing plants, headquarters offices, and assembly operations on the basis of the "comparative advantages"—that favor them at a particular time.[53]

Although the differences between the political economies of the U.S. and the USSR, and between the U.S. and Nazi Germany[54] are considerable ones, the variations among the U.S., Japan, and the U.K. in the manpower realm, alone, are almost as great, their essentially "democratic-Capitalist" and their grossly similar institutional-legal characters quite aside. Thus, employment for

51. We leave aside here the special cases of "mixed" enterprises, "public authorities," federally chartered corporations (like the communications satellite corporation, Comsat, The New York Port Authority, The U.S. Postal Service, and the Tennessee Valley Authority). The question of differences, within the United States, associated with professional versus owner-managers, will concern us in chapter 5.

52. We forego discussion here, for example, of retired military personnel and civilian leaders in military departments in the United States, whose appointments to high posts in supplier firms are favored by government contract writers, and of the allegedly potent roles of top level private managers, in the corridors of Japanese political power, from conglomerate-like enterprises called *Zaibatzu*.

53. For recent studies of "multinational" corporate behavior see Richard J. Barnet and Ronald E. Muller, *Global Reach: The Power of the Multinational Corporations* (New York: Simon & Schuster, 1974); and Raymond Vernon, *Storm over the Multinationals* (Cambridge, Mass.: Harvard University Press, 1977). For specific descriptions of multinationals and unions, see Robert J. Flanagan and Arnold R. Weber (eds.), *Bargaining without Boundaries: The Multinational Corporation and International Labor Relations* (Chicago: University of Chicago Press, 1974).

54. For earlier dissenting views that serve to emphasize commonalities in the U.S. and German Nazi economies, see Franz Neumann, *Behemoth: The Structure and Practice of National Socialism, 1933-1944* (New York: Harper & Row, 1966; originally Oxford University Press, 1942); and Robert A. Bardy, *Business as a System of Power* (New York: Columbia University Press, 1943).

nearly half of all employed Japanese is in principle for life; entry into British and American firms involves a far less permanent commitment in the understanding of both parties to a "labor contract."[55] In Japan there is an important distinction, reflected in their wage and other working conditions, between permanent, "life-time" employees and temporary employees. In England this distinction is almost meaningless, while in the U.S. it is a highly relevant one in some industrial sectors and of relative unimportance in others.

Thus in the unionized manufacturing sector, U.S. employers have chosen to contain the size of their wage bill, by amortizing the costs of what they regard to be expensive collectively bargained fringe benefit programs, to low and stable numbers of relatively well paid workers, by employing overtime rather than "additional hires" to contend with cyclical and seasonal variations in their manpower requirements. In other sectors of the American economy, however, part-time and part-year workers constitute a very sizable part of the work-force, affording employers in more competitive branches of industry, like retailing, much desired orders of flexibility in the uses of people as well as accesses to work force participants whose "dissestablished" attachments to work appear to square well with employer needs.[56]

Japanese employers, meantime, and to a far greater degree than English employers seek to ensure that their permanent employees are selected from the upper reaches of the labor pool's intelligence elite by recruiting procedures in which significance is attached to formal schooling, to academic grades, and to the substantive content of education. In England, relatively speaking, managers provide jobs for and employ men and women from all the rungs on the intelligence ladder and tend to accept, without much ado, their legal quotas of handicapped workers.

Practices in the U.S. on this score vary greatly among employers. Employers place great emphasis on degrees and diplomas in the U.S., especially when the labor market is loose as in periods of economic recession, but far greater emphasis is placed in screening job applicants on the recommendations that come from other employees, their families, and their friends. Thus nearly 50 percent of American job holders in 1970 obtained their jobs through ac-

---

55. The British and Japanese patterns are drawn, almost without exception, from Ronald Dore, *British-Factory-Japanese Factory: The Origins of National Diversity in Industrial Relations.* (Berkeley and Los Angeles: University of California Press, 1973). While Professor Dore's studies were of two British and two Japanese factories in the same industries, they are quite demonstrable of wider-going patterns. Interested readers can pursue the matters treated here in P. Sargant Florence, *The Logic of British and American Industry: A Realistic Analysis of Economic Structure and Government,* 3rd ed. (London: Routledge and Kegan Paul, 1972).

56. The word "appear" is used advisedly. Whether part-time, part-year workers actually prefer such working conditions is a subject of some debate. Cf. Marcia K. Freedman, *The Process of Work Establishment,* (New York: Columbia University Press, 1969); and Dean Morse, *The Peripheral Worker* (New York: Columbia University Press, 1969).

quaintanceships and family associations, rather than through employment agencies, advertisements, or by being what personnel officers call "walk-ins."[57]

Next, English workers tend to be recruited for fairly specific work roles. In the Japanese case recruitment is far more often for a general range of work roles; for permanent Japanese workers there is a reasonably clear "meritocratic" career progression. In the U.S. again, practices vary on both counts from industry to industry and from firm to firm. There is also evidence in the American case that, even where fairly ladder-like career arrangements govern in an enterprise, many of the levels are more nominal than real and appear to be linked, as often, to extant salary differentials (resulting from a mixture of inflation-inspired pay policies, tight labor market conditions, and increments of service) as they are linked directly to actual differences in the functions employees perform. Beyond these worker-selection differences are differences among the three countries regarding training procedures, the roles of governmental and private sectors regarding job training and its costs, and the statuses, in each nation, of nonwork-related or general, post-school educational exposures.

Next, the roles of unions vary considerably in the three countries. Thus English workers in a particular firm may belong to a variety of unions represented in the enterprise depending upon workers' skills and crafts; in Japan, workers belong to unions that are organized on company lines. In the U.S. organized workers in a company belong, typically, to one union in most of the basic industries but the unions, themselves, vary in terms of whether they are organized, overall, along craft or along heterogenous "industrial" lines. (The construction industry, in the U.S. is a large and glaringly different exception. This industry and its unions are organized around a system of subcontracting involving specialized firms and, respectively, their specialized craft workers.)

In both Japan and England union members see their organizations' main functions to be wage bargaining. In both countries this bargaining is centralized in that it is conducted by the parent of a company's "local" union with the parent company's managers. In Japan workers belong to a federation of enterprise unions, in England to national unions. In Japan corporation-wide union federation officials play a role in bargaining. In England the most crucial bargaining takes place between national unions—transport workers, e.g.—and an employers association made up of managers from a variety of distinct firms who must also bargain with other national unions representing their employees. In both nations, unions as such—federated, in Japan, along company lines and national in the U.K.—have ties with (left wing) political parties, though in the Japanese case the party is not, as in the U.K., likely ever to form a government.

In the U.S. collective bargaining is seen by most well informed citizens to focus on wage negotiations and unions are seen to be only nominally "attached" to the democratic party. The facts are vastly more complicated on both counts, however. First, in neither Japan nor England is the *local* grievance

---

57. *Recruitment, Job Search, and the United States Employment Service*, R & D Monograph 43, Dept. of Labor (Washington, D.C.: U.S. Government Printing Office, 1976), pp. 52-67.

machinery, which is highly developed in American shops and factories, nearly as important a component of *regular* collective bargaining procedures as in the U.S. Indeed, grievance handling may be said, with little argument among industrial relations specialists in government, business, or the labor movement, to be a major function of American unions. The processing of grievances, moreover, although rarely made the object of the public's attention is inextricably woven into the more publicized bargaining processes, involving contract negotiations, which the public is aware. Thus, in some very important instances the withdrawal of thousands of formal, unsettled grievances may be among the "quids" that are exchanged for "quos" in even the most notorious of America's post War II labor-management contract settlements that have been made to appear to be solely over wages.[58]

It is highly relevant to note, as well, that in the U.S. labor-management relations have been encumbered by the need for the parties to a contract, in the absence of adequate and fully developed national policies (England) or highly sophisticated and nearly unilateral private-corporate practices (Japan), to negotiate over a full array of health, unemployment and related "fringe" benefits. The results have been challenging to American collective bargaining to a remarkable degree, and have spawned large numbers of specialists in both unions and corporations to study and deal with the essentially nonbusiness issues bearing upon questions unrelated to a firm's economic missions.

Next, America's republican form of government has generated six major parties—a democratic and a republican party at each of the federal, state, and municipal levels[59]—making the associations between unions and the two "national" parties highly problematic; neither of the national political parties are "vertically integrated" on all the issues that interest either American unionists or their union leaders.

There are other remarkable differences among the three nations as well, in the degree to which the enterprise constitutes a highly integrated community, in the classically sociological sense; in the degree to which managements' authority is defined as legitimate; in the extent to which interests are perceived to be in conflict; and in the degree to which wage and salary bills are distributed in terms of market prices for *skills* or market prices for a *lifetime's work*. The schematic outline already presented however, serves to illustrate that important differences characterize the arrangements even among ostensibly "capitalist" economies. The methods of recruitment of a nations's labor force are, after all, intimately connected with the character of a nation's industry-serving educational and training vehicles, of its social and community structures, its "associational" patterns and class structure, of its structure of opportunities, and of its standards of equity.

58. For a highly sensitive discussion, based on case-like materials, see James W. Kuhn, *Bargaining in the Grievance Process* (New York: Columbia University Press, 1961).

59. See James MacGregor Burns, *Presidential Government: The Crucible of Leadership* (Boston: Houghton Mifflin, 1966).

The machinery for settling wage and salary questions, meantime, is a greater or lesser component (depending on the degree of unionization) in the social machinery for distributing incomes and the goods and services they command as among skill, age, sex, ability, and others of the groups into which a society is consequentially differentiated. Finally, the nature and types of linkages among employers, employees, employee representatives, and government in the conventional political sense have direct and immediate as well as indirect and enduring consequences. Trade, fiscal, and monetary policies are among the most obvious of those measurably influenced, or basically determined, by the precise ways in which the linkages become operative. The effects of these policies on a nation's payment balances and its internationally competitive position, its employment and inflation rates, as well as the value and the distribution of its national product among its citizens are unsurprisingly among the hotly debated questions in industrial capitalist societies.

The outcomes of these debates and the labor-managment relationships on which they focus are more than just vaguely reflected in national policies, foreign not less than domestic. A hasty examination of the conflicts among friendly and allied nations, whether over the costs of mutual defense arrangements, over tariffs and trade bills, over manpower embargoes imposed in the interest of protecting a variety of skill categories, over the joint postures to be assumed vis-a-vis ambitions and equally self-serving commodity-controlling "cartels," will assure the reader that an underlying and ever-fervent capitalist commitment is no guarantee of international nor of domestic harmony among and within nations, respectively, with different "employment systems."

CONCLUSION

The Japanese and British cases are especially interesting because their differentiated systems of industrial relations and employment may readily be seen to be related to their histories. Thus Professor Dore, whose thorough comparisons of the two cases were undertaken with the expressed purpose of determining the sources and degrees of "divergence" and "convergence," anchors the considerable differences he reports in the different dates of British and Japanese industrialization. As if to provide the transition to the next chapter, in which some of the sources of convergence are discussed, Professor Dore adds:

> . . . to return to the main thesis . . . the institutional luggage acquired by Britain as the pioneer of industrialization, may slow down the adaptation of institutions to the existence of the giant corporation and to the growing strength of egalitarian ideas, but it does not entirely prevent it. Changes are taking place in the British employment system . . . The changes . . .

might reasonably be characterized however loosely, as "in the Japanese direction . . ."[60]

By "Japanese direction", Professor Dore means away from what he regards as a "market-oriented" in favor of what he terms the Japanese "organization-oriented" employment system. As we shall see in chapter 6, in which several different approaches to shop, office, and factory level work-modes are discussed, the Japanese "organization-oriented" system is very much like the one recommended by a sizable group within each of two generations of American social scientists who have emphasized the virtues of studies (by Harvard Business School investigators in the late 1920s and others in the 1970s) of good "human relations." These develop only, it is argued, when the firm is seen as a social system, the management of which is improved by the application of social science techniques in place of those dictated by the highly impersonal, contractual, calculating values emphasized in economics. Radical enough in their time, these social psychological studies have increasingly emphasized the communal qualities of traditional societies like those that prevailed in Japan, among other places, before industrialization occurred, and which are rather precisely analogous to the qualities of the lives of millions of Japanese who, along with their union leader (!) are not just employees but are *members* of firms that are explicitly conceived of as working *communities*.

It is interesting to ponder, in this connection, whether evolving patterns of convergence and divergence are likely to be around "traditional" or about "modern" models of society and social philosophy. Put another way, one wonders whether a good deal of what was "traditional" is simply transmuted, in some lately industrializing societies, into a synthesis with some elements of the modern mode. In others, meanwhile, the equilibrium between "early modern" and "late traditional" modes persists in a kind of "unstable equilibrium," in which orderly conflict prevails over commitments to harmony. In the next chapter we will assay some of the evidence bearing upon these questions in a discussion that focuses on the sources of convergence in industrial societies.

---

60. Dore, *British Factory-Japanese Factory*, pp. 338-39.

CHAPTER 2
INDUSTRIALISM AND THE MOBILIZATION OF RESOURCES

In this chapter we will move a short analytical distance down our metaphorical mountain in quest of some additional differences as well as some additional commonalities among industrial societies. Our quest is informed by the premise that the citizens and leaders who make national economic histories have made considerable room for different detailed combinations of resolutions of a number of inescapable issues and choices facing them in the industrialization process. These issues, and the choices implied by joining the issues, have to do, most crucially, with (1) the mobilization and disposition of human and other resources; (2) the calculation and distribution of both the social and personal costs and benefits of industrialization; and (3) practical matters of organization and administration. The ways in which the issues are joined, finally, have implications for the character of shop- and office-level relationships discussed in later chapters.

It is the concern with these issues that to a significant degree underlies the debates between industrialism's defenders and its critics: "Are not industrial societies converging? Do not historical and cultural differences among nations give way to the substantially homogenizing effects of large organizations, the sale and utilization of labor, the impersonal ways of science and the relentless demands of machines, schedules, and clocks?"[1] One's assessments of the best answers to these questions will bear upon one's estimates of the capacities of nations to retain their identities and perhaps even of the viability of a differentiated world of nations with different political, social, and

---

1. For a brief and lucid outline of the scholarly side of a fruitful debate over the matter and of the convergence–divergence question, see Wilbert Moore, *The Impact of Industry* (Englewood Cliffs, N.J.: Prentice-Hall, 1965), especially ch. 2.

economic—which is to say moral and political—principles. A search for answers to questions about convergence, however, will not result in the discovery of any immutable rules on the subject. As Moore points out, though some generalizations are possible, the "maximum aim" of establishing highly general laws of economic growth and industrial development is likely to be wide of the theorist's mark. Thus, one may note that the requirements for modern economic development "include the positive side of discontent [with the status quo] . . . the quest for improvement . . . ; [they] also include ironically, a considerable measure of political order, a condition notably lacking in some of the very areas where the demand for economic improvement is articulated to the point of stridency."[2] Beyond these two almost contradictory conditions, which may be said to be primary ones, it is exceedingly difficult to identify the weights and priorities among preconditions.

The questions involved are by no means just academic ones in a restless world in which populations grow, in which the gap between "haves" and "have nots" is actually growing, in which partisan leaders seek to bring developing nations into their own camps as allies, and in which hundreds of billions of dollars are expended by nations and by economic agencies like corporations in efforts to modernize and industrialize rapidly.

We may proceed, then, to a discussion of three prerequisites for industrialization and economic growth that involve sociologically problematical issues: (1) physical capital formation; (2) social and organizational technology; and (3) "human capital" formation. Whether a population seeks to begin or seeks to continue on the road to Huddersfield, it must join and rejoin a series of issues under each of these three rubrics; there are, in our metaphor, critical evaluations on the road at which the relevant populations must make choices and with which they must otherwise come to terms.

CAPITAL FORMATION: "MARKET" AND "PLANNING" APPROACHES

If a society is to produce the needed surplus for industrial development, the excess of value over and above a population's minimum subsistence requirements, it must mobilize the capital necessary for the actual production of this surplus. Such accumulation requires a considerable degree of capital mobility and one or another method for inducing saver-producers to invest the surplus as well. These inducements may take a variety of forms, but the end, capital formation, is a universal requirement.

In some nations savings may be mobilized and allocated by the state which may appropriate them directly through public ownership, or indirectly by tax and transfer programs. In "free enterprise" economies, the profit from produc-

---

2. Moore, *The Impact of Industry*, p. 22.

tion may be reinvested, with greater or lesser inducements from sundry governments (1) that make supplementary and complementary public investments in what economists call infrastructure—from roads and public health programs to airports; (2) whose tax schemes contain incentives to investments; and (3) whose foreign trade policies may include tariffs designed to protect "infant" or vulnerable industries against the chill winds of competition. Whatever the specific machinery, capital formation in a society requires that some—individuals, corporations, governments, or combinations thereof—defer consumption over the short haul. Just as a child is obliged to learn to control its urges as a prerequisite for membership in society, so a population must be encouraged, enticed, or driven to sacrifice the fulfillment of some present wants and needs in favor of the future fulfillment of its or its leaders' aspirations. Decisions about the precise allocations of the sacrifices needed for capital formation and for the mobilization of other resources necessary for industrialization will thus be informed in some measure by dominant ethical and political values and, in greater or lesser degree, by the values of socially dominant groups in a developing society.

Having said this much only about capital formation, and before getting into other resource mobilization issues,[3] a key question relating to a matter that can trigger heated debate over martini lunches in New York pubs or in the offices of the Soviet Politburo's secretariat comes to mind: What *types* of economic planning should be undertaken to assure capital formation in adequate amounts? Note that the question does not ask whether or not there is to be planning; the choice involves gradations, not a dichotomy. Rhetoric on the subject notwithstanding, *all* nations engage in economic planning, the U.S. not a great deal less than the USSR, China, and their "socialist" peers. At the same time, the needs, expressed generally in America, for increased independence of economic enterprises, for profit criteria, and for prices that are set economically (rather than arbitrarily, and therefore with minimal regard to cost and efficiency) are not unique needs in capitalist economies. Indeed, the growing inclination of Soviet economists to separate the debate over capitalism and socialism from the debate over the respective roles of markets and planners is a sensible one and has been documented by Letchie.[4] The separation of these

3. For a theoretical discussion of resource mobilization issues facing sociopolitical *movements* and the modes of their management by the leaders and members of social movements that bears upon the questions here at hand, see Mayer N. Zald and James D. McCarthy, "Resource Mobilization in Social Movements," *American Journal of Sociology*, 82, 6 (1976), 1212-41.

4. J. M. Letchie, "Soviet Views on Keynes: A Review Article Surveying the Literature," *Journal of Economic Literature*, 9, 2 (June 1971), 448. The passage is cited in a most helpful and lucid review of theories and findings regarding the roles of planning decisions and market forces in the development process: Derek T. Healey, "Development Policy: New Thinking About an Interpretation," *Journal of Economic Literature*, 10, 3 (September 1972), 757-97 (emphases added). For a most helpful review of these issues see Gregory Grossman, *Economic Systems*, 2nd ed. (Englewood Cliffs, N.J.: Prentice-Hall, 1974). For a definitive set of comparisons of the roles of "nationalization," income distribution, and a number of aspects of property in industrial systems, see Frederick Pryor, *Property and Industrial Organization in Communist and Capitalist Nations* (Bloomington: Indiana University Press, 1973).

debates refers in part to the distinctions among "isms" that concerned us in chapter 1. As American readers may gauge from current arguments over interest rates, tax policies, unemployment, and inflation, we are knee deep in economic planning efforts in the U.S. though it has been our inclination to plan in respect of each of these programmatic issues quite separately.

At one extreme, in an absolutely (and only theoretically possible) free, competive market system, profit is recognized as both the aim and, ultimately therefore, the regulator of economic activity: At another extreme the detailed planning of *all* of a nation's economic activities is regarded as the means (and the end, some would add) of economic activity. Industrial countries actually fall at the outer edges of a very large middle ground between these extremes, however, whereby (1) the *predominantly* free market systems of unfettered buyers, sellers, savers, and investors are assisted by a large number of public policies— regarding both investment and regulation, while (2) the *predominantly* planned economic systems make room for increasing orders of market activity.

Thus, although he eschews any belief in the need for private property as an essential lubricant for the efficient operation of the "market mechanism," Lieberman, a most influential Soviet economic theoretician, writes of older and newer economic policies in the USSR:

> The substitution of voluntarism and naked administrative fiat for economic stimuli produced distressing disproportions, a lower efficiency in utilizing [Soviet] fixed assets, deterioration of the quality of goods, and, as a result, insufficient growth of the working people's property. . . . The essential principle of . . . reform . . . is that which is advantageous for each industrial enterprise. Toward this end a number of measures are being adopted, including: increasing the independence of enterprises; appraising their work by the criterion of profitability; . . . and establishing economically based, as opposed to arbitrarily set, prices.[5]

A Hungarian economist-planner writes in the same vein that on January 1, 1968 his country embarked successfully on a system of reforms designed to "organically combine" central control with "the functioning of the self-regulating market mechanisms."[6]

George Feiwel, finally, writes of the roles of market forces in Czechoslovakia.

> Past achievements were at the cost of extensive utilization of the labor force and ever-increasing investments and material inputs, with little concern for efficiency. . . . Moreover, the path of development pursued resulted in deleterious unbalanced growth, with considerable fluctuations

---

5. Cited in Healy, "Development Policy," p. 761.

6. T. Nagy, "The Hungarian Economic Reform: Past and Future," *American Economic Review Papers and Proceedings,* 61, 2 (May 1971), p. 430 (emphases added).

in the growth rates of production. [Also] the traditional planning system was conducive to waste of investment, not only because it was void of criteria for evaluating investment efficiency, but because micro units squandered capital offered to them virtually *cost* free.[7]

While Eastern European—and Chinese—planners increasingly contemplate the utilities and values that are served by the selective but substantial introduction of market-determined price systems, Americans and others in the west have acquiesced, to a remarkable degree, in the need for greater orders of planning in *their* economies! The managers of large economic enterprise, for example, have joined hands with government policy makers to design and implement many laws and regulations whose practical effect it is to eliminate "destructive" competition, and to insulate owners, managers, and (sometimes) employees against some of the risks that huge investments—capital formation—made at one time, will not come acropper at the time, much later, when they should begin to bear fruit.

The results in the U.S., though uneven in their effectiveness and controversial in their implications, are reflected directly and indirectly in subsidy programs, investment guarantees, consumer protection regulations, labeling requirements, government stockpiling and procurement schedules, minimum wage, fair labor standards and labor relations laws, as well as in long lists of tariffs, customs, and import restrictions, in zoning, patent, licensing, and copyright laws, and in legal prohibitions against conspiracies, against trusts, against securities frauds, and against air and water pollution. Directly and indirectly these measures impinge upon investment decisions, on the capital formation process.

In addition, sizable legions are daily at work in America examining ways to increase the confidence of investors by "countercyclical" fiscal and monetary policies. These policies are designed, sometimes fictively, to introduce compensations in the economy for the often untoward and unpredictable consequences of the private behavior of hundreds of large investors and of millions of buyers and sellers. The fickleness and whimsy of the two latter groups at the retail level are regularly reflected in fashion and other shifts, no less than in their reasonableness in pursuit of their self-interests. Just these whims can lead to intolerable disjunctions and discontinuities in the economy. Consider that a fleeting affection for small cars in 1955—an affection that lasted for one year—led to a half-billion dollar loss when Ford's Edsel automobile "failed." Twenty years later, OPEC, the oil "cartel," led to a boom, once again, for small automobiles. And, by summer 1976 in the early stages of an energy crisis of monumental significance, there was actually a *glut* of small and a *dearth* of full-size

---

7. George R. Feiwel, "The Inverse Economic Miracle: Sources of Growth and Retrogression in Postwar Czechoslovakia," *Economic Development and Cultural Change*, 19, 3 (April 1971), 368-70, cited in Healey, "Development Policy," p. 761 (emphasis added).

automobiles as consumers sought to undo the efforts of government officials and the judgments of auto company planners who had made their own judgments about the 1976 utilization of the industry's plant and equipment in 1974. Radical shifts in the tastes of whimsical consumers can thus have quite immediate effects on industries' capital requirements, and thus on job opportunities.

Capital Formation: Sectoral Tradeoffs of Cost and Benefit

Our purpose here is not to imply that commitments to *private property* lie around the next eastern European economic corner. Neither do we suggest that the "bulls" and "bears" in "the fortresses of capitalism," as the sociologist Max Weber called New York's financial district, will soon be pleased to eliminate the market system entirely, in favor of even higher orders of planning. The purpose, rather, is to highlight the inherent and common problems in the industrialization process (1) of articulating market with planning processes and mechanisms; (2) of establishing the economic and the social costs and benefits of the articulations; and (3) of identifying incentives capable of enlisting support for a socioeconomic system within which investments, consumption, savings, and production are in such a balance that public and private decisions will lead to economic performance patterns that are responsive to a society's preferences.

For long periods the specific problems attending capital formation were widely seen to be subordinate to problems attending efforts to *initiate* industrialization. Increasingly the problem of capital formation has come to be regarded as crucial in *sustaining* economic growth, as well. The international rule of thumb, so to speak, has been to control the import of goods into a nation for which markets already exist—a policy called import substitution—in favor of home industry. The results of such policies have profound income distributive— and redistributive—effects, and therefore social structural consequences, as a moment's reflection will suggest. Consider that successful import substitution at one stage generates policy questions at later stages to the precise extent to which some domestic producers, earners and investors rather than others are the beneficiaries' of early economic growth. These beneficiaries' incomes, in turn, spark new demands for more imports. In general, in this circumstance, import substitution is attempted anew. One result is to provide too much capacity at the final and too little at the intermediate stages of production,[8] leading to unequal sacrifices for the population in each of the production stages. When imports exceed exports the resulting imbalances in a nation's trade payments lead to the underutilization of capacity at the final stages of production. A sense then develops that import substitution has gone too far, in the sense:

---

8. Ian Little, Tibor Scitovsky, and Maurice Scott, *Industry and Trade in Some Developing Countries* (London: Oxford University Press for the OECD Developing Countries, 1970), cited and discussed in Healey, "Development Policy," p. 761.

that it appeared because protection, through distorting prices, raised the prices of stimulated manufacturers in relation to the prices of outputs from other sectors. In some instances, the contribution to value added of the economy of a particular industry [is] actually negative.[9]

A closely related byproduct of this long-favored route to industrialization resides in the fact that tariff arrangements in support of domestic production are not cost free. Thus, the real contribution of domestic agriculture to an economy is significantly obscured when no discount (in the amounts of tariffs on manufactures) is applied to the value of goods produced by protected industries. The results—seen around the world—are the highly charged disputes among the members of the different sectors of an economy—its managers and particularly their employees and their families. Protection of manufacture through tariffs constitutes a domestic "tax" on farmers to the extent to which tariffs raise the price of industrial as compared to the agricultural products *they* export and, therefore, farmers' incentives to produce for export and their economic capacities to consume domestic products!

We need not detain ourselves here to review all the evidence in support of a growing suspicion that "import substitution" is a problematic policy for developing or developed nations. The technical economic issues involved in this and the larger dispute over capital formation have boggled and will continue to boggle the minds of the best planners and economic theoreticians, public and otherwise, in Washington, Moscow, Tel Aviv, Iowa City, and Paris, and in the innumerable new capitals in Africa. Thus, lengthy studies have dealt with questions, within the "pro-industry" school, of the *types* of capital industries to be fostered. Our present interest in these interrelated matters, and the larger growth and development imperatives, lies in the fact that the cluster of questions involved relate to the important matter of social choice.[10] The point is that these choices, in turn, have consequential effects upon the distribution of income and therefore most other rewards, as well as upon the distribution of sacrifices and ordinary costs, among population groups.

Housing and Credit:
An Illustrative Case

The banker-authors of one of America's most influential economic reports allude to the macroscopic economic questions implied in the discussion so far very well. Although the report in question was descriptive of the recessionary

---

9. Healy, "Development Policy," pp. 761–62.

10. For a fine overview of the literally hundreds of pros and cons by a sociologically sensitive economist, see Gunnar Myrdal, *Asian Drama: An Inquiry into the Poverty of Nations,* 3 vols. (New York: Pantheon, 1968). It is interesting to note that "leftist" governments in developing nations have endorsed investments in labor intensive industrial activities, the better to spread employment opportunities. The effect is

and inflationary circumstances in the second half of the 1970s, the assessments therein have a generic quality, a timelessness, that helps us to identify a series of industrial-sociological issues. Thus, the economic group of Chase Manhattan Bank, argues that there is a capital shortage in America because our requirements exceed what "American business and the American people have financed out of their savings."

The bankers' concerns are that governments have been obliged, because of their operating deficits, to borrow money, thereby increasing the demand for funds. Reductions in public outlays, revisions in government regulations and in corporate taxes, the bankers argue, are necessary to reduce inflation-producing demand for what otherwise would be cheaper investment dollars.[11] Liberal—not necessarily radical—critics would agree that new investment is needed but that the necessary savings would flow from higher employment levels and the greater utilization of the nation's existing physical capacity facilitated by public spending and from the loosening of tight credit policies by the U.S. Federal Reserve.[12] The arguments go to the very philosophical heart of political issues revolving around the roles of private investors and public policy makers, and of the effects on economic well being of diverse incentives, of different unemployment and employment levels, of different interest rates, and much more.

Consider that while the "national habits of savings and investing" that concern the Chase bankers may, indeed, be subject to change, they are not, like childrens' cereal-eating preferences, subject to the frivolous influence of artfully drawn television ads. Indeed, savings are influenced by a complex of fairly stable institutional arrangements. Thus, expenditures supported by credit are listed in (America's) national accounts as savings; among America's larger credit-based expenditures are mortgages on private, single-family dwellings, the interest payments on which are deductible from the income tax payments of home owners.[13] Leaving aside the extraordinary large effects of these "tax expenditures" on income distribution, we should note here that the subsidies involved are to individuals. In many other industries equivalent subsidies are allocated to producers, not to consumers. It could well be argued that the home-building industry, with its large numbers of relatively small builders, owes its unusual production structure (a structure not unlike that of the cottage or

---

to split the lesser-skilled workers of competing nations into conflicting camps and to reduce prospects for collaboration in an "international working class."

11. *Business in Brief* (New York: Chase Manhattan Bank, June 1975), no. 122, p. 1.

12. See, for example, James Tobin, "Who is Crowding Out What?" *Challenge*, 18, 5 (November/December 1975), for a treatment that goes beyond current news events in its implications.

13. For a detailed discussion, see Henry J. Aaron, *Shelter and Subsidies: Who Benefits from Federal Housing Policies* (Washington, D.C.: Brookings Institution, 1972), p. 57.

"putting out system) to the particular "saving habits" encouraged by public tax policies so strongly favoring custom-made, i.e. relatively unique, homes.

A brief conversation with congressmen will assure one that neither their home-building nor their home loan-making constituents are likely soon to change the now deeply ingrained habituation to tax deductible mortgage interest arrangements, though these habits help considerably to assure a building industry made up of relatively inefficient small firms. Other key constituents, meanwhile, have interests in housing "starts" that become the scene of consumption decisions—carpeting, lawn mowers, refrigerators—which, in turn, are significant in shaping the quantities and types of demands for skills in firms across the land and, in some cases, in other lands. We may remind ourselves, for example, that the "second car," a byproduct of the postwar growth of suburban housing developments, sustains a very large segment of the demand for workers in the auto industry.

On another side, saving habits are amenable to some influence by the government agencies to whom the Chase bankers appeal. Thus the bankers argue that governments whet the public's tastes for expensive public programs that force public officials to borrow in the markets in which private producers also seek to make loans with which to purchase more efficient machines. The point is that we are talking, once again, about *differential* demands for *different* outputs provided by people of *differentiated* skills who work in (or manage) economic entities that provide *different* goods and services to *diverse* population groups with *differential* incomes and with *differential* accesses to subsidies and the rest. Some citizens will wish, in the absence of earning opportunities, to receive goods and services directly from the government. Others (builders?) will be pleased to obtain these goods and services indirectly from government through tax expenditures favoring house buyers. Still others will prefer only to earn their own incomes, and to engage in consumption activities without publicly endowed inducements. Most of us, however, want all we can get of both private earnings and what may be termed public largesse,[14] and many of us do: publicly financed "GI Bills" and subsidized student loans expended in proudly private institutions of learning, public highways and private cars, private airlines and public airports, private dwellings and (in 1966) $7 billion in home purchase subsidy-like tax expenditures.

We may summarize this section by saying that although there is considerable room for detailed choices to be made in the course of a nations's industrialization, they are made in respect of a handful of overarching requirements. The choices made regarding the modes of capital formation has a long series of sociologically consequential "spillover" effects affecting economic organizations' managers and their workers, the larger economic structure of which they are among the key agents, and thus the numbers and types of jobs as well as

---

14. For a treatment of economically valuable rights and claims the entitlements to which are created by law, see Charles Reich, "The New Property," *Yale Law Review*, 73, 5 (April 1964), 733-81.

the incomes, status, and prospects of individual actors. In the next section we turn to a few specific social arrangements that either facilitate, accompany, or reflect the industrialization process.

SOCIAL TECHNOLOGY

Moore identifies three sets of preconditions that fall under the second of our resource rubrics. The resources in question, he writes, are "organizational, institutional and ideological-motivational" in character.[15] Thus, in addition to stable creditable financial institutions that facilitate the necessary balances and flows of savings and investments along one or another of the lines we have discussed, industrial development requires that a population and its leaders have available and can draw effectively upon what Stinchcombe calls "social technology."[16]

Social Technology in Temporal Perspective

According to Stinchombe, the capacities of a population for organizing itself and its activities, like those for planning various kinds of rationally administered economic enterprises, are quite strictly limited at any given time. These capacities multiply over long time periods as the result of accumulated experiences in problem solving, as do the organizational forms through which a population may perform economic and related industrial activities. It is accordingly of particular relevance, in order to understand the industrial-developmental process, to identify differences in a population's organizational capacities, especially differences that ultimately lead to different labor force characteristics in different economic periods.

Stinchombe groups 33 industries according to whether they appeared in the "prefactory" period, the "early nineteenth century," or in what he calls the "railroad and the modern ages." He reports evidence showing, first, that as one moves from the earlier to the last of these periods, one finds industries with fewer persons who are self-employed or employed by their families and, specifically, fewer unpaid family workers. Second, the evidence shows an increasing proportion of clerical workers as a percentage of all "administrative workers," and an increasing proportion of "professional workers" in positions of organizational authority as well.[17] The labor force shifts are attributed to changes in the social technology available to industry organizers in the different

15. Moore, *The Impact of Industry*, pp. 21-24.

16. Arthur Stinchcombe, "Social Structure and Environment," in James G. March (ed.), *Handbook of Organizations* (Chicago: Rand McNally, 1965), pp. 142-93.

17. Ibid., p. 158. The data are from the 1952 census.

historical periods in which the industries are founded. Stinchcombe's thesis is a suggestive one because the particular labor force indicators he has chosen are those that mirror the industrialization process itself: The separation of the production process from household activities, an ever more refined and differentiated division of labor and the increase of administrative, technical, and clerical workers as economic units become more rationally bureaucratic.

The important point is that organizational discoveries, like "breakthroughs" in physical technology, most likely have a cumulative quality: Just as organization builders are aided by the spirit of rationalism that informs their exploitation of physical resources and of legal arrangements (like tariffs, charters and incorporation laws) they are aided by their reason and a certain empiricism, a certain opportunism, in designing organizations.[18]

The thesis can, of course, be pushed rather too far. We may note, for example, that some of the most modern contemporary industries have adapted organizational forms that were basic 200 years ago! The results of putting very old wine, so to speak, in new bottles, are not really reflected in data on labor force characteristics as the Census Bureau classifies these data, and as Stinchcombe uses them. Consider, for example, that if one diagrammed the system of franchises used in the *distribution* systems in the gasoline, automobile, motel, fast food, and many other industries in modern times, one would produce a near carbon copy of the organizational chart that would describe the *production* process known as the "putting-out" system, or the cottage industry system in the English midlands in the late eighteenth and early nineteenth centuries.

Thus enterprising merchants of that age "put-out" raw materials to cottage workers,[19] and their apprentices and their skilled journeymen who operated "mules," spinning frames, and "jennies" in the production of textiles. The merchant would return at a later date to fetch the finished goods, then sell them in the European markets. Later (and critical in this context) some "putters

---

18. We will be obliged to return to bureaucratic organizational forms, so-called, in a later chapter. For a useful discussion, meanwhile, see Charles Perrow, *Complex Organization: A Critical Essay* (Glenview, Ill.: Scott, Foresman, 1972), ch. 4. For a review of the efforts of several well-known corporate efforts to design (and redesign) organizations the better to contend with problems and to exploit opportunities, see Alfred D. Chandler, *Strategy and Structure* (Garden City, N.Y.: Doubleday, 1963). For a detailed discussion of the organizational adjustments undertaken by one of America's largest and most innovative organizations, see Alfred P. Sloan, *My Years with General Motors* (New York: MacFadden-Bartell, 1965). For a dissection of the essentially uncritical ways in which organizations have been analyzed by social scientists, see Shermann Krupp, *Pattern in Organization Analysis* (New York: Holt, Rinehart and Winston, 1961).

19. These cottage workers later contracted privately with journeymen and apprentices, on the one side, and with factory owners in an evolutionary process that ended with "foreman" being workteam *leaders* of employees, rather than their employers. For a sociological treatment of this historical process, see Reinhard Bendix, *Work and Authority in Industry, Ideologies of Management in the Cause of Industrialization* (New York: John Wiley, 1956), pp. 211-26.

out" expanded their operations by leasing machinery to cottage workers, just as oil companies and fast food companies nowadays invest in promising properties, build service stations or restaurants on them, and then lease the "outlets" to our "independent" friendly neighborhood dealers. And, just as oil companies apply pressures on their lessee dealers by raising rents (as gasoline sales increase) in efforts to earn returns on their property investments), so the "putters out" did when their markets were reduced by Napoleon's naval blockade of Europe, called the continental system, a blockade that sealed off profitable continental textile markets and reduced the putters-outs' profits.[20]

In Stinchcombe's analysis, nonpayroll personnel, like service station dealers and the owner-managers and their sales and repair personnel in retail automobile outlets, or the managers, cooks, and attendants in fast food establishments, are excluded from calculations of the leasing companies' labor forces though they are far from being truly independent small businessmen for being off corporate payrolls.[21] If these workers were added to those attributed to the industries in Stinchcombe's calculations for the modern age, these industries would look a good deal less different, in organizational terms, from earlier industries: in 1969 franchized outlets numbered 383,908 of which 315,045 were franchise-owned; in 1976 there were 463,482 of which 376,355 were franchise-owned. These outlets sold $4 billion of food ingredients, supplies, and merchandise in 1975 and employed 3.5 million full and part-time workers.[22]

The first point of this discussion is that although the industrialization process involves finding satisfactory solutions to a number of overarching problems—the need for transportation and communcation modes are among the more critical ones—it is by no means obvious how one goes about identifying the correct chicken-and-egg sequences involved in the processes themselves. Thus it is not obvious how one distinguishes between the prerequisites and the

---

20. The increased rents were paid by the cottagemasters from funds saved through the abridgment of higher-wage apprenticeship rules and by wage reductions applied to journeymen. The resulting violent, late-night attacks on the master's rented machines, called "Luddism," after a certain Ned Ludd, has mistakenly been attributed for generations by cliche-prone writers to workers' resistance to machine technology—to change per se—rather than to workers' outrages over the violations of protective apprenticeship rules, of labor-management wage agreements, and of the hostility to their unions. It could indeed be argued that it was the early employers who were "luddites" in their antagonism toward unions, which, after all, were new forms of social technology at the time. See William Felkin, *A History of the Machine-Wrought Hosiery and Lace Manufacturers* (London: Longmans, Green, 1867), p. xiii and ch. 16. For more recent discussions, see F. O. Darvall, *Popular Disturbances and Public Order in Regency England* (London: Routledge & Keegan Paul, 1934); and Malcolm T. Thomis, *The Luddites: Machine-Breaking in Regency England* New York: Schocken Books, 1972).

21. See David Rogers and Ivar Berg, "Occupation and Ideology: The Case of the Small Businessman," *Human Organizations*, 20, 3 (Fall 1961), 103-11.

22. *Franchising in the Economy 1975-77,* Department of Commerce (Washington, D.C.; Government Printing Office, December 1976), pp. 30, 32, 33, 40.

correlates of industrialization. The significance of the point, for the moment, inheres in the fact that we can hardly draw specific lessons, for planning purposes, of the most efficacious sequence to commend to nations embarked on industrialization.

The second point is that many of the developments that appear to be solutions to generic problems inhering in the industrialization process—the asserted needs to fulfill prerequisites—are, in fact, sometimes solutions to problems that are *not* intrinsically industrial in character. The widely used retail franchise distribution system in modern America, as an exemplary case, clearly did not evolve from a reading of histories of the "putting out" system by rational and innovation-bent modern automobile, petroleum, and fast food company executives who sought literally to capitalize upon and extend the state of the organizational arts. In the auto and petroleum industry the franchised dealer system, first called the "Iowa Plan," was a response by auto and oil producers (1) to chain store taxes imposed by antibusiness reformers among Iowa's state leaders in efforts to protect that state's smaller merchants from competition by mass distributors,[23] and (2) to labor laws. The putting out system was thus unwittingly rediscovered by managers who sought to deal with public sector innovations designed to protect more traditional social values and to deal, as well, with trade unions, a long-time corporate bugaboo; trade unions, as we have seen, were a bother to the original putters-out as well.

Inventive uses of social technology, meantime, are important to developers—and often to their creditors—as part of the building, the maintenance, and the regulation of industrial societies. To attempt to sort out the causes and effects, the initiatives, and the responses in the industrialization process is to attempt to identify choices and opportunities and to distinguish them from explicit and implicit limitations on decision making. Even if such attempts are likely to confront numerous anomalies that frustrate clear dispositive cases of cause and effect, they can help to illuminate what might otherwise be significant issues that may be joined if not fully resolved from a scientific point of view.[24]

Social Technology in Institutional Perspective

It is fairly clear that one of the major differences between industrial and other societies inheres in the gradual separation of economic institutions from all others and, ultimately, the ascendancy to preeminent status of the network of

---

23. For a discussion of the other benefits to large corporations of the use of franchise systems designed in part to decentralize and "deorganize," see David Rogers, *The Automobile Dealer* (Ph.D. thesis, Harvard University, 1960). See also Sloan, *My Years With General Motors,* passim.

24. For an effort to derive lessons about development that takes account of difficulties in linking specific causes and effects, and that stresses the need to look at cultural values, institutional arrangements, and trade-offs among social-technological modes of organization, see Myrdal, *Asian Drama: An Inquiry Into the Poverty of Nations* (New York: Pantheon Press, 1966), Vol. II, pp. 959-1530.

social-legal arrangements that dominate economic activities. Thus Adelman and Morris have conducted inventive statistical analyses of a host of social, political, and economic indicators from countries at the "lowest," the "intermediate," and the "high" level of socioeconomic development. They report that development does not "proceed continuously and uniformly from tribal conditions to the fully developed status," but that the process can nevertheless be reduced to a coherent picture.

> In the long transition during which a society evolves from tribalism to self-sustained economic growth, the closely woven political, social and economic strands of the social fabric change their pattern and their relationships. Our research suggests that one may look at the entire process of national modernization as the progressive differentiation of the social, economic, and political spheres from each other and the development of specialized institutions and attitudes within each sphere.[25]

The evidence suggests that there are three nearly universal steps involved: First there is separation of the economic sphere from the complex of social organization and the traditional norms governing this complex. This process of differentiation hastens at the intermediate level, until "the diffusion of economic concepts has extended throughout the society to the point where market attitudes and values color the outlook of even those who participate only peripherally in market transactions."[26] In this second step the economy is separating or is being separated from political constraints. In the last phase, during which economic development can proceed in earnest, the economic aspects of a social system, once the tail, have effectively come, in the cliche, to wag the dog: "Economic consideration becomes a powerful force in shaping national behavior."[27]

The model thus derived squares very well with theoretical conceptions of the interplay of social and political with economic institutions by Hoselitz, by Smelser and Parsons, and by Smelser, conceptions deriving in turn, from the work of Max Weber and Emile Durkheim.[28] These and other writers' positions diverge essentially only on the specifics of the wider process by which "noneconomic" institutions (i.e. political and social arrangements) are adapted,

---

25. Irma Adelman and Cynthia Taft Morris, *Society, Politics and Economic Development: A Quantitative Approach* (Baltimore: Johns Hopkins University Press, 1971), p. 266.

26. Ibid., p. 267.

27. Ibid., p. 267.

28. Bert F. Hoselitz, *Sociological Aspects of Economic Growth* (New York: Free Press, 1960); Talcott Parsons and Neil J. Smelser, *Economy and Society* (New York: Free Press, 1956); Neil J. Smelser, *Social Change in the Industrial Revolution* (Chicago: University of Chicago Press, 1959), and *The Sociology of Economic Life*, (Englewood Cliffs, N. J.: Prentice-Hall, 1976), pp. 141–47; Max Weber, *A General Economic History*, trans. Frank H. Knight (New York: Greenberg, 1927); Emile Durkheim, *The Division of Labor in Society* (New York: Free Press, 1949).

violated, or retained only in forms best described as symbolic in the evolving phases of development. The practical relevance of these theoretical discussions, stems from the fact that some major social conflicts occur precisely over whether particular institutions should enjoy a legitimate place or whether they are undergoing "too rapid" change in one or another of the stages. Thus, readers will be able to see for themselves, in the future, whether angry attacks against liberal abortion laws, in which the sanctity of the life of fetuses and a host of related values concerning the family are stressed, will continue to have much force in the face of the fact that pregnant women, with new employment rights, are demonstrably victimized by industrial chemicals. The probability that tradition-oriented opposition to abortion will more likely yield to the logics of employers whose employees seek to abort their poisoned fetuses than it has to the parallel logic of women's rights groups is, in historical terms, not small. (It is worth noting, in this context, that Sunday closing of "blue" laws and liberal attitudes toward the absenteeism of church-goers from Sunday (and Saturday) work assignments are gaining fewer endorsements in courts of law.)

Social Technology and Legal Institutions

The history of the continuation of the industrialization process in the USSR, which began in the reign of Peter the Great, gives proof that the absence of "private property" incentive arrangements, respecting capital, is no bar to development, even though the whole of the story of alternative incentive systems cannot yet be written. The point is that the role of property ownership may be easily exaggerated. It is arguable, thus, that whether or not many of the economic organizations in a developed economy are privately owned, a great many of them will be what Max Weber called legal-rational bureaucratic ones. In such organizations almost every position's ownership is separated from its incumbent, and its members are drawn from a formally free work force; workers are legally free to stay or leave. In these organizations, furthermore, rules and regulations govern the organizationally relevant actions of members, and members gain their positions more by virtue of their technical competencies than by virtue of organizationally irrelevant qualities and associations. We will examine some of these analytical characteristics in chapter 6.

The conduct of these organizations as component parts of social systems will be influenced—and even constrained—by growing bodies of public laws and regulations in developed societies, laws about property quite apart. The contents of these laws have substantial implications for the rights, liberties, privileges, immunities, and obligations of organizational members and for the margins of choices of their ostensibly responsible employers as well.[29] These contents, in turn, will reflect a population's traditions and its conceptions of the role of legal rules. These conceptions, finally, will assign various weights, even in the most

---

29. For a classic analysis of law, private property, and capitalism, see John R. Commons, *The Legal Foundations of Capitalism* (Madison: University of Wisconsin

developed societies, to economic and noneconomic, to market and nonmarket values, and to the balances that the population wants—or will tolerate—between emphases on efficiency and emphases on justice and equity.

The specifics of industrial social technology—the particular traits of economic organizations—are thus not totally predictable from the elemental facts either of property ownership or of production and distribution seen in technical, operational terms. The most obvious illustrations occur as such older, preindustrial, local modes of social integration as extended kinship groups give way to newer types of groups with "integrative significance."[30] Clubs, political parties, labor unions, and other voluntary agencies, in some developed nations, also come readily to mind. Indeed, as Smelser points out, some of these are "precipitated" in the industrialization process; in some instances, they can even be mobilized as social movements, or components of larger interest group efforts to limit or undo what some in a society will deplore among industrialization's real and threatened consequences. In the process, these groups may augment deficient applications of some social technologies, or they may seek to introduce social technologies they feel have been neglected in the industrialization process. In the best known cases in the U.S., those involving unions and corporations, one may observe "nonmarket" considerations—fairness, due process, and expectations of reciprocal favor-granting arrangements—borrowed from tradition and interlaced with narrower considerations of economic rationality.[31]

The cemeteries of several industrial societies, meanwhile, contain the bones of property owners who argued with impunity that the "public be damned." These cemeteries are also the permanent homes of fair numbers of dreamers, reformers, and revolutionaries whose mission ran afoul of the contesting, property-holding, industrial power groups who sought to tame people even as they tamed nature. In these cases one readily apprehends the fact that citizens in industrial societies invent a variety of forms for tempering economic forces as well as a variety of forms for the conduct of economic activities. In all of this one also sees that a variety of social technologies are available to many of the parties as competing clusters of people use laws, organizations, conspiracies, vote trading, the threat of terror, union federations, cooperatives, proprietary arrangements, and voluntary pressure groups to establish, pursue, protect, and expand their interests.[32]

Press, 1959). For a recent examination of law and the modern corporation, see Christopher D. Stone, *Where the Law Ends* (New York: Harper & Row, 1975). For an overview of the interactions of selective legal arrangements and economic activities see Fred L. Pryor, *Property and Industrial Organization in Communist and Capitalist Nations* (Bloomington: Indiana University Press, 1973).

30. Smelser, *The Sociology of Economic Life*, p. 159.

31. For a discussion of different meanings of economic rationality, see ibid., pp. 34-36.

32. For an early but not dated examination of the competing strategies of the Communist party, the military establishment, and the industrial apparatus in the

Social Technology and Physical Technology

Technical features of production—and distribution—the use of machines and of "intellectual techniques"—research methods, leadership techniques, accounting procedures, and merchandising tactics, for example—have five basic effects. They (1) set the demands for physical exertion, (2) influence the degree to which work is paid, and (3) shape the skill hierarchies of economic and related organizations, while (4) they substantially define the division of labor and authority therein. Finally, (5) these technologies also influence the character of on-the-job social relations.[33] To put it succinctly, physical and intellectual technologies have measurably significant effects on the choices among social technologies, in the widest sense of the term, that may be made by the people in industrial societies. Indeed the interactions, so to speak, of social with other technologies is the core of the subject matter in industrial sociology. In the next section, meantime, we move from a consideration of the mobilization of social technology to the mobilization of human resources.

"HUMAN CAPITAL" FORMATION

Just as there are well-defended scientific, academic, and public policy arguments about the whys and wherefores of physical capital formation and about the efficacy and appropriateness of sundry social technologies, there are arguments about how best to invest in human beings. Basically these questions focus on investments in health, welfare, education, and training. Although the details of these arguments are hotly disputed in national legislatures no less than in academic settings, few will take exception to the proposition that for industrialism to work, conventional capital investments must be accompanied by public and private investments in people. There are lively disputes among manpower economists and others about the social and personal rates of economic return on such investments, but the disputes are over technical-analytical details, not over the principle involved.

Consider that there has been a most important and interesting debate for well over a decade, among manpower specialists, over the appropriate discount rates to be applied in calculating the life-time income streams of differentially educated persons, over the relative roles of their ability and their educational

---

USSR, see Barrington J. Moore, *Terror and Progress: USSR* (Cambridge, Mass.: Harvard University Press, 1953). Each of these sectors, Moore points out, are organized about different logics and interests that affect the characters and capacities of their respective structures.

33. Note that we use qualifying words to avoid giving the impression that technology is totally determinative. For a brief discussion, see Smelser, *The Sociology of Economic Life*; and William A. Form, *Problems of an Industrial Society* (New York: McGraw-Hill, 1968), pp. 39–83.

achievements in determining personal income returns, and over the validity of the use of incomes allocated to differentially educated persons as an indirect measure of education's productivity in a society. There has in short, been a spirited debate over what education's economic value really is, and over the optimal (and the equitable) distribution of whatever education's product is conceived to be. The terms of the debate bear directly on students, a fact that assures that the topic runs little risk of being sidetracked as an overly "academic" one, as annual discussions of tax credits for tuition expenditures have demonstrated.

In recent times it has been mainly economists who have concerned themselves with the question of economic development's manpower prerequisites, but the issue relates to an old sociological chestnut. Thus a long-time sociological question reemerged in 1962 when two economists, Denison and T. Schultz, reported separate but very similar estimates of the proportion of U.S. economic growth attributable to investments in education. These investigations revolved about the fact that international differences in the growth of national income and in growth of per capita income could not be as readily attributed to differences in the more familiar physical forms of capital investments as the received wisdom suggested: Nations with similar investments in physical capital have in fact exhibited markedly different growth rates.[34]

Put another way, the fact that high rates of capital formation by themselves do not necessarily produce high economic growth rates has led students of growth (1) to emphasize, instead, the manner in which capital is accumulated, produced, and utilized in their discussions of growth, and (2) to point to what one of them characterizes as the "host of economic and social conditions which sometimes permit attainment of high rates of growth with little capital, but at other times impede the growth inducing effect of even large amounts of capital."[35]

It is noteworthy that Professor Kuznets, whose recognition of the "host of . . . social conditions" underlying growth is based on a careful review of historical trends in capital formation, first invented and developed the concept of gross national product, the measure of the value of a nation's total output of goods and services. The GNP concept, by now a familiar one, does not, for example, for a variety of reasons, include the value of the "work"—the productive efforts—involved in raising children. The exclusion is noteworthy because Professor Kuznets would unquestionably recognize the extraordinary importance of the labors that contribute to the formation of "human capital"

---

34. Edward F. Denison, "The Sources of Economic Growth in the United States and the Alternatives Before Us," supplementary paper no. 13 (New York: Committee for Economic Development, 1962); and Theodore W. Schultz, "Investment in 'Human Capital,'" *American Economic Review*, 51 (1961), 1–17.

35. Cited in Moore, *The Impact of Industry*, p. 26, from Simon Kuznets, "Quantitative Aspects of the Economic Growth of Nations: VI. Long-term Trends in Capital Formation Proportions," supplement to *Economic Development and Cultural Change*, 9, 4 (July 1961), 56.

in the family, even were we to consider only the inculcation of language skills in children as the family's greatest "input."

Mention of the GNP omission helps direct attention to one cluster of the social conditions alluded to by Professor Kuznets. Thus, child-rearing processes will facilitate economic growth more or less to the degree—in modern terms—to which clusters of economically relevant attitudes, aptitudes, values, and skills are imparted to and cultivated in society's neophytes on their way to the adult roles they will fill. The general influence of schools in these respects is, of course, well known. There is room, however, for significant debate about the *degree* of education's influence and about the reversibility, through education, of traits generated by preschool experiences that are rather less than more conducive to the fulfillment of role demands in a modern industrial society.[36] The formulation of the more general question by modern economists is not unfamiliar to sociologists, whose studies of economic development have long been cast along the lines staked out first by Karl Marx and later by the German economic historian and sociologist, Max Weber, and by Emile Durkheim.

It was Weber's view, contra Marx, that capitalism emerged as, when, and where it did, with the substantial assistance of the Protestant ethic. This ethic was conceived by Weber as a cluster of beliefs anchored in Puritanism, beliefs about the preconditions for salvation and the nature of sin that simultaneously made a highly regarded virtue of the economic necessity for work and for saving. Specifically, Weber rejected Marxian notions of ideologies as simply apologetics, so to speak, for the interests of actors within different segments or "economic sub-structures." It was Weber's view that the ideological tenents organic to predestrinarian religion could serve as powerful social mechanisms in their impacts on the motivations of sizable population segments. Weber thus added to the other prerequisites for capitalist growth he had identified—like orderly and therefore predictable political-legal systems—the subscription of critical population groups to out-and-out preachments regarding the virtues of hard work, the deferred gratification of hedonistic impulses, and the saving, the mobilization of capital, the results from such efforts and sacrifices.

Very few social scientists outside of economics have pursued the Marxian and Weberian initiatives in respect of the "prerequisites" question with anything like rigorous empirical methods. Most pertinent in the immediate context is the question of how social systems bent upon industrializing (or bent upon maintaining, in later periods, the momentum of their growth) secure from their populations the appropriate combination of behavior patterns that are consonant with modernization in general, and with industrialization in particular. In the modern age, meantime, there has been considerable todo in the U.S., in western Europe, and in the USSR about the problematic consequences for industrial society of the allegedly errant ways of youth, of the demise of the

---

36. See Orion White, Jr. and Gideon Sjoberg, "The Emerging 'New Politics' in America," in M. Donald Hancock and Gideon Sjoberg (eds.), *Politics in the Post-Welfare State* (New York: Columbia University Press, 1972).

so-called work ethic, and the hostile attitudes toward economic growth by adherents to a "counterculture perspective."

**Beliefs, Structures, and
Concomitant Variations**

Weber postulated the need for an "ethos," a "geist," a "spirit" like the one he inventively and perceptively captured in his notion of the spirit of capitalism.[37] While few social scientists would impute the same weight to this spirit that Weber accorded it in his comparative sociological investigation of economic development, most are disinclined to write off, entirely, the role of the types of population predispositions that favor industrialization and modernization.

In one of the most popular theories of the early 1960s great weight was assigned to the needs, transmitted through the child-rearing process, for achievement: Variations in the economic development of nations can be explained, according to the view presented by McClelland in 1961 to variations in the numbers of persons a population produces with highly developed "needs for achievement."[38] A scant year after McClelland's essentially social-psychological thesis was presented, Hagen, an economist, argued that economic theories of growth were peculiarly fragile or peculiarly removed from reality . . ."[39] and that the ". . . analysis of societies in an analysis of human behavior, and such analysis which omits the clues provided by current personality theory is unnecessarily crippled."[40] Hagen aspired to develop, "piece by piece, a fully defined model of society, a model which stresses the chain of causation from social structure through parental behavior to childhood environment and then that from childhood environment through personality to social change."[41] With the formal assistance of leading American social scientists, he applied this model first to traditional society and then to the process of transition from traditional conditions to economic growth.[42]

Efforts like those by McClelland and Hagen are both bold and inventive but they are flawed because of their dependence on highly schematic historical materials. Such dependence denies analysts the opportunity to test the degrees

---

37. Max Weber, *The Protestant Ethic and the Spirit of Capitalism* (trans. Talcott Parsons) (New York: Scribner's, 1958).

38. See David C. McClelland, *The Achieving Society* (Princeton, N.J.: Van Nostrand, 1961).

39. Everett E. Hagen, *On the Theory of Social Change* (Homewood, Ill.: Dorsey Press, 1962), p. 36

40. Ibid., p. 5.

41. Ibid., p. 9.

42. Ibid.

and types of social changes, like modernization and industrialization, that are incident to prior changes in individuals' psychological structures, and in their propensities. Such models are suggestive of the processes by which the human social psychological prerequisites to industrialization are met in smaller or greater degree and equally suggestive of explanations for variations in developmental styles and growth rates because they elevate psychological propensities into prime causes of change, but these causes are not vulnerable to rigorous scientific study; The policy implications to which they point are accordingly not clear.

An alternative model, proposed by Inkeles, is more firmly grounded because it shifts attention from personal propensities as causes of social change, and from historically important social changes, to the contemporary impact of social change on the individual.[43] The general problem is to identify how far, and in precisely what manner, individuals' psyches are altered as a consequence of their exposures to social institutions. Thus one may ask whether the democratic, fascistic, or communistic patterns of industrialization[44] are linked to equivalent personality configurations in particular populations, a question that has concerned many among the world's literate people in the wake of Hitler's rise to power[45] and in the face of recurrent east-west tensions.

Inkeles' logic is straightforward: The greater are individuals' exposure to modernizing institutions, the more likely they will be, by disposition, to have a sense of personal efficacy and to be open to new experiences; the more hospitable they should be to the *values* of planning and fixed schedules; the more they should show an interest in current events and in acquiring knowledge of public figures and their doings; the more they should strive for economic-occupational success; and the more they should have such affective qualities as optimism and trust.[46] A six-nation study permitted extensive tests of this formulation, and the results were essentially consistent with the view that

---

43. Alex Inkeles, "Continuity and Change in the Interaction of the Personal and Sociocultural Systems," in Bernard Barber and Alex Inkeles (eds.), *Stability and Social Change* (Boston, Mass.: Little, Brown, 1971), p. 275 (emphases in original).

44. For an assessment of the various crystallizations of political and legal arrangements of different strata in societies emerging from the early stages of economic development associated with each of these ideologies, see Barrington Moore, *Social Origins of Dictatorship and Democracy: Lord and Peasant in the Making of the Modern World* (Boston: Beacon Press, 1966). For alternative assessments see Richard A. Peterson, *The Industrial Order and Social Policy* (Englewood Cliffs, N.J.: Prentice-Hall, 1973), pp. 11-32.

45. See, for example, Erich Fromm, "Individual and Social Origins of Neurosis," in Clyde Kluckhohn and Henry A. Murray (eds.) *Personality in Nature, Society, and Culture* (New York: Knopf, 1949), p. 409. For an assessment of social science findings on the American "character" and their implications for the nation's structure and functioning, see David M. Potter, *People of Plenty: Economic Abundance and the American Character* (Chicago: Univeristy of Chicago Press, 1954).

46. Inkeles, "Continuity and Change."

certain institutions central to the definition of "modern" and "traditional" society do influence the personal psychological systems of individuals. Thus, exposure to urban living does not significantly produce individual modernization, nor does "the vigor with which an individual holds to his kinship obligations, nor the inclination to practice his religion, decline markedly with increasing contact with modernizing institutions."[47] On another side, however, the effects of formal education and factory experiences are notably "modernizing" in the effects. Indeed, the factory is second only to formal schooling in producing psychological changes among adults.

It is clear that we are not able, with such findings, to address questions regarding either the prime historical causes of, prerequisites for, or obstacles to modernization and industrialization. Nor do such findings help us to dispose entirely of many questions regarding variations among social structures, since nations differ in the degree of their institutional modernization. The fact, meanwhile, that no traditional society bent upon modernization need start from scratch, that there are numerous templates available to modern nation builders and industrializing elites, reduces somewhat the significance of causal questions having to do with industrialism's prerequisites. To put it another way, comparative studies provide us with a model for studying industrial societies *in being*, if they do not instruct us in methods for *starting* the modernization-industrialization process; They help us to forecast separately the consequences of industrialism in the narrow sense, and the consequences of modernization, more generally. These forecasts, in turn, are of relevance to understanding economic policy prospects, international trade relations, and the quality of relationships between native populations and those who lend funds to, invest in, or advise these population's economic developers.

The evidence suggests, for example, that industrial modernization, once underway, can help societies to generate *both* the traits in people required for further industrial development and perhaps (and as interestingly) some of the very traits that lead industrial citizens to tame or temper—and even traduce—those elements of industrial life they come, eventually, to contest. Inkeles thus offers the following suggestive answer to romantic critics of industrialization suggested by his findings:

> There is a widespread belief, almost a fundamental conviction among many intellectuals, that the process of industrialization inevitably brings with it great, indeed excessive, social disorganization, the disruption of social ties, and the consequent disorganization of the individual. . . . Our belief is that work in industry not only could be, but in many parts of the world actually was, an educational and liberalizing influence on the men who experienced it. We feel that it has the capacity to broaden their

---

47. Ibid., p. 277; Alex Inkeles, "The Role of Occupational Experience," in C. S. Brembeck and T. J. Thompson, *New Strategies for Educational Development* (Lexington, Mass: D.C. Heath, 1973), pp. 97-98.

horizon, to increase their initiative. to widen their participation in society, even to increase their sense of personal worth and dignity.[48]

Inkeles' research and related research on the modernization of institutions by Lerner, Hirschman, Adelman and Morris, Liebenstein, Coleman et al., and by Lipset[49] directs our attention to many problematic issues attending the mobilization of human resources that are of an essentially sociological and social-psychological character. To begin merely to identify these problematic issues is already to go well beyond the economists' formulations of these issues in terms of the narrower human capital or the physical capital formation approaches mentioned earlier. The latter approaches focus on the most obvious of the social arrangements that are implicated in the course of modernization and industrialization, but they beg questions of social and social-psychological import. To broaden the questions is not, of course, to disallow the view favored in economic analyses of education's role, for example. Thus it is clear that industrial operations require that a large number of citizens can read, write and calculate and that a goodly number can deal at high levels of abstraction with very complex materials.[50]

Policy makers will find no sure guide in the social science literature, however, on how much schooling is required for the nonprofessional jobs in an industrial economy. There is some evidence that the elevation in education requirements for jobs in the period 1950-1968 was more a reflection of employers' and thus others' beliefs that if a little education is good, more simply has to be better, than it was a reflection of hard evidence on the subject.[51] The

48. Alex Inkeles, "Becoming Modern" in et al., 2, 3 (1970), 59-60.

49. Daniel Lerner, with L. W. Persner, *The Passing of Traditional Society* (New York: Free Press, 1958); A. O. Hirschman, *The Strategy of Economic Development* (New Haven, Conn.: Yale University Press, 1958); Adelman and Morris, *Society, Politics and Economic Development* p. 49 ff.; Harvey Liebenstein, *Economic Backwardness and Economic Growth* (New York: John Wiley, 1957); J. S. Coleman (ed.), *Education and Political Development* (Princeton, N.J.: Princeton University Press, 1965); S. M. Lipset, "Some Social Requisites of Democracy: Economic Development and Political Legitimacy," *American Political Science Review*, 53 (March 1959), 69-105.

50. For basic statements on the subject see Frederick Harbison and Charles K. Myers, *Education, Manpower and Economic Growth* (New York: McGraw-Hill, 1964); E. F. Denison, *The Sources of Economic Growth in the United States* (New York: Committee for Economic Development, 1962); Theo. W. Schultz, "Reflections on Investment in Man," Supplement, October 1962, *Journal of Political Economy*, 70, Part 2 (1962), 1 ff; OECO Study Group on the Economies of Education, *The Residual Factor and Economic Growth* (Paris 1964); Gary Becker, *Human Capital* (New York: Columbia University Press, 1964).

51. For some reasonably reliable estimates of the relationships between real and putative changes in job requirements and thus for educational credentials in this period, see Ivar Berg, *Education and Jobs: The Great Training Robbery* (New York: Praeger, 1970). Updated estimates (1960-1975), and projections are reported in Ivar Berg, Marcia Freedman, and Michael Freeman, *Managers and Work Reform: A*

personal returns to higher education have recently begun to decline, a fact that suggests that some education per se, as evidence of either real abilities or as a "screening" device, has limited value.[52] The implications of the educational achievements being "underutilized," a formulation that avoids the unfortunate term "overeducated," will be explored later.

CONCLUSION

One of the major themes of this and the preceding chapter has been that industrial development both borrows from and contributes to the more general process of modernization and modernism. A second theme holds that the survival quotient of a nation's preindustrial cultural heritage, its older values, and even a number of its institutions, its values, its norms, and its roles is higher than might be inferred from an overly deterministic view of the impacts of complex machines, of modern production methods, and of modern distribution techniques. In general the older ways of a society are adapted to newer imperatives though substantial changes in some of a people's older ways can occur over relatively long periods of time.

Next, societies are often usefully conceived, in heuretical terms, to be systems in the Newtonian-mechanical sense.[53] The further implication is often drawn from such a conception that social systems, as aggregates of subsystems, may be disaggregated, that they may be readily divided up into functionally interdependent parts, for purposes of either analysis or policy making. When the heuretical notion is pushed to its logical extreme, however, the metaphor of a mechanical system fails us for the implied imagery simply does not square very well with the palpable fractionation in social systems documented in the work of social analysts.[54] Consider, in this connection, that factories in Inkeles' six-nation study—essentially economic organizations—engender social, political,

---

Limited Engagement (New York: Free Press, 1978), ch. 6. For a neo-Marxist critique of the use of education by American employers, see Samuel Bowles and Herbert Gintis, *Schooling in Capitalist America* (New York: Basic Books, 1975).

52. See Richard B. Freeman, *The Overeducated American* (New York: Academic Press, 1976). For a recent review of the entire economic issue and a critique of the assumed role of education as a "screening" device for employers, see Mark Blaug, "The Empirical Status of Human Capital Theory: A Slightly Jaundiced Survey," *Journal of Economic Liberation*, 14 (September 1973), 827–55. For an analysis in which actual job requirements are juxtaposed with the educational achievements of the labor force and the resulting underutilization of American's educational achievements in sociological and economic terms, see Ivar Berg, Marcia Freedman, and Michael Freeman, *Managers and Work Reform: A Limited Engagement* (New York: Free Press, 1978), ch. 6.

53. See Talcott Parsons, *The Social System* (New York: Free Press, 1964).

54. N. Smelser, *The Sociology of Economic Life*, 2nd ed. (Englewood Cliffs, N.J.: Prentice-Hall, 1976), esp. pp. 159–64.

and psychological predispositions having to do with many more aspects and subsets of society than those bearing alone upon production. It is especially noteworthy that factory experiences augment those of formal education in generating what are in some degree liberal progressive political attitudes, attitudes often linked to the urge for reforms in the ways in which industrial wealth, political power, and social welfare are distributed in a society. Indeed these attitudes can also inspire urges that manifest themselves in out-and-out conflicts in society. Preindustrial and industrial[55] values, institutions, roles and norms thus interact in ways that must contribute to modesty in all but the least responsible of policy advisors among social analysts.

One reasonably responsible way to avoid the obstacles to clean decisive prescriptions for conducting the industrialization process is simply (1) to stress the considerable interplay among industrializing and modern forces in society; (2) to emphasize the constant interpenetrations of social systems' institutional and structural components; but (3) to urge upon readers the proposition that there are limited degrees of variations in the separate social, cultural, and psychological realms in a given society. The effect of following such a route is effectively to beg many of the vexed questions of causes and effects and to seek to discover, instead, the ranges of smaller diversities in larger unities. As we descend from the analytical heights from which we made our observations in this and the first chapter, it is judicious to avoid problematical simplifications rather than to mislead ourselves by formulations (or by imagery) suggesting more linear relationships among institutions-in-flux. We should thus resist the implication that there are highly limited degrees of "fit" among discrete clusters of population traits, and among the key features of social structures in industrial systems. Thus we may focus on a series of institutional arrangements common to industrial nations and content ourselves with assessments that are less directed to the detailed isolation of causes and effects than to the contingent quality of the grosser relationships among industrial societies' institutions, and among their populations' and their structures' traits. It is to these arrangements that we turn in the next chapter.

---

55. The question of whether some industrial societies become what has recently been termed "postindustrial" societies will detain us in the concluding chapter.

CHAPTER 3
OCCUPATIONS AND INDUSTRIAL STRUCTURE

Few of us deal directly with the issues joined in chapters 1 and 2, the majority of citizens being content to let elected and appointed officials and the leaders of industry, labor, and other major collectivities in the social system stake out the main directions of our industrial social systems. We are a good deal less sanguine, however, about specifically distributive questions. Most of us have reasonably well formed conceptions about the degrees of essential justice and equity in the ways in which our society's output of goods and services are allocated among social-economic sectors, segments, and strata in the system, the overall character of the system aside. We have fairly well developed ideas, in short, about our economic interests, and our individual rights, privileges, and immunities.

Our interests in the specifically distributive correlates of the industrial system reflect focal concerns about the returns distributed to occupations, about the effects of technological and related changes on our jobs, about the framework of rules within which the "system" operates day by day, and about our numerous governments' roles in affecting, at least, the character of all of these social tangibles. These interests and concerns, moreover, are not shelved between elections. Thus while there may be considerable consensus on the overall versions of industrialism favored in a nation, there are larger and smaller disagreements about the nittier and grittier questions at the middle levels of social analysis—disagreements that occur on an almost daily basis in relations among owners, managers, regulators, buyers, sellers, and employees.

There is, regrettably, no readily available model of the institutional arrangements on the social terrain that comprehends the linkages tying producers and social product on the one hand, to worker and consumer beneficiaries in industrial societies on the other. There is, in short, no convenient intellectual or theoretical apparatus that helps us to organize our thinking about the *detailed* ways in which equity, justice, fairness, and efficiency are to be served *within* the vague "social contracts," the social consensus, the loose agreements that prevail in an industrial society. Short of such a model, but suggestive of the issues that need to be pursued in the ultimate construction of such a model, is the outline that guided nearly 90 social scientists who set out in 1952 to identify the contingent relationships among social, political, and economic structures and, thereby, to uncover what they conceived to be the main "logics of industrialization."[1] Although it would be fatuous to attempt to distill the contents of the three dozen books and an even larger number of scholarly articles generated by a formidable international intellectual cadre, it is useful to outline the themes emanating from this exhaustive multidisciplinary effort to identify the correlates of industrialization, and to augment the discussion with others' findings. Thus, it is pertinent to consider some of the main traits of the occupational structures in our industrial society, and especially the role of technology and technological change in shaping these structures. It is also pertinent to examine the interplay of social and technical factors in the allocation of occupational roles, the "web of rules" governing work, the emergent role of government, and the character of industrialism's impact on community structure. These are all issues that are joined, quite visibly, before industrial citizens' very eyes.

THE WORK FORCE

Although industrialization may follow different patterns in respect of details, as we have already noted, Dunlop and his colleagues identify the central elements of what they term the "logic of industrialization." Their summary description of the first of these elements merits close attention:

> . . . a concentrated, disciplined industrial work force with new skills, a wide variety of jobs and occupations, and a hierarchy of skill levels

---

1. See the final report of the Inter-University Study of Human Resources in National Development: John T. Dunlop, Frederick H. Harbison, Clark Kerr, and Charles Myers, *Industrialism and Industrial Man Reconsidered: Some Perspectives on a Study over Two Decades of the Problems of Labor and Management in Economic Growth* (Princeton, N.J.: The Inter-University Study of Human Resources in National Development, 1975), pp. 6-40. This slim volume contains a detailed project bibliography. For a far longer discussion of their own version of many of the notions pursued here, see Clark Kerr, John T. Dunlop, Frederick H. Harbison, and Charles A. Myers, *Industrialism and Industrial Man* (London: Penguin Press, 1973). This is the most up-to-date version of four English editions, the first of which appeared in 1960. The Penguin edition contains a valuable "Postscript to Industrialism and Industrial Man," first published separately in *International Labor Review*, 103, 6, (June 1971).

OCCUPATIONS AND INDUSTRIAL STRUCTURE   59

broadly distributed through the work force . . . [and] the necessity of frequent changes in the skills, responsibilities and occupations of the work force as a consequence of the dynamic science and technology that accompanies industrialization, leading to a more mobile and open society.[2]

Tables 3-1 and 3-2 provide the most current capsule data for the U.S. bearing upon several of the points in the cited passage.

It is noteworthy that where 1 of every 4 U.S. workers was in agriculture in 1920, only 1 in 25 was thus occupied in 1970. The fact that agriculture is highly mechanized and otherwise made more efficient, by the use of potent fertilizers and pesticides, for example, is one that needs to be stressed. Thus agricultural workers, especially family workers, have declined in absolute, as well as in relative terms, from nearly 5 to 1.5 million, while the man-hours required for farm production has been reduced in the period 1950-1975 by two-thirds.[3] Somewhat the same may be said about the mining industry which, like agriculture, is a far more productive industry than it was even as recently as 1960. Indeed, coal output has increased by more than 40 percent since 1960,[4] while the ranks of coal miners have been thinned by nearly 22 percent.[5]

Noteworthy also, however, is the stable character of the proportion of employed persons needed in the manufacturing sector of the American economy over a 70-year period. This sector, like agriculture and mining, nevertheless can also produce at far higher levels—thus with fewer people-per-unit of output—nowadays because of the increased productivity of workers. In all, the increases in productivity reflect investments in people, across-the-board, as well as increases in physical capital formation, refinements in social technology, and improvements in transportation, communications, and in materials-handling methods.

Next, we may note that during the most recent 50-year period it is the so-called service sector, not the goods producing sectors, that has come to absorb the bulk of the better than four-fold increase in the U.S. labor force's numbers, a point we considered in a somewhat different perspective in chapter 1. At first blush it may seem a bit strange that it is the service sector, the relatively least bureaucratic, the least union-organized, the least "large-scale," the least mechanized, the least high-energy-consuming, and the most labor intensive sector of an industrial economy that gains most rapidly as an industrial society matures! These sectoral traits, after all, are the opposite of those that come most readily to our minds when we think stereotypically of industrialized societies,

---

2. Dunlop et al., *Industrialism and Industrial Man Reconsidered*, p. 6.

3. U.S. Bureau of the Census, *Statistical Abstract of the United States: 1976*, 97th ed. (Washington, D.C.: Government Printing Office, 1976), Table 1106, p. 653.

4. Ibid., Table 1200, p. 705.

5. Ibid., Table 1207, p. 710.

Table 3-1 Occupation as a Percentage of Industry Group, 1970

Occupational category and group	GOODS-PRODUCING					SERVICE-PRODUCING					TOTAL OCCUPATIONAL CATEGORY AND GROUP	
	Agriculture, forestry, and fisheries	Mining	Construction	Manufacturing	Total goods-producing	Business services	Personal services	Transportation, public utilities, and communications	Health, education, research, and government	Total service-producing	Percent	Number (000) omitted
White-collar												
Professional and Technical	2.9	10.6	4.5	9.9	8.4	7.5	3.1	7.6	42.2	18.6	14.2	11,351
Managers and Administrators	0.9	6.0	9.5	5.2	5.5	14.7	12.6	7.3	5.9	10.0	10.5	6,371
Sales Workers	0.4	0.1	0.8	2.7	2.2	19.1	18.0	1.3	0.3	10.0	6.2	5,445
Clerical Workers	1.8	9.6	6.3	12.5	10.2	35.7	14.2	24.3	23.5	22.4	17.4	13,748
Total White-collar	6.0	26.3	21.1	30.3	26.3	77.0	47.9	40.5	71.9	61.0	48.3	36,915
Blue-collar												
Craft Workers	1.5	25.0	55.9	19.7	23.9	5.8	9.9	22.1	3.3	8.1	12.9	10,609
Operatives	2.0	42.1	8.8	43.1	33.2	8.7	10.3	26.0	1.8	8.6	17.7	13,456
Laborers, Except Farm	6.4	4.1	13.2	4.6	6.2	3.2	4.6	7.3	1.2	3.5	4.7	3,431
Total Blue-collar	9.9	71.2	77.9	67.4	63.3	17.7	24.8	55.4	6.3	20.2	35.3	27,496
Service Workers	0.6	1.5	1.0	2.3	1.9	5.3	27.3	3.1	21.8	18.8	12.4	9,773
Farm Workers	83.5	—	—	—	8.5	—	—	—	—	—	4.0	2,367
Total Percent	100.0	100.0	100.0	100.0	100.0	100.0	100.0	100.0	100.0	100.0	100.0	76,553
Total Number	2,840,488	630,788	4,572,235	19,837,208	27,880,719	8,221,668	17,507,255	5,186,101	17,712,856	48,627,880	—	76,553
Industry Group Percent	3.7	0.8	6.0	25.9	(36.5)	10.7	22.9	6.8	23.1	(63.5)	100.0	—

Sources: Adapted by Paul D. Montagna, Occupations and Society: Toward a Sociology of the Labor Market New York: John Wiley, 1977), pp. 58–59, from: U.S. Department of Commerce, Bureau of the Census, Detailed Characteristics: United States Summary, 1970 Census of Population (Washington, D.C.: Government Printing Office, 1973), Table 232, pp. 788–97; and Department of Labor, Bureau of Manpower Administration, Manpower Report to the President, 1973 (Washington, D.C.: Government Printing Office, 1973), p. 142.

Table 3-2 Profile of the American Labor Force, 1900-1980 (in percent)

MILLIONS OF WORKERS	(29) 1900	(49) 1930	(62) 1950	(67) 1960	(79) 1970	(95) 1980
White-collar						
Professional and Technical	4	7	9	11	14	16
Managers and Proprietors	6	7	8	11	11	10
Clerical	3	9	12	15	17	18
Sales	5	6	7	6	6	6
Total	18	29	36	43	48	50
Blue-collar						
Skilled Workers	10	13	14	13	13	13
Semiskilled Workers	13	16	20	18	18	16
Unskilled Workers	13	11	7	6	4	4
Total	36	40	41	37	35	33
Service Workers						
Private Household Workers	5	4	3	3	2	a
Service Workers, Other than Private Household	4	6	8	9	10	a
Total	9	10	11	12	12	14
Farm Workers						
Farmers and Farm Managers	20	12	7	4	2	a
Farm Laborers and Foremen	18	9	4	4	2	a
Total	38	21	11	8	4	3

[a] No figures given.

Sources: Adapted by Paul Montagna, Occupations and Society: Toward a Sociology of Labor Markets (New York: John Wiley, 1977), p. 22, from: David L. Kaplan and M. Claire Casey, Occupational Trends in the United States, 1900 to 1950, Bureau of the Census, Working Paper No. 5 (Washington, D.C.: U.S. Department of Commerce, 1958); Statistical Abstract of the United States, 1961, and Statistical Abstract of the United States, 1971 (Washington, D.C.: Government Printing Office); U.S. Department of Labor, Bureau of Manpower Administration, Manpower Report of the President, 1972 (Washington, D.C.: Government Printing Office, 1972), p. 259; U.S. Department of Labor, Bureau of Labor Statistics, The U.S. Economy in 1980 (Washington, D.C.: Government Printing Office, 1970), Bulletin 1673.

with their mass production industries, their large conglomerate structures, their complex organizations and their blue-collar hordes. In fact, however, one must go back more than two decades, the entire lifetime of the average American college undergraduate, to come upon a year in which blue-collar workers outnumbered white-collar workers in America.[6]

It is indeed the case, then, as Dunlop et al. write, that one of the significant hallmarks of industrial societies is frequent change. In early developmental stages, agricultural workers are both displaced and redistributed; in the middle stages the urbanized, factory-type blue-collar force expands very substantially. In the later stages it is the service sector—especially government—that grows most explosively. Demographic changes are accordingly attributable, in significant measure, to the byproducts of material technology, including machinery, communications, and transportation, and to byproducts of intellectual and social technology. Furthermore, as Zald has pointed out, material technology "enables the invention of new products and leads to the creation of specialized organizations to manufacture and market them."

> Increased levels of productivity, higher per capita income, and, through increased discretionary income [i.e., the income available for household and personal expenditures after the purchase of food and shelter], the support of organizations and products that a poorer society could not afford are general effects of both material and social technology.[7]

Occupational Structures

The state of technology not only affects the distribution of labor force participants as between agricultural and nonagricultural activities and between "goods" and "services" sectors, but affects the distribution of persons within these sectors, as well, as the data in Table 3-2 clearly suggest. Tables 3-1 and 3-2 also indicate that significant changes take place in the kinds of particular occupations that emerge—or virtually disappear—as production and work processes change within the "goods" and "services" sectors. Thus one finds the old-time crotch sawyers (who split the hindquarters of cattle) only in small slaughter houses, as the large meat packing companies have turned increasingly to machines in the processing of beef, pork, and sheep carcasses. Bookkeepers have been displaced by accountants skilled in the collection and analysis of

---

6. Women undergraduates, resentful over the discriminatory treatment often accorded their peers in the labor force, will take only slight solace (given the disproportionately large numbers of women in most paid clerical and sales jobs) from the fact that blue-collar males outnumbered white-collar males by 15 percent even in 1972; there were, meanwhile, more than four times as many white-collar as blue-collar women in that year. See *Statistical Abstract of the United States: 1972*, p. 230.

7. Mayer N. Zald, *Occupations and Organizations in American Society: The Organization-Dominated Man?* (Chicago: Marham Publishing, 1971), pp. 6-7.

complicated tax, organizational control, and wage data. And engineers, with costly academic degrees, have displaced hundreds of thousands of technical school graduates who are still qualified, for example, to perform as draughtsmen.

Collectively, these changes are among the "constants" in industrial societies and involve highly intellectualized techniques as well as innovations in the specific ways work is accomplished in offices, mines, mills, and foundaries, in road-grading projects, in machine tool shops, on assembly lines, and in laboratories. On one side, these changes force questions about the most equitable and efficient ways of mobilizing work force cadres competent to perform skillfully in the jobs that emerge within the gross occupational classifications.

We mention *both* equity and efficiency in connection with *both* job displacement and the creation of new job opportunities for the important reason that earnings from their work is the major source of income for most persons and for the dependent families of many breadwinners. Their social-economic circumstances, in turn, have strategic implications for the attitudes, activities, and actions of persons and the interest groups to which they belong,[8] a proposition that appears to hold up well even when tested across national boundaries.[9] The upshot is that while technology and technological changes are not, in and of themselves determinative of them, they are among the important components in influencing a society's values as well as its political and social structures. Through their impacts on occupational structures, occupational tasks, and the resulting claims, rights, entitlements, and benefits that accrue to the members of occupations and their dependents, these changes also influence the conduct of a society's institutions.

One of the arguably grosser effects of technological developments, by virtue of the skill demands they imply, is to differentiate a nation's markets for labor into segments of differentially protected or sheltered groups. Put another way, the differentiation of occupations is linked to the differences in the skills accompanying "good" and "bad" jobs. Whether one should adopt the premise, for analytical purposes, that industrial societies are thus "dualistic," or that these societies are more fractionated and differentiated than a two-way

---

8. For an overview of occupation's and stratification's socially significant correlates, see Edward B. Harvey, *Industrial Society: Structures, Roles and Relations* (Homewood, Ill.: Dorsey Press, 1975), pp. 291–331. See also, for example, R. Hodge, P. Siegel, and P. Rossi, "Occupational Prestige in the U.S., 1925-1963; *American Journal of Sociology*, 60 (November 1964), 286–307; C. K. Riesman, "Birth Control, Culture and the Poor," *American Journal of Orthopsychiatry*, 38 (1968), 693-99; W. Goode, *The Family* (Englewood Cliffs, N.J.: Prentice-Hall, 1972); Melvin Tumin, *Social Stratification* (Englewood Cliffs, N.J.: Prentice-Hall, 1965); and Herbert Hyman, "The Value Systems of Different Classes" in S. M. Lipset and R. Bendix, *Class Status and Power*, 2nd ed. (New York: Free Press, 1966), pp. 488-99.

9. See, for example, Alex Inkeles, "Industrial Man: The Relation of Status to Experience, Perception and Value," *American Journal of Sociology*, 66, 1 (July 1960), 1-31, and A. Inkeles and P. Rossi, "National Comparisons of Occupational Prestige," *American Journal of Sociology*, 61, 4 (January 1956), 329-39.

hierarchical classification suggests, is subject to considerable dispute.[10] There is little dispute, however, over the point that, in general, the more complex the technology and techniques associated with a job, the better the pay, the fringe benefits, and the bargaining power of the incumbent, and the higher the prestige attaching to the job especially in the short and medium runs.

Over the long run, of course, technical changes can reduce the benefits and even the "shelters" of once better situated workers. Thus the members of the different brotherhoods of railroad workers were once the "aristocrats of labor," an aristocracy whose proud place has been completely undermined by the car, the truck, the sea-going tanker, by gas and oil pipelines, and by the large jet-powered airplane.

Skill Hierarchies and Labor Market Stratification

The notions of "good jobs" and "bad jobs," of better and worse situated workers, are useful in considering the circumstances of workers distributed both within and across occupations, and both within and across the individual organizations in which they are employed. The connecting conceptual linkage between and among occupations and organizations may be identified with the fact that workers are differentiated by their skills. Thus employees can be placed in stratified skill hierarchies, usually shaped like pyramids (1) in their own employment settings—a fact that will concern us in chapters 5 and 6, (2) in their occupations more generally, and (3) in both the local and national labor markets in which labor services are sold. In general the circumstances of these skill hierarchies are influenced in similar ways by events in the economy that reverberate across these three levels, though disjunctions in some instances between events in local and national labor markets do occur. Such a disjunction occurred during the recessions of the early 1970s when the overall national demand for many skills, at all levels of the occupational structure, was problematical while the demands for most skills were booming, for example, in most large Texas communities. In general, however, the patterns of labor market developments tend to be similar and pervasive in their consequences; the American economy increasingly takes on the character of an integrated system in which sectoral tremors ripple through the economy.

One consequence of skill differentiation in labor markets is a preoccupation among Americans with increasing their claims to skills that are least vulnerable to risks induced by changing economic circumstances. These claims may be embodied in apprenticeship rules, in government-supported licensing

---

10. For an empirical discussion of the virtual insulation of some from, and the vulnerabilities of others to an economy's ups and downs, and from other changes, see Marcia K. Freedman, *Labor Markets: Segments and Shelters* (Montclair, N.J.: Allenheld, Osmun, 1976). For a more general discussion of theories of labor market stratification in sociological terms, see Paul D. Montagna, *Occupations and Society: Toward a Sociology of Labor Markets* (New York: John Wiley, 1977), pp. 65-96.

arrangements, and in the application to aspirants of formal training requirements and associated accrediting procedures.[11] Americans, like the citizens of other industrial countries, have been notably ambivalent about the application of principles of free competition to the job allocation process. Although American labor unions do more or less affect the experiences of competitors for approximately 23 percent of all jobs held by unionized workers,[12] the overriding majority of Americans' 90-odd million jobs are filled with nonunion employees whose eyes, for all that, are similarly fixed on one or more exclusionary criteria that serve essentially to protect job incumbents. Sometimes, as in the licensing of neurosurgeons, electricians, and teachers, exclusionary criteria may also serve an occupation's or a skill group's clients against incompetent predators. (The hue and cry over successful medical malpractice suits in recent years reminds us, however, that outright charlatans and incompetents are not the only persons who may offend the clients of a fairly scrupulously licensed occupation's members.)

Occupations and Social Group Memberships

In addition to basically legitimate and more or less rational screening devices for jobs and occupations are those that are rooted entirely in the social, the social psychological, and the perceived economic needs of some citizens to discriminate against others, usually minority group members. Thus, immigrant laborers, their so-called guest workers, are disproportionately to be found in the least desirable jobs, for example, in France, Sweden, Norway, and Germany, even as Mexican nationals are obliged to look up, in the U.S., from the lowest rungs on the American occupational ladder. Even more familiar, of course, are the often unhappy occupational circumstances of native American Indians, blacks, and those with Spanish surnames, as well as those of women, "older workers," members of some groups of physically handicapped workers, and youths. The complex mechanics and dynamics of bigotry and discrimination—which are overlapping but not necessarily identical terms—need not detain us in the present context,[13] but it is important to note that the aforementioned groups' members are systematically disadvantaged, compared to members of other population groups, both in terms of the types of skilled jobs to which

---

11. See Harold Orlans et al., *Private Accreditation and Public Eligibility* (Lexington, Mass.: D.C. Heath, 1975) for a history of accrediting developments in the U.S.

12. The number of "union jobs" is not, of course, as great as the number of union members since, except in wartime, not all union members are employed. For detailed breakdowns by industry, state, and by sex, etc. see U.S. Bureau of the Census, *Statistical Abstract of the United States,* 1976, pp. 383-86.

13. For a useful outline of these mechanics and dynamics of prejudice and discrimination, see Metta Spencer, *Foundations of Modern Sociology* (Englewood Cliffs, N.J.: Prentice-Hall, 1976), pp. 266-85.

they gain access and in terms of the security and other returns that accrue to their labors.

These groups' members, for example, are disproportionately under represented in professional and technical groups while persons in clerical, sales, craft, and agricultural jobs are from twice to ten times more likely to suffer unemployment.[14] Montagna has consolidated the detailed unemployment figures, for example, as follows:

> The semiskilled (operatives) and unskilled (nonfarm laborers) have the highest rates of any occupational groups—6.9 percent and 10.3 percent, respectively. In the early 1970s the black-to-white ratio of unemployment stayed at about 1.8 to 1; that is, there were 1.8 black workers unemployed for every white worker. However, it has increased to more than 2 to 1 as unemployment rates have gone up during the mid-1970s. The rate for women is higher than for men: in 1970 it was 5.2 versus 3.9 percent for men. For young people (ages 16 to 24) it was one-one-one-half times the national rate (9 percent). For teenagers, it was 12 percent, twice the national average. Thus, if one happens to be female, nonwhite, and young, one's chances of being among the unemployed are very high. In 1972, the jobless rate for young black teenagers was 33.5 percent; for young black teenage girls it was 38.6 percent.[15]

One one side, the raw statistics on unemployment represent (1) the "frictional" or unavoidable temporary layoffs of workers in seasonal jobs or in industries that shut down for annual model and other production changeovers, and the joblessness of workers who are moving between old and new jobs; (2) the effects of somewhat longer-term shifts in the demands for goods and services among fickle or fashion-conscious consumers; (3) job-displacing technical changes; (4) increased labor force participation rates of particular groups, as in the case of American women in recent years; (5) failures in public and private policies directed at full employment, policies having to do with wages, salaries, governments' expenditures, saving, taxes, investments, and economic regulations and with the resulting levels of confidence among consumers, investors, income earners, and managers.

The allocation of skills, and hence of work benefits, among identifiable population groups, on the other side, represent both real and purported differences in these group members' "human capital" value. These differences, in turn, reflect the discriminatory values and preferences of the citizens of a society as well as objectively demonstrable variations in the economic value, the so-called productivity, of disadvantaged groups. Consider that American blacks

---

14. See data from 1958-1973 in Department of Labor, Bureau of Manpower Administration, *Manpower Report of the President, 1974* (Washington, D.C.: Government Printing Office, 1974), p. 275, Table A-17.

15. Montagna, *Occupations and Society*, p. 83.

as a group are less well educated than their white peers, a difference that reflects many of the other circumstances distinguishing blacks from whites and a difference that accounts for some of the differences in the earnings of blacks and whites. As Thurow points out, the differences in the employment experiences between the two groups have by no means disappeared as a result of the erosion, in recent decades, of political and legal barriers to equality:[16] The fact that blacks (and women, for that matter) have political legal rights does not automatically put them into a competitive position with workers who have traditional entitlements to their jobs through custom, for example, and the benefits that accompany seniority. The theoretical information cost "savings" to white employers who avoid allegedly high risk employees by discriminating against groups whose work attendance records, when aggregated, are slightly higher than others, is not by itself adequate to explain discrimination. The *belief*, however, that a given black applicant's performance will mirror the group's record is of no small relevance to black job applicants' prospects, prospects influenced by the interlocking effects of income, housing, and schooling.

In none of these differentiated realms, absent equal opportunity laws and their enforcement, does the do-it-yourself, individualistic principle operate in accordance with the person-centered conceptualization of occupational and economic success favored in the American myths. As Thurow puts it

> Each type of [race] discrimination makes it easier to enforce other types. Less schooling leads to fewer job skills. . . . Together, all of these forms of discrimination lead to low incomes. . . . Together, they reduce black political power and make schooling discrimination possible. No matter what type of discrimination is examined, it is reinforced by other types. They exist in a system of mutual support. When all viewed together, no white perceives great economic losses from discrimination. Consequently, there are only minor economic pressures to put an end to it.[17]

The story is not fundamentally different when one turns to the differences in earnings of men and women. Thus Bibb and Form have compared the role of differences in the "human capital investments" made in men and women in blue collar labor markets, as discussed in chapter 2, with an eye to identifying the relative roles of these investments and of discriminating hiring and placement practices. The comparison was conducted by equalizing mens' and womens' human capital investments and then distributing women among industry sectors, locations, and occupational groups as men are distributed. They discovered that if women's educational attainments were raised to those of men, these attainments would yield women an added $21 per annum; if women received

---

16. L. Thurow, *Generating Inequality: Mechanisms of Distribution in the American Economy* (New York: Basic Books, 1975), passim.

17. Ibid., pp. 169-70.

vocational training on a par with blue-collar males, they would, in analytical terms, earn another $82. If women suffered no discrimination in their quests for differentially skilled jobs, however, and were thus distributed in locations, sectors, and occupations as men are distributed among them women "might expect an average earnings increase of about $430."[18] Bibb and Form conclude that

> human capital investments are less crucial in the income biographies of blue-collar women than industrial and occupational stratification.[19]

Taking stock, we may state that technology is one important factor in shaping labor markets, but the effects of technology and technological changes may be significantly countered and exaggerated by the practices of individuals and groups, and by the policies and practices of larger collectivities and formally organized public and private agencies. These practices and policies reflect social tastes about the relative places, in value terms, of justice, efficiency, and equity. The tastes in question, along with narrow economic criteria, will significantly influence decisions about how many and what kinds of workers of different skills and backgrounds are needed in the economy, technology aside.[20] These tastes and preferences will also affect the distribution of opportunities for preparation and for entry into jobs and occupations and the conceptions, in society, of the social esteem and thus often the economic value of particular skills. Readers may ponder the question in this context (as Paul Samuelson, the Nobel Prize-winning economist, once urged) of why plastic surgeons have higher incomes than cardiac surgeons.

TECHNOLOGICAL CHANGE

After affirming the strategic role of values in the stratification of occupations and labor markets, and the frequent arguments to which the resulting inequalities give rise, we should point out that social more than technical factors influence the rate of change in the development and application of technological innovations. And social forces are, by definition, caught up in the ways in which the members of occupations and organizations contend with technological changes. To put it differently, technological developments influence social

18. Robert Bibb and William H. Form, "The Effects of Industrial, Occupational, and Sex Stratification on Wages in Blue-Collar Markets," *Social Froces*, 55, 4 (June 1977), 991.

19. Ibid.

20. See Eliot Freidson, "The Division of Labor as Social Interaction" in Marie R. Haug and Jacques Dofny (eds.), *Work and Technology* (Beverly Hills, Calif.: Sage, 1977), pp. 13-25; and Herbert Blumer, *Symbolic Interactionism: Perspective and Method* (Englewood Cliffs, N.J.: Prentice-Hall, 1969).

relations directly to some degree, to be sure, but these developments are not "uncaused causes," for they are themselves shaped by industrial leaders and by industrial citizens. Consider, first, that great concern was expressed in the 1950s, on all sides in the U.S., and in other industrial nations as well, that "automation" would, by the 1970s, become the order of the day. The implications for organizations, for skill hierarchies, and for the work experiences of their management and other members, it was widely argued, would be as radical as they would be rapid. The modern computer, it was further argued, would have especially spectacular direct effects on the worlds of both production and distribution, its widespread employment as a central element in so-called servomechanisms, or tool control systems, quite apart.

As it turns out, "automation" and "computerization" have had relatively few novel social-economic consequences. Put another way, automation has had almost no consequences not noted earlier in the U.S. history in connection with earlier breakthroughs in the mechanical extentions of managers' and workers' skills and capacities. (The impacts of technological changes on managers' careers, on ownership patterns, and upon the experiences of workers will be discussed in chapters 5 and 6.) In the aggregate and in balance, new-fangled technology has increased the productivity of managers and their charges as did old-fangled technological changes. It has, in many instances, also improved the quality of products.

Automation and computerization have, of course, caused specific dislocations in the demands for specific groups of workers, dislocations that have long been noted in conjunction with technological changes. As Simon has pointed out, "society as a whole benefits from increased productivity, but often at the expense of imposing transient costs on a few people."[21] And "transient costs," like costs incident to business failures, are not trivial costs. But as Simon puts it, "The sensible response to this problem is not to eschew the benefits of change; it is rather to take initial steps to shift the burden of the transition from the individual to society;[22] these steps, meanwhile, are among those over which there are likely to be debates, over which specifically distributive values become involved. These steps have been the subject of arguments, in the wake of technological changes, on many of the roads to many of the world's Huddersfields.[23] That we have typically been slow by some standards to take burden-sharing steps is not, however, to concede that the grimmer forecasts about automation's deterministic effects were right! Rather, in the U.S. we tend to move rather circumspectly in dealing with the "external costs" of change, a fact that is echoed in the complaints of those who are immediately victimized. We may accordingly argue that technological change, as such, is as

21. Herbert Simon, *Science*, 195, (March 18, 1977), 1186.

22. Ibid., p. 1188.

23. Ibid. Huddersfield was seen as the "seat" of the Industrial Revolution. See chapter 2.

technological change does, not more and not less; people, not machines, make policies, including policies covering manpower needs, the disposition of workers in work settings, and the care and feeding of those whose skills command no fees.

One can contemplate the possible effects of changes, furthermore, without disproportionate emphases upon discontinuities perceived to attach to large qualitative change in the particular character of an industry's capital equipment. The gradual if relentless quality of the shift of people out of capital-intensive manufacturing production operations comes readily to mind in this context. Indeed, it is the nonmanufacturing or "service" sector, nowadays, that is becoming increasingly capital intensive, as in banking, transportation, and hospital-based health service delivery arrangements. The technological changes in the service sector are typically obscured, however, by the expanded demand there for clerical and kindred workers even as the goods producers have hired more and more service-type workers. The frequently heard phrase, the "post-industrial revolution," offered as a description of the service-oriented society, further distracts attention from the real role of technology in society.

The 1966 report of the National Commission on Technology, Automation and Economic Process provides apposite data. Its authors pointed out that while the pace of technological change had increased after World War II, the increase in the rate of productivity and of productivity's growth—perfectly useful indirect measures of the hard-to-gauge rate of technological change—was not consistent with the assumption that "a veritable technological revolution has occured [through] the *increase* itself is nevertheless substantial."[24] The Commission went on to point out that "Growth at 2 percent a year doubles in 36 years . . . growth at 3 percent a year doubles in about 24 years. The notion that the product of an hour of work can double in 24 years—not much more than half a working lifetime—is quite enough to justify the *feeling* of continuous change that is so much a part of the contemporary environment. The time scale has shrunk visibly,"[25] but is has by no means contracted to the vanishing point.

The Commission, meanwhile, sponsored one and cited another study on the speed with which technological developments move from discovery to commercial application, and concluded that the time gap has indeed been shortened, but the lags involved are not inconsiderable: ". . . major technological studies may wait as long as 14 years before they reach commercial application even on a small scale, and perhaps another 5 years before their impact on the economy becomes large. It seems safe to conclude [in 1966] that most major technological discoveries which will have a significant economic impact within

---

24. *Technology and the American Economy: Report of the National Commission on Technology, Automation and Economic Progress* (Washington, D.C.: Government Printing Office, February 1966), p. 2.

25. Ibid.

the next decade are already at least in a readily identifiable stage of commercial development."[26] Horowitz and Herrnstadt examined detailed job descriptions for five industries for the period 1940-1965—a quarter century—and reported that "There was considerable change in occupational requirements and content, but on balance, it was inconsequential or inconclusive with respect to overall skill levels."[27]

Unfortunately, we have available no more adequate assessment of what innovations are in an "identifiable" but not commercially developed stage now than the forecasters of 1956 had about 1966! It is interesting to note, in this context, that we do not know very much about whether and how technological changes, as such, affect either organizational members generally or occupational groups in particular. Thus Mueller and her colleagues conducted a survey of 2,662 labor force participants in 1967, in accordance with multistage probability sampling techniques, and discovered that the jobs of about 1.5 to 2 million members of the work force—that is to say a scant 2 to 3 percent of all employed Americans—changed to a significant degree by technological changes in the course of a year. Over the five-year period preceding the study, the investigators report, "about 10 percent of the labor force underwent one to more changes in machine technology which (in their view) altered their work significantly."[28] This is not to deny that the members of the labor force are not often buffeted or staggered by changes of other sorts in organizations, that jobs, job classifications, skill hierarchies, disciplinary and supervisory arrangements, work group membership patterns, and organizational rules are not subject to substantial revisions. Indeed, these important issues deserve the separate treatment we will accord them in chapter 6.

Nor do we deny, for example, that many occupations have not been substantially altered in consequence of new equipment. We wish simply to point out that the untoward effects of technological changes are generally selective in their incidence, generally slow-moving, and usually caught up together with parallel

---

26. Ibid.

27. Morris A. Horowitz and Irwin L. Herrnstadt, "Changes in the Skill Requirements of Occupations in Selected Industries," in *The Employment Impact of Technological Change, Appendix Volume II, Technology and the American Economy, Report of the National Commission on Technology, Automation and Economic Progress* (Washington D.C.: Government Printing Office, 1966), p. 287.

28. Eva Mueller et al., *Technological Advance in an Expanding Economy: Its Impact on a Cross-Section of the Labor Force* (Ann Arbor: University of Michigan, Institute for Survey Research, 1969) p. 10. One possible reason for the basically modest amount and slow rate of technological changes: Nearly two-thirds of all dollars expended in the U.S. in 1976 for research and development ("R and D") were spent for development, not for more radically change-making, research activities. See National Science Foundation, *National Patterns of R & D Resources NSF 76-310* (Washington, D.C.: Government Printing Office, 1976), p. vi.

and intervening forces that often temper what might otherwise be the more predictably unsettling correlates of technological changes, per se.

The specifics of public interventions, like the Pension Reform Act of 1975, that facilitate the occupational mobility of afflicted workers by making pensions portable, meanwhile, are not more readily predicted, and some interventions do not even involve formal, macropolicy innovations. Thus locomotive firemen sought to protect themselves against the threats posed by "dieselization," *long* before the railroad managers disowned the old puffing steam locomotive, by rationally exchanging wage demands for employers' promises that firemen would be guaranteed seats on diesel locomotives should these machines ever become the order of the day.

To take two other cases, typographers traded their controls over wages in the printing trades to employers in the early years of the present century, in exchange for work guarantees like the "bogus type rule" which still affords a very few typographers the right to reset advertising matrices prepared and delivered to publishers by advertisers. These guarantees were finally and quite literally bought back from workers in the late 1960s as employers agreed to provide early retirement plans for workers—most of whom were over 50 years of age—who were displaced by "computerized" electrotypesetting machinery. And, in 1960, west coast longshoremen traded away work rules restricting the use of larger sling loads on loading booms, of "containerized" cargo, and of fork-lift trucks in the holds of merchantmen, for profit-sharing arrangements that supported workers' early retirements on the heels of change-induced manpower reductions. In each case the parties shared the fruits of changes. Note, meantime, that the changes in loading procedures on the docks—involving heavier duty booms, cranes, and forklift trucks—were hardly exotic.

To put a blunt point on the matter, American workers and American managers have most often, and most inventively and rationally, adapted existing and bilaterally made arrangements by schemes designed to meet emerging mutual needs. These arrangements are not generally understood by forecasters who overlook the fact that organizational and institutional systems are social systems, systems with histories and, not uncommonly, with well developed *modus operandi* for incorporating many if not all challenges to their systems' integrity, their systems' rationality, and their systems' quality. It is worth noting that the systems permitting the interventions to which we allude are familiarly written off by hard-nosed citizens as work rules protecting "featherbedding." The facts of the needs of the parties, for both change and for rational change-assimilating arrangements, however, support somewhat more complicated if not exactly imaginative interpretations! (We will return to the work rules question in chapter 5.)

In this section we have emphasized a number of essentially nontechnical considerations that must be taken into account in weighing the specific effects of the employment of technical means to productive ends. In the following section we will consider a number of secondary and tertiary developments that help to put industrialism's equipage in even clearer perspective.

OCCUPATIONS, INDUSTRY, AND COMMUNITY

That economic organizations can have great impacts on community life has long been recognized by sociologists. As two noted contemporary industrial sociologists remind us, Karl Marx, Max Weber, Emile Durkheim, and Thorstein Veblen are only among the best known of those who have most forcefully described this impact. They cite one of the founders of the institutional school of economics, Thorstein Veblen,[29] on the subject in the following helpful summary statement:

> Any community may be viewed as an industrial or economic mechanism, the structure of which is made up of what is called its economic institutions. These institutions are habitual methods of carrying on the life process of the community, in contact with the material environment in which it lives. When given methods of unfolding human activity in this given environment have been elaborated in this way, the life of the community will express itself with some facility in these habitual directions.[30]

As Form and Miller make clear, the image of a community orbiting about its economic institutions is, at best, a suggestive one because the life of a community is a composite of many institutional forces.[31] At the same time, the impact of economic institutions in general, and of their modern industrial variants in particular, especially upon occupational and therefore labor force characteristics, may be shown at the community level of social structure in a most dramatic fashion. Consider, in this vein, the graphically descriptive Tables 3-3 and 3-4 which are of particular interest in the present context because the data upon which they are constructed apply to the period immediately *before* America truly became "a service society" in occupational and organizational terms.

By way of background, Form and Miller point out that the size of a community depends largely on the size of its industrial base. This base they conceive as having two parts, the basic activities and the service activities that the basic activities support.[32] The ratios of basic-to-service activities will vary in accordance with cities' sizes and functions and with the classifications used in respect of the two types of activities; in addition, these ratios may vary over

---

29. For present purposes, the perspectives of the institutional school in modern economics may be likened to those of sociologists who concern themselves with macrosocial policies.

30. Cited in William H. Form and Delbert C. Miller, *Industry, Labor and Community* (New York: Harper & Row, 1960), pp. 20-21.

31. Ibid., p. 20.

32. Ibid., pp. 26-27.

Table 3-3 Illustration of the Effect of the Multiplication Factor on Supporting Workers and Population of a Community

POPULATION OF THE COMMUNITY

Basic Workers	100,000	Service Workers	200,000
Dependents	200,000	Dependents	400,000
Total	300,000	Total	600,000
Grand Total	900,000		

ESTIMATED NUMBER OF SERVICE WORKERS REQUIRED IN SOME SELECTED OCCUPATIONS

Jobs	Number	Jobs	Number
Truck Drivers	5,500	Gas Station Attendants	900
Department Store Clerks	5,500	Tailors, Furriers	900
Stenographers, Typists	5,000	Firemen	800
Mechanics, Machinists	5,000	Welfare Workers	800
Bookkeepers, Cashiers	4,000	Cabinet Makers	600
Teachers	4,500	Clergymen	500
Cleaners, Laundrymen	3,500	Dentists	500
Waitresses	3,500	Printers	500
Food Clerks	3,000	Shoe Clerks	500
Carpenters	3,000	Real Estate Agents	400
Painters	2,800	Shoe Repairmen	400
Beauticians, Barbers	2,400	Florists	300
Postmen	2,300	Plasterers	300
Nurses	2,000	Roofers	300
Bank Clerks	1,500	Librarians	300
Cooks	1,500	Photographers	300
Druggists	1,500	Conductors	250
Electricians	1,500	Writers, Editors	250
Watchmen	1,500	Highway Workers	220
Plumbers	1,300	Newsboys	200
Policemen	1,300	Entertainers	200
Insurance Agents	1,200	Architects	100
Phone Operators	1,200		
Musicians	1,100	Outside Services Included:	
Hardward Clerks	1,000	Farmers	40,000
Bakers	1,000	Miners of Raw Materials	
Dressmakers	1,000	Including Fuel	5,000
Lawyers, Judges	1,000	Federal and State Employees	
Doctors	950	Including Armed Forces	24,000

Source: Adapted by William H. Form and Delbert C. Miller, Industry, Labor and Community (New York: Harper & Row, 1960), p. 26, from Better Living (May-June 1954) pp. 10-14. Data represent estimates which are useful for illustrative purposes only.

Table 3-4 Every 100 Jobs in Industry Create These Additional Jobs

Jobs	Percentage	Jobs	Percentage
Bus Drivers	.42	Architects	.06
Department Store Clerks	2.5	Electricians	.22
Lawyers and Judges	.44	Miners	2.2
Waitresses	1.6	Real Estate Agents	.16
Plumbers	.13	Nurses	1.0
Doctors	.57	Shoe Repairmen	.16
Painters	1.0	Teachers	.50
Firemen	.30	Pharmacists	.25
Dressmakers	.44	Editors and Reporters	.25
Bank Clerks	.66	Florists	.13
Stenos, Typists	2.2	Plasterers	.13
Cleaners, Laundrymen	1.6	Mechanics, Machinists	2.2
Carpenters	2.6	Postmen	.50
Musicians	.44	Bookkeepers	2.0
Truck and Tractor Drivers	4.0	Dentists	.20
Gas Station Attendants	.40	Telephone Operators	1.0
Printers	.22	Technical Engineers	.14
Beauticians, Barbers	1.0	Shoe Clerks	.20
Policemen	.57	Photographers	.14
Highway Workers	.10	Entertainers	.13
Librarians	.14	Bakers	.33
Food Clerks	1.3	Farmers	28.5
Cooks	.66	Tailors, Furriers	.40
Newsboys	.09	Hardward Clerks	.44

This table is based on a ratio of civilian jobs in manufacturing to the number not in manufacturing. In the table that ratio is assumed to be 1 to 2.6. This is higher than the multiplication factors which are described because of the classification of all jobs not in manufacturing as supportive. Many nonmanufacturing jobs which produce goods and services for export are basic activities.

Adapted by William H. Form and Delbert C. Miller, Industry, Labor and Community (New York: Harper & Row, 1960), p. 27, from Better Living, Employee's Magazine of E.I. DuPont Co. (May–June 1954), p. 14.

time within a given city. A multiplication factor does arise, however; it is not accidental and it has a specificable range of values.[33] Thus

> the ratio for cities over 10,000 population appears to be between 1 to .5 and 1 and 2. . . . In small cities from 10,000 to 120,000 the ratios range between 1 to .6 and 1 to .9. As larger cities are examined, the ratio of service employees to basic increases. . . . New York City comes to 1 to 2.29. In a large city with a 1 to 2 ratio of basic to service employment,

33. Ibid.

every new plant employing 100 workers would support 900 total new population.[34]

In Table 3-3, the ratio is assumed to be 1 to 2.6, a ratio that is higher than the multiplication factor for the largest cities discussed by Form and Miller because all the jobs not in manufacturing are classified as supportive; such classification subtracts many nonmanufacturing jobs from the basic activity category that do in fact produce goods and services that are exported from the city, jobs that were, for that reason, included in the "basic" category in the earlier commentary. In Table 3-4 we see the effects of the multiplication factor on a mythical city of 100,000 basic workers in which there are, among other agencies, ". . . 15,000 business establishments, 100 charitable organizations, and 150 professional athletes. There are 92 elementary and 19 high schools. Churches number more than 400."[35]

One point of this discussion is that the industrial base is among the critical variables in determining the overall size of the surrounding community. Next, the character of this base, the types of firms, and the base's internal composition, or industry mix, will also be an important determinant in the future growth and stability of a community (1) because some industries grow faster than others within different periods, and (2) because individual industries are differentially vulnerable to or aided by changes in business conditions, in technology, and in international trade relationships. Finally, industry mix will have direct effects upon (1) a community's occupational composition; (2) whether or not it is significantly influenced by the policies and practices of trade unions; (3) the patterns of land use in the community; and (4) the community's power and class structure. Some of these effects have been diagrammed as follows:

Industrial composition of the community → Occupational composition of the community → Income and educational levels of the community → Health, housing, education, cultural institutions[36]

Data on correlates of an industrial society's differentiation at the community level thus underscore the fact that there are some fairly predictable patterns associated with industrialization, growth, and economic development. Of particular note are the effects of different industry mixes—the types of firms in the community—on the types of jobs, skills, and occupations to be found there. These employment patterns are also influenced by ". . . changes in the skills, responsibilities and occupations of the work force as a consequence of the dynamic science and technology that accompanies industrialization,

---

34. Ibid., p. 27.

35. Ibid., p. 29.

36. Ibid., p. 49. The possible effects of shifts in many American communities, from locally owned to absentee ownership of employer-firms will be discussed in chapter 4.

leading to a more open society."[37] In the next section we consider some additional implications of this differentiation process for national occupational structures and therefore the social structures of nations.

THE SERVICE SECTOR

In chapter 1 we stressed the fact that the rate of growth in the numbers of service workers in the U.S. has been greater than the not inconsiderable growth rate descriptive of goods-producing workers; a major component of the former group's growth, we indicated, is attributable to expansion of government activities at all jurisdictional levels.

Industry, Government, and Employment

Among the fastest growing governmental services are those in the areas of health and education. And in the U.S. the expansion of governmental payrolls at the state and local levels in the recent American past has actually surpassed that at the federal level. Together, all U.S. governments "employ 13.5 million persons, or nearly one of every six employed persons."[38] In Table 3-5 we may see some of the personnel breakdowns in the period 1950 to 1975, a breakdown that helps one to sense (1) the rippling effects on manpower management and on occupational structures that emerge in highly industrialized nations, and (2) the roles of governments as agencies of both production and distribution.

The table tells us, among other things, that where federal civilian employment went up approximately 35 percent over a quarter of a century, state employment grew more than two and one half times, and local governments' payrolls went up by almost the same factor. The entries under "education," "teachers," and "health and hospitals" give an indication of the source of the latter two payroll expansions. Health and education, we will recall, are strategic elements in human capital formation, though the specifics of their importance, as we noted in chapter 2, are not readily measured.

In Table 3-6 the personnel breakdowns and their monthly costs are shown in aggregate form for state and local government for the period 1960-1975.

Services and Goods-Producers

Service-rendering agencies of government have not simply succeeded or displaced goods-producing private corporations as users of service workers. Indeed, privately owned corporations, including the numerous large ones in the

---

37. Dunlop et al., *Industrialism and Industrial Man Reconsidered*, p. 6.

38. Eli Ginzberg, *The Manpower Connection, Education and Work* (Cambridge, Mass.: Harvard University Press, 1975).

Table 3-5 Governmental Employment and Payrolls: 1950 to 1975

YEAR AND FUNCTION	EMPLOYEES (1,000)					OCTOBER PAYROLL (MIL. DOL.)				
	Total	Federal (civilian)[1]	State and local			Total	Federal (civilian)[1]	State and local		
			Total	State	Local			Total	State	Local
1950	6,402	2,117	4,285	1,057	3,228	1,528	613	915	218	696
1960	8,808	2,421	6,387	1,527	4,860	3,333	1,118	2,215	524	1,691
1965	10,589	2,588	8,001	2,028	5,973	4,884	1,484	3,400	849	2,551
1967	11,867	2,993	8,874	2,335	6,539	6,056	1,842	4,213	1,106	3,108
1970	13,028	2,881	10,147	2,755	7,392	8,334	2,428	5,906	1,612	4,294
1971	13,316	2,872	10,444	2,832	7,612	8,911	2,529	6,382	1,742	4,641
1972	13,759	2,795	10,964	2,957	8,007	9,950	2,710	7,240	1,937	5,303
1973	14,139	2,786	11,353	3,013	8,339	11,027	3,012	8,015	2,158	5,857
1974	14,628	2,874	11,754	3,155	8,599	12,086	3,294	8,792	2,410	6,382
Total, 1975	14,986	2,890	12,097	3,268	8,828	13,243	3,584	9,659	2,651	7,008
Percent of Total	100.0	19.3	80.7	21.8	58.9	100.0	27.1	72.9	20.0	52.9
National Defense[2]	1,051	1,051	(x)	(x)	(x)	1,295	1,295	(x)	(x)	(x)
Postal Service	692	692	(x)	(x)	(x)	846	846	(x)	(x)	(x)
Education	6,294	22	6,272	1,400	4,872	4,985	24	4,960	1,022	3,939
Teachers	3,524	(x)	3,524	407	3,118	3,560	(x)	3,560	482	3,078
Highways	609	5	604	275	329	497	8	489	251	238
Health and Hospitals	1,447	247	1,200	592	608	1,188	281	907	471	437
Police Protection	664	55	609	69	540	669	83	585	75	510
Fire Protection	291	(x)	291	(x)	291	250	(x)	250	(x)	250
Sanitation and Sewerage	213	(x)	213	(x)	213	172	(x)	172	(x)	172
Parks and Recreation	218	(x)	218	(x)	218	125	(x)	125	(x)	125
Natural Resources	454	253	201	165	36	473	313	160	137	23
Financial Administration	390	105	285	113	172	347	130	217	100	118
All Other	2,664	460	2,204	654	1,549	2,397	604	1,794	595	1,200

For October. 1950 excludes Alaska and Hawaii. See also Historical Statistics, Colonial Times to 1970, series Y 272–289.
X Not applicable.
[1] Includes employees outside United States.
[2] Includes international relations.

Source: From Statistical Abstract of the United States, 1976 (Washington, D.C.: Government Printing Office, 1976), p. 284, Table 452.

Table 3-6 State and Local Government Employment and Payrolls: 1960 to 1975

ITEM	STATE AND LOCAL					LOCAL[1]				
	Total	Average annual percent change	Education	Other	State	Total	Counties	Municipalities	School districts	Townships[2]
EMPLOYEES (1,000)										
Full-time equivalent:										
1960	5,570	4.3[3]	2,525	3,045	1,353	4,217	738	1,447	1,729	302
1965	6,937	4.5	3,337	3,600	1,751	5,186	893	1,638	2,287	368
1967	7,455	3.7	3,658	3,797	1,946	5,509	973	1,715	2,449	371
1970	8,528	4.6	4,258	4,271	2,302	6,226	1,098	1,922	2,786	420
1972	9,237	4.1	4,585	4,651	2,487	6,750	1,242	2,029	2,981	498
1973	9,578	3.7	4,751	4,827	2,547	7,031	1,318	2,109	3,074	530
1974	9,852	3.2	4,901	4,950	2,653	7,199	1,343	2,127	3,183	545
1975	10,111	2.6	4,952	5,159	2,742	7,369	1,408	2,158	3,243	560
All employees, 1975	12,097	(x)	6,272	5,824	3,268	8,828	1,563	2,521	3,969	775
Full-time	9,410	(x)	4,471	4,939	2,538	6,872	1,332	2,053	2,971	516
Part-time	2,687	(x)	1,802	885	731	1,956	231	468	998	259
OCTOBER PAYROLL (mil. dol.)										
1960	2,215	8.5[3]	1,095	1,120	524	1,691	254	583	735	118
1965	3,400	8.9	1,778	1,623	849	2,551	377	818	1,189	167
1967	4,213	11.3	2,244	1,969	1,106	3,108	465	972	1,475	196
1970	5,906	11.9	3,170	2,737	1,612	4,294	640	1,361	2,032	262
1972	7,240	10.7	3,814	3,426	1,937	5,303	857	1,654	2,428	364
1973	8,015	10.7	4,185	3,830	2,158	5,857	952	1,855	2,623	427
1974	8,792	10.2	4,580	4,212	2,410	6,382	1,057	1,985	2,882	458
1975	9,659	9.9	4,960	4,699	2,651	7,008	1,183	2,150	3,160	514

For October. 1955 excludes Alaska and Hawaii. For payrolls, see also Historical Statistics, Colonial Times to 1970, series Y 274–289 and Y 292–307.
X Not applicable.
[1] Except for 1967 and 1972, subject to sampling variation.
[2] Includes special districts.
[3] Change from 1959.
Source: From Statistical Abstract of the United States, 1976 (Washington, D.C.: Government Printing Office, 1976), Table 453.

manufacturing sector, employ 73 percent of all *service*-rendering American workers. There is of course no gainsaying the increasing size of American taxpayers' public sector work force: In 1974, 27.3 percent of all employed Americans held jobs in governments or held government contract connected jobs. If we added the private sector doctors, lawyers, and accountants involved directly in tasks engendered by government, especially by government regulations, we could quite probably account for one-third of America's labor force. The point is that many "private sector" beneficiaries of government contracts and other public economic initiatives, no less than many public servants, though involved directly in production, are involved in the industrial system as such: Antitrust specialists in oil companies, accountants who prepare reports for federal regulatory agencies, and private physicians who receive fees from state workmen's compensation boards for the workers' injuries they treat come readily to mind.

The character of American government thus shapes—and is shaped by—the facts of modern industrial life, even though the lines between goods and services workers become fuzzier, and even while proportionately fewer and fewer of an industrial society's citizens are engaged in stereotypically industrial work, whatever their sectors. Once again, we note that industrialization engenders parallel structures and occupations, even as the industrialization process modifies and is modified by these developments, many of which are quite remote from the lathe, the bench press, and the combustion engine, the foundry, the forge, and the assembly line. Even a cursory examination of the so-called not-for-profit-sector is persuasive: This sector accounted for well over one quarter of the purchases of goods and services tallied in the gross national product for the U.S. as long ago as 1963.[39] Machine technology is a critical factor to consider in its own right in examining the character of life in modern industrial societies as we noted in chapter 1; but it contributes, as we have now seen, to the development of other characteristics that substantially blur the singular effects of machines.

That "technical determinism," as discussed in chapter 1, is a tempting concept we may, however, well understand, expecially when we link machine technology, in our minds, with large firms. Thus, if we lump nonmanufacturing firms, banks, and insurance companies together with manufacturing firms, for example, we find that 31 percent of *all* employed Americans worked for the 1,250 largest corporate employers in 1973. Consider also that nearly half of all employers in manufacturing alone, may be found in America's 100 largest manufacturing firms. These few manufacturing firms employ fully 12.2 percent of all wage and salary workers, while the 500 largest American corporations, by themselves, accounted for about 25 percent of the value added to the republic's

---

39. For the latest thorough treatment of America's "nonindustrial" sector, see Eli Ginzberg, Dale L. Hiestand, and Beatrice G. Reubens, *The Pluralistic Economy* (New York: McGraw-Hill, 1965). The figures cited have been calculated from data reported in *Fortune*, 88, 5 (May 1974), 232-51; 89, 6 (June 1974), 162-81; 91, 5 (May 1975), 210-29; and 91, 6 (June 1975); 121-41.

gross national product in 1973. The story of the machine's and the factory's places in contemporary American life is, in short, by no means a simple one.

If the process of economic growth in industrial development so often necessarily triggers expansions of nations' service sectors, the magnitudes of these expansions are typically the subject of lively intranational political debate. Consider, first off, that the productivity of the goods-producing sector's members is far more readily measured than that of the service sector's, a fact contributing to great arguments among the leaders of different occupations and of the social classes or strata into which they may be crudely allocated. These arguments focus on questions of equity in respect of income distribution—the dividing of the economic pie—among those who live by salaries and those who live by hourly wages. It is a good deal easier to claim that people should be paid in accordance with their productivity than to measure the relevant variables in such an equation!

Next, consider that the more of the gross national product—the total value of a nation's output—that is expended upon services, the less in most cases there is seen to be for our old friends, physical and human capital formation. Thus an argument that overlaps to some degree with the distributive argument among the members of occupations and classes develops in industrial societies over the needs for savings and investment, on one side, and the expenditures for expanded public services, on the other. The fact that a host of services are financed by government tax collections and public borrowing leads additionally, in so-called market economies, to particularly sharp debates over the effects of competition between the "public" and "private" sectors for funds, as we noted in chapter 2. Quotes are used here because the distinction is a somewhat controversial one in countries in which many privately held firms and industries, as in the case of defense production, are heavily involved in government contracting, just as many of the greatest private universities derive substantial shares of their annual operating incomes from public contracts and grants.

In recent years, the competitive demands of these sectors for labor and capital in the U.S. have been held by many to be critically important sources of notoriously high levels of inflation by driving up the cost of money; inflation issues, in turn, have been joined with the income distribution issues to which we have already alluded, as consumers of *all* goods and services seek to use their respective market positions—their economic power—to protect their income shares from erosion by inflation. The point is that industrialism creates, as one of its most significant products, what might be termed large *para*industrial population groups, groups whose members may indeed be in the numerical majority in societies we are accustomed to thinking of as industrial! Indeed, most of us in the work force rarely see the paraphernalia and equipage of industry, in either the romantic or any other sense. Indeed, for most of us, the terms "hardware" refers to computers; "machines" to Selectric typewriters and tape recorders; and "production" to the output of TV empressarios, the content of trade fairs, and the demonstrations to their clients of Madison Avenue admen's prowess. Few of us will ever see a forge, a turret lathe, an oxygen steel furnace, a drill punch or a printing press, a coal cutter, an electro-plating machine, a rivetting device, or a helium welding apparatus.

Many services are of course indispensable to continued economic growth—e.g., research and development activities; some are needed to guide and regulate the course of growth; some, like security guards, vendors, and purchasing officers, are needed by industry and society to help them protect, sell (and resell), as well as to buy industry's awesome physical output. And some services are needed to deal, as families once sought to (and now continue to, in more traditional societies), with the sick and the aged whose numbers are directly associated with the degree of industrialism. Finally, corps of specialized personnel, including teachers, are needed to educate and to train neophytes, helping thereby to form "human capital" and more or less successfully to socialize—to prepare—the young for their adult roles in society.[40]

In this section we have again stressed the differentiation of industrial societies. In the next section we consider a few dimensions of the social contracts in industrial societies that help to define the limits of disagreements among key population groups that arise out of the differentiation process. These social contracts may be conceived as integration-serving "webs of rules."

THE "WEB OF RULES"

The concept of a network or a "web of rules," in accordance with which a nation's actual work is conducted, was first delineated by Kerr and Siegel in 1955 in a discussion of the structuring of industrial labor forces,[41] and was elaborated later by Dunlop. Dunlop's work is of particular sociological interest because as this distinguished labor economist, government advisor, and former Secretary of Labor points out, his efforts to lay out the essential characteristics

---

40. For one provocative treatment of relevant materials regarding education's social functions by sociologists, see Christopher Jencks et al., *Inequality* (New York: Basic Books, 1972). For an equally controversial treatment (from the left) of America's educational system as a socializing agency, see S. Bowles and H. Gintis, *Schooling in Capitalist America* (New York: Basic Books, 1975). For a long-term view of the "consumption" benefits of education to individuals as knowledgeable persons and citizens, rather than simply as economic agents, see Herbert Hyman, Charles Wright, and John Shelton Reed, *The Enduring Effects of Education* (Chicago: University of Chicago Press, 1975). The role of education as a "human capital" building institution, meantime, was discussed in chapter 2.

41. "The Structuring of the Labor Force in Industrial Society: New Dimensions and New Questions," *Industrial and Labor Relations Review* (January 1955), and J. Dunlop, *Industrial Relations Systems* (New York: Holt, Rinehart and Winston, 1958).

of industrial systems as subsets of social systems "may be viewed in the general framework for analyzing social systems developed by Talcott Parsons."[42]

The rules, which evolve in the gradually institutionalized relationships among managers, workers, and the political states' representatives, affect job classifications, compensation, and the relative rights and duties of the three "actors." The process of rule setting, in turn, is affected by given industrial relations system's larger national environment, "in terms of several 'contexts': technology, market and/or budget constraints, and the power relations among the [three critical groups of] actors."[43] Thus, technological features of the work place, features that are often common to whole industries, whole economic sectors of an economy (and sometimes common to industries and sectors across national boundaries) are of considerable importance. Cross-national similarities among sectors may be especially common in white-collar workers' worlds of work, influenced as these are in any nation by typewriters, telephones, computers, duplicating devices, and the like. The differences among particular blue collarites' work worlds may, in many respects, be more different within national boundaries than among them, though the "web of rules" governing their workaday lives tend to have some clearly identifiable national characteristics. The technological features referred to also include the types of products or services involved; these play a part in determining

> . . . the size of the work force, its concentration in a narrow area or its diffusion, the duration of employment at one locale, the stability of the same working group, the isolation of the work place from urban areas, the proximity of work and living quarters, the contact with customers, the essentiality of the product to the health and safety or to the economic development of the community, the handling of money, the accident potential, the skill levels and education required, the proportions of various skills in the work force, and the possibilities of the employment of women and children.[44]

The next "givens" in shaping the rules, whether in socialist or market-oriented countries, are environmental constraints and those imposed by the challenges and opportunities present in markets and by budget constraints.[45] Put in simplest terms, managers, workers, and the public's representatives have different problems and options in their interactions depending upon the ways in which the most elementary of economic forces are seen to impact (or *not* to impact) upon them. These forces, meantime, may be "local, national or inter-

42. Dunlop, *Industrial Relations Systems*, p. 29.

43. Dunlop et al., *Industrialism and Industrial Man Reconsidered*, pp. 6, 6-17.

44. Dunlop, *Industrial Relations Systems*, pp. 9-10.

45. Ibid., p. 10.

national depending on the industrial relations system; the balance of payments [for example] constitutes the form of the market constraint for nationwide systems."[46] Observant readers will recall that we have already encountered one aspect of these contraints in our brief treatment of protective tariffs and their effects on the "rules" governing the disposition of incomes as between the agricultural and industrial sectors and therefore upon the population groups and classes engaged in the occupations in these sectors.[47] The slow growth in productivity (output per man hour) meanwhile has been linked in many minds to the American dollar's questionable value in international exchange in recent years. Arguments about the dollar's health have thus had a substantial impact upon union contract negotiations, for example.

Dunlop sought to illuminate further the context within which the web of rules in industrial relations systems are spun by postulating that industrial relations complexes are subsystems of societies in which the loci of power are always of great moment. Thus "the prestige, position and access to the ultimates of authority within the larger society shapes and constrains an industrial-relations system," and "relative distribution of power among the actors in the larger society tends to a degree to be reflected within the industrial-relations system."[48] Though it does not directly determine the interactions of the actors within the industrial-relations system, the distribution of power in society

> . . . is a context which helps to *structure* the industrial-relations system itself. The function of one of the actors in the industrial-relations system, the specialized governmental agencies, is likely to be particularly influenced by the distribution of power in the larger society.[49]

Among the most important strands in the webs of rules, meantime, are the procedures for establishing rules, and the procedures for identifying the occasions for applying the rules once they are established.[50] Consider for example, the U.S. Supreme Court's efforts in 1960 and 1974 to balance the conflicting

---

46. Ibid., pp. 10-11.

47. For a discussion of the efforts of large corporations to avoid the effects of short-run market vacillations on their investments programs, see Walter Adams (ed.), *The Structure of the American Economy*, (4th ed.) (New York: Macmillan, 1971); and John Kenneth Galbraith, *The New Industrial State* (Boston: Houghton Mifflin, 1967), chs. 2-5.

48. Dunlop, *Industrial Relations Systems,* p. 11.

49. Ibid, p. 12 (emphasis added). For examples in the U.S. of governmental agencies whose doings directly affect the industrial-relations system and which are highly vulnerable to national political and economic developments, consider the Council of Economic Advisors, the Department of Labor's several bureaus, and the various wage and price councils and commissions of recent years.

50. Dunlop, *Industrial Relations Systems,* p. 13; and Kerr and Siegel, "The Structuring of the Labor Force" pp. 151-68.

interests of union members and employers that often lead to disruptions in the economic order, on the one hand, with the interests of the multitudes of third-party bystanders in society, on the other. Mindful that the parties to a labor *agreement* are obliged to live with each other, week in and week out, the court has elevated arbitration proceedings into component parts of a system of "industrial common law."[51] This interpretation enjoyed the Court's implicit sanctions in the two cases referred to here. In the initial landmark case, in 1960, the Court ruled that disputes over the arbitrability of a dispute ought to be resolved by arbitrators in favor of arbitrability. In the Court's judgment, arbitrators were in better positions than judges, who are bound by formal jurisprudential requirements (regarding the rules of evidence, for example) to help interdependent parties work out local and often unique labor-management problems. The thrust of the decision was to obligate managers to *bargain* in connection with an *agreement* rather than to *litigate* in connection with a *contract*.[52]

A later decision, in 1974, pushed the point rather further than once-enthusiastic labor leaders have liked, by obligating the parties to a labor agreement to submit disputes over legal requirements regarding mine safety to arbitration. This decision, also of landmark importance, virtually takes a federal safety law's enforcement components *out* of the hands of Labor Department specialists and enmeshes law enforcement in the "common law of the shop."[53]

Although the web of rules within organizations is most readily discernible in situations that involve collective bargaining, i.e. in situations in which much of rule-making thereby becomes relatively stylized,[54] there are analogous "webs" in other situations as well, among which perhaps costly white-collar coffee breaks are only the most notorious if pedestrian examples. Thus a "fair share" notion often operates compellingly among the members of office typing pools concerning whatever clerical chores, like typing tables, are defined by a particular work group as onerous. Students, too, are bound by "work rules,"

---

51. The term was coined by Archibald Cox in "Reflections Upon Labor Arbitration," *Harvard Law Review*, 72 (1959); and Charles Summer of the Yale Law School, in "Reason, Contract and Law in Labor Relations," *Harvard Law Review*, 68 (1955), 999 ff.

52. Actually there were three cases, collectively called the Trilogy Cases, that were decided as one; *United Steelworkers of America v. American Manufacturing Co*, 363 U.S. 564 (1960); *United Steelworkers of America v. Warrior and Gulf Navigation Co.*, 363 U.S. 574 (1960); and *United Steelworkers of America v. Enterprise Whee and Car Corp.*, 363 U.S. 593 (1960).

53. *Gateway Coal Co. v. United Mine Workers*, 94S. Ct. 629, 1974. In this case the court held against workers' right to strike (and in favor of arbitration) over the alleged falsification of mine records on the adequacy of air flow into a deep coalmine by three Gateway Co. foremen.

54. Even under collective bargaining in the basic industries, as we will see in chapter 7, there are still wide margins for much highly informal bargaining over work place specifics.

as sophmores discover at registration time when seniors and juniors have crowded them out of irregularly offered but sorely needed "elective" courses in their fields of concentration.

Indeed, a moment's reflection will lead thoughtful readers to recall many formal—and more informal but equally binding—rules governing the bigger and smaller questions of organizational lives in their own experiences. Many of such informal rules could well be listed under a rubric first formally identified in the sociological literature by Emile Durkheim as the "non-contractual elements of contract." These emerge in the interactions of people involved in tasks, the contingencies and exigencies concerning which even the most prescient of the parties to formal relationships would not be able to make forecasts. Often these rules operate as the grease that lubricates what would otherwise be friction-full and cumbersome bureaucratic machines.

The point is that there are discrete local or "proximal" sources of variations in particular rules to be found in the shops, offices, laboratories, meat packing plants, shipyards, coal mines, and other sites in which people work. Thus, individual plant superintendents, deans, chiefs of surgery, factory foremen, steamfitters, crotch sawyers, and computer programmers play important parts in writing local rules in which particular organizational and interpersonal rewards and sanctions are meted out, and by which the specifics, the equities, of work are defined and redefined—including such important rules as those affecting job rates, the pace of jobs, the equitableness of restrictions on personnel, and the "due" in "due process."

CONCLUSION

In this chapter we have focused on a series of questions having to do with labor markets, occupational structure, and the "web of rules" that help to accommodate an industrial society's differentiated parts to each other. These questions we have identified specifically as those one encounters at the middle-level altitudes in our mountain metaphor because the issues involved may be abstracted out, for analytical purposes, from other ongoing and wider developments in a society.

In the next chapter we move down another analytical level to consider the place of corporations on the institutional landscape and the roles and experiences of their leaders.

CHAPTER 4
CORPORATIONS
AND
MANAGERS

INTRODUCTION

Numerous allusions to corporations and unions in earlier chapters have already served to suggest that these intriguing specimens of social technology cast rather long shadows on the institutional landscapes of Japan and of the western democracies. As we move down to lower elevations it becomes necessary to single out several clusters of materials about these collectivities for detailed examination.

In the first cluster are studies of the political and economic powers of corporations. The issues joined therein have to do with the influence of businessmen in general, and of those in the larger corporations in paticular, upon the nation's public policies, its economy, its regulatory apparatuses, and finally upon the well-being of its communities.

In the second cluster are studies of business leaders themselves. Of critical interest here are questions attaching to the possible implications of the facts (1) that corporate managers have become increasingly separated from corporate stockholders-owners, and (2) that a great many managers function as the top- and upper-level incumbents of what Max Weber called legal-rational bureaucratic organizations, organizations that are built around (1) highly specialized tasks, (2) technically-given standards, (3) career and merit-type personnel systems, (4) routinized procedures, and (5) impersonal rules and regulations.

The third cluster of studies includes those by investigators who have sought to explain older and newer versions of businessmen's beliefs and ideologies. These beliefs and ideologies are of particular interest insofar as they help us to understand the tensions in a social system in which balances must regularly be struck between the legitimate exercise of power in its private and public spheres.[1] Their possession of power and their considerable authority over people, meanwhile, compels business leaders, like other power holders, to identify a rationale for their social votes and their actions.

CORPORATE POLITICAL AND ECONOMIC POWER

An economist caught the essential flavor of the concerns of many social scientists about business leaders in the title of an early monograph on the insidious efforts of trade associations in Germany and the United States to serve their corporate constituents by subverting democratic institutions: *Business as a System of Power*.[2] In the period before World War II concerned analysts borrowed to a great extent from theoretical ideas associated with Marxists' critiques of capitalism,[3] and their expositions were heavily influenced by empirical studies conducted under the aegis of the Temporary National Economic Committee in the years prior to 1941. These studies of "the structure of the American economy" essentially blamed the managers of large banks and manufacturing companies for decisions that resulted in the great depression of the 1930s.

The Influence of Corporations on the Federal Government

In a widely held view, managers mobilize their abundant resources, almost like leaders of social movements, to use government in what they perceive to be their interests—especially against regulatory and other reforms favoring consumers, smaller enterprises, and labor.[4] The more or less opposite view has

---

1. Many of the themes in this chapter, and some of the specific materials related thereto, are discussed in much abbreviated form in Ivar Berg and Mayer Zald, "Business and Society" in *Annual Review of Sociology,* vol. 4 (1978), pp. 115-143.

2. Robert A. Brady, *Business as a System of Power* (New York: Columbia University Press, 1943); for a parallel study of business in the Nazi period in Germany, see Franz Leopold Neumann, *Behemoth: The Structure and Practice of National Socialism, 1933-1944* (New York: Octagon Books, 1963).

3. For an unsympathetic but nevertheless useful overview of a variety of critiques cast in theoretical terms that may be thus grouped, see Sidney Hook, *Marx and the Marxists: The Ambiguous Legacy* (New York: Van Nostrand, 1955). For a sympathetic and equally useful overview, see Paul Sweezy, *The Theory of Capitalist Development: Principles of Marxian Political Economy* (London: Dennis Dobson, 1946).

4. For a convenient collection of what are termed left-liberal critiques by the editor, along the lines mentioned, see selections by Miller, Bennet, and Alapatt; Magdoff, Dye, and Zigler; Mills; Hacker; Dornhoff; O'Connor; and Reynolds and

enjoyed more popular support than is encouraged in systematic social scientific studies. Representative studies of a general nature reporting the limits on corporate leaders' political and economic powers have been made by Chamberlain, Jacoby, Epstein, and Nadel; the most recent discussion of the powers and the limits on the powers of American-based multinational corporations on other nations' politics and economies is by Vernon.[5] A thoughtful review of these and an apposite though limited body of related materials will suggest that the picture of corporate political power in American society is not a clear one.

One of the important access routes to political power—that is, to the shaping of legislative resolutions and of executive decisions that bear upon industry—is through partisan political involvement. Thus one might expect that businessmen reputedly interested in reducing regulatory infringements on their freedom of actions; in constraining the options of labor unions; in particular fiscal and monetary policies; and in procorporation policies in such important areas as environmental protection, pension regulations, minimum wage scales, and in occupational health and safety rules would support the national republican party and that "labor" would support the national democratic party.

The facts about party finance, about the recruitment of officials and about the alliances formed by legislators, however, support no such inference, as Epstein, Ladd, Nadel, Lowe, and Weidenbaum have shown.[6] Indeed, the facts show that while business leaders share a number of highly general beliefs about the role of government, as we will see, their actual political activities reflect many important differences in their specific interests in particular statutes, regulations, and public policies; the fact that they belong to different industries with different interests almost dictates that businessmen will differ among themselves on a large number of issues. The piecemeal evidence suggests that the consensus in

---

Smolensky, in Maurice Zeitlin (ed.), *American Society, Inc.: Studies in the Social Structure and Political Economy of the United States*, 2nd ed. (Chicago: Rand McNally, 1977). Radical critiques, taken by themselves, have been synthesized in Charles Perrow (ed.), *The Radical Attack on Business* (New York: Harcourt Brace Jovanovich, 1972). For an updated overview of American economic development in neo-Marxist perspective, see Douglas F. Dowd, *The Twisted Dream: Capitalist Development in the U.S. since 1776* (Cambridge, Mass: Winthrop, 1974).

5. Neil W. Chamberlain, *The Limits of Corporate Responsibility* (New York: Basic Books, 1973); Neil H. Jacoby, *Corporate Power and Social Responsibility: A Blueprint for the Future* (New York: Macmillan, 1973); Edwin M. Epstein, *The Corporation in American Politics* (Englewood Cliffs, N.J.: Prentice-Hall, 1969; Mark V. Nadel, *Corporations and Political Accountability* (Lexington, Mass.: D. C. Heath, 1976); Raymond Vernon, *Storm over the Multinationals: The Real Issues* (Cambridge, Mass.: Harvard University Press, 1977).

6. Epstein, *The Corporation in American Politics;* Everett C. Ladd, Jr., "The Unmaking of the Republican Party," *Fortune*, 95, 3 (1977), 91ff, and "The Democrats have their Own Two-Party System," *Fortune*, 96, 4 (1977), 212ff; Nadel, *Corporations and Political Accountability;* Theodore J. Lowi, *The End of Liberalism: Ideology, Policy and the Crisis of Public Authority* (New York: Norton, 1969), p. 322; Murray Weidenbaum, *Government Mandated Price Increases* (Washington, D.C.: American Enterprise Institute for Public Policy Research, 1975).

business circles, such as it is, is reflected in the public relations and public opinion-molding efforts of the Committee for Economic Development, the Business Council (a presidential advisory group), and the Business Roundtable, and, in some measure, the Advertising Council and the Council of Foreign Relations; the consensus discernible in the work and the productions of these agencies and of peak trade associations is organized essentially about highly general themes, not often about many specific issues.[7]

Of particular interest to industrial sociologists are the political issues that might be expected to divide labor and business. And some degree of division there has been, over minimum wage legislation, for example, and over the exemption of unions from antitrust laws after the passage in 1936 of the National Labor Relations Act and over the needs for restrictions on unions in the Taft-Hartley and Landrum-Griffin Acts. These differences—sometimes involving deeply held values and heated debates—have not been totally divisive however, as when truckers sided with Teamster Union leaders in opposition to labor-management disclosure requirements contained in the Landrum-Griffin Act. Otherwise, note may be made of carefully executed joint lobbying efforts by the biggest steel comapnies and the United Steel Workers Union, in pursuit of import restrictions, and by the Big Three auto companies and the United Auto Workers Union in pursuit of duties on foreign car imports. Both of these unions have supported corporate efforts directed against rising costs and the allegedly declining sales and job reducing effects of environmental protection requirements. Corporate attorneys have also joined labor and civil liberty groups in blistering attacks on the use, by federal tax and security agencies, of secret surveillance techniques. And, in one of the most notorious cases, in the 1940s involving businessmen's conspiratorial efforts to limit price and other forms of competition, the offending corporations in the heavy electrical equipment manufacturing industry, were working hand-in-glove with the International Brotherhood of Electrical Workers. The case had a number of political overtones partly because it was encouraged by industry-wide, i.e., multiemployer, collective bargaining, and partly because it had its origins in price-setting arrangements endorsed in the National Industrial Recovery Act, an act later held to be unconstitutional.[8] These, and literally countless parallel instances of corporate needs for help from

---

7. For a general description of the agencies mentioned, and their effort to establish "ideological hegemony" against social change, their interrelationships, and their relationships to business corporations, see Glenn K. Kirsch "Only You Can Prevent Ideological Hegemony: The Advertising Council and Its Place in the American Power Structure," *The Insurgent Sociologist*, 5, 3 (Spring 1975), 64–82. For a recent review of trade associations, the results of which may be compared with those of Brady on American peak trade associations, see David Rogers and Melvin Zimet, "Business and the Local Community," in Ivar Berg (ed.), *Business of America* (New York: Harcourt Brace Jovanovich, 1968), pp. 39–80. For a discussion of public relations efforts by a sociologist, see Kenneth Henry, *Defenders and Shapers of the Corporate Image* (New Haven, Conn.: College and University Press, 1972).

8. The reference is to the Alan-Bradley case, 325 U.S. 797 (1945).

Foreign Policy

Although America's hegemony in foreign policy has been limited in the past decade, there is no denying its location at the center of the international stage. An assessment of self-serving corporate influences over policies vis-à-vis other nations needs to take a number of facts into account before conclusions about corporate power may be drawn. First it must be recognized that business leaders are for the most part internationalist in their orientations, a fact that links up with a generally internationalist position on matters of foreign trade and therefore on matters of foreign policy.[9] Indeed, as Vernon shows, the older, more nationalist position of conservative corporations has recently been adopted by radical leaders in the developing nations who view the presence of foreign corporations in their economies as a threat, in their political systems, to their reform programs.[10] At the same time many American workers have become concerned that corporate ventures overseas involve the "export" of jobs to workers in lower-wage countries.

Second, though many corporations have sought to help "stabilize" friendly governments in other lands, their record has been a mixed one; the publicity recently given to these efforts and to corporate alliances with government agencies—especially the publicity surrounding ITT's collaboration with the Central Intelligence Agency in the overthrow of the Allende government in Chile—may reasonably be expected to make business leaders highly skeptical of interventionist techniques, even as legislators continue to look more closely at the activities of federal executive agencies in foreign affairs. The apparently clearest cases of corporations' capacities to influence American foreign policy involve the major oil companies, capacities that are also under close scrutiny in the wake of the worldwide energy crisis. The activities of the so-called Seven Sisters—the major international oil companies—are clearly of immediate interest because these activities have direct effects on prices and upon employment developments in the U.S., both of which areas are of obvious and critical importance to the structure and functioning of industrial democracy and therefore of great interest to industrial sociologists. Thus the actions of the OPEC, the energy producers' cartel, and their oil company partners have become the objects of concern in the White House, the Treasury, Justice, and State departments, in the Congress, in the Federal Reserve, in offices of corporate resource mobilization task forces, and in union headquarters across the land. The fact that the major oil companies

---

9. Raymond A. Bauer, Ithiel D. S. Pool, and L. A. Dexter, *American Business and Public Policy: The Politics of Foreign Trade,* 2nd ed. (Chicago: Aldine-Atherton, 1972).

10. Vernon, *Storm over the Multinationals.*

92 CORPORATIONS AND MANAGERS

have substantial holdings of gas, coal, and uranium resources has added to the public's interests in their political efforts. That these companies have well developed arrangements, at least, for influencing public policy is demonstrably clear.[11]

The Military Industrial Complex

When President Eisenhower issued his warning, upon leaving the White House in 1961, against the power of what he labelled the military-industrial complex, he quickened the interest of many who had otherwise ignored the alarms sounded by many Americans over what were thought to be the too highly effective and intimate linkages between the military services and their civilian suppliers in industry. The fact that some unions, too, with interests in defense-related jobs, had vested interests in defense expenditures had the effect of adding to the restiveness of many observers. That the links between some corporations and their leaders, on one side, and the generals, admirals, and the civilian leaders in the Pentagon are well forged, is by now well known, as is the fact that many former military leaders have moved into the firms with whom they did business as government procurement officers upon their retirements from military service.

Formal investigations of the implications of these linkages ignore some of the relevant issues, however. Whatever one's sympathies and fears, a thoughtful scientist's conclusions about the military-industrial complex must be cautious ones. There is, of course, no dearth of data on the magnitudes of the dollar-and-job stakes involving corporations, the armed forces, foreign military allies and weapons customers in foreign lands. Melman thus provides us with the mind-boggling parameters of defense and defense-related expenditures, though his emphasis is on the weight—the opportunity costs incident to the forgone outlays for "peaceful" purposes—of these expenditures in economic, not in political terms.[12] Whether or not one believes, as Sweezy and Magdoff argue, in Marxist-Leninist styles, that capitalist America needs defense expenditures for its economy to operate without staggeringly high unemployment levels,[13] the employ-

11. For empirically informed discussions, see Robert Engler, *The Brotherhood of Oil: Energy Policy and the Public Interest* (Chicago; University of Chicago Press, 1977); James M. Blair, *The Control of Oil* (New York: Pantheon, 1977); and Anthony Sampson, *The Seven Sisters: The Great Oil Companies and the World They Shaped* (New York: Viking Press, 1975). For a detailed analysis of oil companies' political efforts see a consulting firm's report to the Marine Engineer's Beneficial Association, *The Energy Cartel: Big Oil vs. The Public Interest,* by Norman Medrin, Iris J. Low, and Stanley H. Ruttenberg (Washington, D.C.: Ruttenberg and Associates, 1975).

12. Seymour Melman, *Pentagon Capitalism* (New York: McGraw-Hill, 1970). See also James L. Clayton (ed.), *The Economic Impact of the Cold War* (New York: Harcourt Brace Jovanovich, 1970).

13. U.S. Bureau of Census, *Statistical Abstract of the United States: 1976,* 97th ed. (Washington, D.C.: Government Printing Office, 1976), Table No. 527, p. 333.

ment implications are truly huge: Defense workers, many of whose skills would be redundant in the short run, at least, were defense contracts suddenly terminated, numbered 26,620,000 in 1975.[14]

When space-military contracts dry up, white-collar professionals as well as production workers are affected, as were many engineers and scientists at work on the celebrated stretch of Route 128, Boston's Circumferential Highway. Indeed, whole communities and local labor markets have been severely affected by contract expirations, shifts in procurement policies, and changes in the favored weapons preferences of particular military branches,[15] as in Seattle and San Diego—cities that are hosts to giant airframes manufacturing companies with wildly gyrating budgets. Many of the personnel in these and other military hardware companies have had to make major career changes involving drastic reductions in income and living standards. Elected officials representing what are called impacted areas understandably act to protect their constituents' defense-related interests with the result that these interests color their representatives' foreign policy positions and add to sometimes angry divisions, among the principals in the federal apparatus, as well as in corporations, that cut straight across conventional partisan lines.

Though some do not admire its precise character, others hold that the pluralistic quality of America's brand of industrial democracy may actually be enhanced by the differentiated nature of the military-industrial complex. Thus accusative reports on the subject rarely attend to questions of whether executives of powerful conglomerate firms, made up of nondefense as well as defense-related subsidiaries, compete with each other over corporate policies.

The view that the military-industrial complex is monolithic does not take account, furthermore, of the fact that most defense contractors are linked to a particular branch of the armed forces or to particular subgroups within one of the branches; the battles among and within these branches over defense strategy, military tactics, and weapons systems, meanwhile, are regularly described in the nation's news media. Defense budgets are huge, but they are not at all clearly the packaged results of simple-minded and coherent conspiracies of military and business decision makers.[16] The evidence of inter- and intraservice rivalries does not yield a brand of pluralism that will please all citizens, to be sure. But such evidence is at least pertinent to a thoughtful appraisal of the short-run effects of

---

14. For a recent specification of the argument that the U.S. needs defense expenditures as a way of staving off unemployment of depression period proportions, see Paul M. Sweezy, "Capitalism for Worse" in Zeitlin (ed.), *American Society, Inc.* pp. 280–81 and Paul M. Sweezy and Harry Magdoff, "Economic Stagnation and the Stagnation of Economies," *Monthly Review* (April 1971).

15. For an analysis of an intramural debate over weapons within the "defense establishment," see Robert J. Art, *The TFX Decision: McNamara and the Military* (Boston: Little, Brown, 1968).

16. For dramatic illustrations of rivalries, see Art, *The TFX Decision:* and A. Ernest Fitzgerald, *The High Priests of Waste* (New York: Norton, 1972).

defense policies on the industrial sector of a democratic society, its occupational structure, its stability, and the welfare of the persons and communities involved directly and indirectly with defense jobs.[17] In the most methodical assessment available on the subject, finally, Lieberson reports that the existence of easily identifiable linkages between military and corporate leaders by no means proves that an industrial-military elite *unilaterally* determines policies regarding defense expenditures, and therefore the shape of defense impacts on the industrial system.[18]

Corporate Power and Industrial Rights. Few citizens believe, with much conviction, that competitive market forces by themselves will force anxious managers to seek to please employees by attending to the rights of individuals; labor markets even when the demand for workers is very great simply do not operate with such rapid and punitive effects on arrogant employers that we are content to let them be the main vehicles for the protection of personal rights and immunities. Protracted periods of relatively high unemployment, meanwhile, reduce further the effectiveness of market forces on managers as employers, as the inverse relationships between turnover and unemployment rates suggest.[19] The result is that we have come to depend upon the law as an instrument of social control, in augmentation of market pressures, to discipline the otherwise considerable powers that managers have over their largely dependent charges.

Thus Vollmer showed that managers have voluntarily become more benign as human relations preachments have come to influence management thinking,[20] but no statistical profiles are available from which one may make judgments about the disciplinary effects of social-legal interventions or constitutional guarantees. Blades, Blumberg, and Blumrosen have conducted careful

---

17. For contrasting appraisals see B. Pyadysher, *The Military-Industrial Complex of the USA,* translated by Yuri Sdobnikov (Moscow, USSR: Progress Publishers, 1977); and Adam Yarmolinsky, *The Military Establishment: Its Impacts on American Society* (New York: Harper & Row, 1971). Yarmolinsky is a former Assistant Secretary of Defense.

18. Stanley Lieberson, "An Empirical Study of Military-Industrial Linkages," *American Journal of Sociology,* 76, 4 (January 1971), 562-84.

19. "Quit rates" are not entirely explicable in business cycle terms, but they are clearly influenced by the cycle's turns. See John H. Pencavel, *An Analysis of the Quit Rate in American Manufacturing Industry, Research Report, no. 114* (Princeton, N.J.: Industrial Relations Section, Princeton University, 1970); Llad Phillips, "An Analysis of the Dynamics of Labor Turnover in United States Industry" (Ph.D. dissertation, Harvard University, 1969); B. W. Anderson, "Empirical Generalizations on Labor Turnover" in Richard Pegnetter (ed.), *Labor and Manpower* (Iowa City: Center for Labor and Management, College of Business Administration, University of Iowa, 1974); Fred L. Fry, "A Behavioral Analysis of Economic Variables Affecting Turnover," *Journal of Behavioral Economics,* 2 (1973), 247-95; and Robert J. Flanagan, George Strauss, and Lloyd Ulman, "Worker Discontent and Workplace Behavior," *Industrial Relations,* 13 (May 1974), pp. 101-23.

20. Howard Vollmer, *Employee Rights and the Employment Relationship* (Berkeley: University of California Press, 1960).

analyses of law cases, however, and it appears that the powers of corporate managers to discipline employees who act, as employees, to unilaterally serve their interests are gradually becoming more limited; Selznick and Ginzberg and Berg have reached similar conclusions.[21] The powers of corporations over individuals are nevertheless very great. When employees' rights are protected in any meaningful sense at all it is almost always the case they they are parties to formal restrictions—usually focused on "due process" like those included in collective bargaining agreements.

Recent legal restraints on managers' have included what Stone calls "invasions of corporate structure" and "organizational adjustment measures," some of which involve employee rights. Affirmative action—equal employment opportunity requirements, for example—requires that monitoring groups be established within employment settings to observe the treatment accorded to persons whose membership in "protected groups" assures them a number of new entitlements.[22] Similarly, recent disclosure requirements prevent some possible abuses of employee recordkeeping activities, though there is no available evidence on the net effects of these requirements. Like others, these regulations are ultimately effective in proportion to which injured parties actually avail themselves of their rights and remedies.

We have been concerned here with corporations and the larger political system. We turn in the next section to a few timely questions about the impact of corporate power in local communities.

The Corporation and the Local Community

Paralleling studies of the impact of industrial development upon communities and their occupational structures are studies of the roles of corporations in their power structures. In the view of some, including Dahl[23] and his followers, business leaders are among elites each of which has functionally

---

21. Dean Blades, "Employment at Will vs. Individual Freedom: Or Limiting the Abusive Exercise of Employer Power," *Columbia Law Review,* 67 (1967), 1404; Phillip Blumberg, "Corporate Responsibility and the Employees' Duty of Loyalty and Obedience: A Preliminary Inquiry," in D. Votaw and S.P. Sethi (eds.), *In The Corporate Dilemma: Traditional Values Versus Contemporary Problems* (Englewood Cliffs, N.J.: Prentice-Hall, 1973). A. E. Blumrosen, "Employer Discipline: United States Report," *Rutgers Law Review,* 18 (1964), 428; Philip Selznick, *Law Society, and Industrial Justice* (New York: Russell Sage, 1969); Eli Ginzberg and Ivar Berg, *Democratic Values and the Rights of Management* (New York: Columbia University Press, 1974).

22. Christopher D. Stone, *Where the Law Ends: The Social Control of Corporate Behavior* (New York: Harper & Row, 1975); and "Controlling Corporate Misconduct," *The Public Interest,* 48 (Summer 1977), 55-71.

23. See, e.g., Robert A. Dahl, *Who Governs? Democracy and Power in an American City* (New Haven: Yale University Press, 1960).

specific interests in community decisions; the members of these elites thus interact in connection with community decisions about which two or more of these separate groups' members have specific interests. In the view of others, including followers of Floyd Hunter,[24] the heads of major local corporations and banks are among the members of a small undifferentiated elite group whose composition is determined through studies of leaders' reputations among citizens. The two approaches—"pluralist" and "elitist"—have been the subject of a number of theoretical and methodological controversies about how one best measures power and influence and how one defines "power" and related concepts. The fact that many decisions of significance in a community are not really in the purview of community residents or their leaders, as such, but are public *and* private decisions, makes for questions about both approaches; whether there is an elite or plural group involved in shifting alliances in a community, many decisions are made by public *and* private representatives acting both together and separately. Questions and decisions about the locations of retail shopping districts, for example, are public-private decisions though they directly affect occupational structures, and the demand for and provision of a large number of services—decisions that may have as great or greater impact on community life as the more "purely" public decisions.[25] The fact that many public decisions affecting communities, meanwhile, are dependent upon the policies or programs involving contingent funding requirements, and upon publicly established standards, further complicates efforts to comprehend the role of local power wielders, corporate and otherwise. As recent developments in New York City illustrate, New York and other bankers who closed their ears to city hall leaders' cries for short-term loans, can be very potent, indeed. The role of New York's and others' bankers, earlier, in encouraging municipal borrowing needs also to be recognized as an influential one in the original genesis of New York's and other big cities' fiscal problems, problems that involve a city's capacity to provide public services and to contribute to the demand for labor.

More typically, however, the picture of corporations' influence upon communities is rather more fuzzy than corporate critics would like. The leaders of local corporations have no special purchase, for example, on the innumerable decisions in which state or federal policies are preeminent. Added problems, in research, stem from the ways agendas are set and public policy questions

---

24. See, e.g., Floyd Hunter, *Community Power Structure: A Study of Decision Makers* (Chapel Hill: University of North Carolina Press, 1953).

25. For a discussion from which this section borrows, see Ivar Berg and Mayer N. Zald, "Business and Society," *Annual Review of Sociology,* vol. 4 (1978). On the specific point, see Harvey Molotch, "The City as a Growth Machine: Toward a Political Economy of Place," *American Journal of Sociology,* 82 (1976) 309-32. The most recent critique of the "pluralist" view argues that Dahl's study of New Haven was incomplete and that newly discovered evidence is descriptive of a powerful single elite group in that city. See G. William Domhoff, *Who Really Rules? New Haven and Community Power Revisited* (Santa Monica, Calif.: Goodyear, 1978).

are phrased, problems which have been shown by Bachrach and Baratz, and by Crenson, to influence the conclusions one may draw about corporate influences.[26] Others have demonstrated the value of looking at specific issues, thereby to observe that corporate actors do have power and that they exercise this power, but they do so not as members of a power elite but specifically as corporate leaders. These leaders' business decisions, *as such,* and linkages to other leaders set aside, thus affect the allocation of community resources, the demand for different types of skills, the interactions of groups in the community, and the character of community networks which, in turn, effect decision making in the community.[27]

The methodological and conceptual difficulties outlined here not only frustrate efforts to get a firm grasp on suggestive answers to questions about corporations and communities; they also plague some efforts to ask questions about the possible implications for communities of the mixes of owners and nonowners among the top managers of their local firms. Thus, statistical analyses of the effects of local or absentee-ownership arrangements on communities' general welfare, their expenditures on public services, and a host of other community characteristics, yield no unambiguous overall results supporting the commonly held belief in the critical importance of the distinction.[28] The distinction between owners and managers refers to an important dimension of the structural differentiation that has occurred in a number of industrial settings, and has frequently been singled out for attention by sociologists, economists, and public policy makers. In this section we have been concerned with corporations and the polity. As we will see, the correlates of what is termed the "separation of corporate ownership from control" will continue to concern us in some of the subsections of the next section of this chapter, in which we look at evidence bearing upon corporations' and managers' powers in the economy.

26. See P. Bachrach and M. S. Baratz, "Two Faces of Power," *American Political Science Review,* 56 (1972), 947-52; P. Bachrach and M. S. Baratz, "Decision and Non-Decision: An Analytical Framework," *American Political Science Review,* 57 (1973) 632-34; and M. A. Crenson, *The Un-politics of Air Pollution: A Study of Non-Decision Making in the Cities* (Baltimore: Johns Hopkins University Press, 1971).

27. For assessments of some of these developments, see J. S. Coleman, "Loss of Power," *American Sociological Review,* 38 (1973), 1-17; R. Perucci and M. Pilisuk, "Leaders and Ruling Elites: The Interorganizational Bases of Community Power," *American Sociological Review,* 35 (1970), 1040-56; and H. Turk, "Interorganizational Networks in Urban Society: Initial Perspectives and Comparative Research," *American Sociological Review,* 35 (1970), 1-18.

28. See M. Aiken and P. Mott (eds.), *The Structure of Community Power* (New York: Random House, 1970), especially M. Aiken, "The Distribution of Community Power: Structural Bases and Social Consequences," pp. 487-526; Paul Mott, "The Role of the Absentee-Owned Corporation in the Changing Community," pp. 170-79; Robert Mills French, "Economic Change and Community Power Structure: Transition in Cornucopia," pp. 181-92; and Roland J. Pellegrin and Charles Coates, "Absentee-Owned Corporations and Community Power Structure," pp. 163-69.

CORPORATIONS, MANAGERS, AND THE ECONOMY

Paralleling questions about managers' and corporations' impact on the political structure of society are questions of their powers to shape the structure and to influence the functioning of the economy. The specific questions to be addressed in the present section derive from the emergence of a relatively small number of very large, resource-rich corporations and from the emergence of a large cadre of professional managers within these and within smaller firms who are effectively the dependent satellites of "big business."

The causes and alleged consequences of big business and "managerialism"—the emergence of a professional manager corps—have been the subject of study for a very long time. Indeed, a fully developed analytical tradition has grown up around the early work of Karl Marx and Frederich Engels who saw individual capitalist managers driven inexorably to make investments and acquisitions that would increase the surplus value produced by their workers, the better to beat down competitors determined to do as much to them. The expenses of capital plant and equipment, they argued, forced them to expropriate what had earlier been the workers' means of production and to accumulate the financial capital that would enable them to survive competitive wars. This model of the economy is only a little bit different from one in which a number of modern analysts have made intellectual investments, the more radical Marxist and neo-Marxist critiques of the twentieth century quite apart. Thus it is widely believed that the costs of modern capital equipment needed to assure a competitive advantage in the marketplace force managers to perfect the social (organizational) technology of production. The results are large aggregations of physical capital managed by the professional leaders of organizations that are structured along highly legal—rational bureaucratic lines.

Among the specific questions growing out of this formulation are the following:

1. Do modern economic-technological-organizational processes lead to expansions in the size of the biggest corporations beyond that needed to achieve the economies in production that generally accompany increases in the scale of operations?

2. Are democratic institutions and the legitimate economic interests of millions of consumers threatened by the presence of large corporate enterprises whose economic powers are less than fully tempered by beneficially high levels of competition?

3. Does the succession to leadership of the professional managers in large corporations that are insufficiently buffeted by the chill winds of the marketplace lead to a kind of self-serving "managerialism," at the expense of owners and others, that threatens both economic efficiency and the "open" occupational system favored in democratic theory?

4. If the answers to the foregoing questions are affirmative ones, is it possible, at least, to set limits on self-serving managerialism, on managers

who help themselves and their careers, and on the predatory economic behavior of large corporations, by public regulatory arrangements? Can regulatory arrangements, in short, help to restore something of a balance between the power of industry, striving for efficiencies associated with large scale, and the power of society to protect itself against economic victimization?

These questions, which apply to the remaining sections of this chapter, are important because even approximate answers to them ultimately bear upon the nature of relations and options among owners, managers, community residents, and workers and consumers. It is to these questions that we now turn.

**The Concentration
of Economic Power**

The question of the degree to which so-called dominant firms in key industries can effectively avoid the forces of competition has preoccupied a number of investigators and public policy makers for several decades. Landmark studies sponsored by the Temporary National Economic Commission in the period before its Congressional mandate expired in 1941 provided rich empirical evidence that in highly concentrated industries, industries in which the eight or four of the largest firms hold more than 70 percent of the market, can earn persistently high profits; the barrier to the entry of new firms into these industries are also quite significant. These, as Caves points out, are signals "that resource allocation has gone wrong." It is the case, moreover, that "the pricing practices used in concentrated industries . . . make it harder to use public policy to maintain full employment without inflation,"[29] issues that have been of chronic concern in the U.S. and of grave concern in the 1970s. The argument is that large corporations in concentrated industries can set their prices as they will, the results of which are inflationary.

The evidence since the TNEC studies shows that tnere is considerable market concentration but that in the critical manufacturing industries, such concentration since World War II "has shown no marked tendency to increase or decrease," and is "moderate" or "relatively low in the greater part of manufacturing."[30] In appraising the meaning of the concentrated industries one should note that (1) it is increasingly difficult to define an "industry"; concentration is more significant if its companies' products are entirely or mostly free

---

29. Richard Caves, *American Industry: Structure, Conduct, Performance* (Englewood Cliffs, N.J.: Prentice-Hall, 1964), p. 111.

30. Walter Adams, "Public Policy in a Free Economy" in W. Adams (ed.), *The Structure of American Industry*, 5th ed. (New York: Macmillan, 1977), pp. 493, 497. See also Alfred S. Eichner, "Business Concentration and Its Significance," in Ivar Berg (ed.), *The Business of America* (New York: Harcourt Brace Jovanovich, 1968), pp. 169-200; and F. M. Scherer, *Industrial Market Structure and Economic Performance* (Chicago: Rand McNally, 1970), pp. 39-71.

of competition from products of other industries; (2) some firms are enumerated as members of one industry though their assets are distributed over a number of other industries; (3) the effects of imported products on industry sales are generally not considered in the calculations of industry concentration ratios; (4) some firms are "dominant" in a region or specific local market but do not appear as dominant in aggregated national estimates; and (5) in some cases a few or even only two firms engage very actively in competition with each other.

Although it is difficult to minimize the extent to which the American economy is concentrated in structural terms, it may be said that the issues involved in proving the case are extraordinarily complicated. The complications result in large measure from the difficulties in measuring the social costs and benefits, that is, the economic and social significance of concentration. Such measurements involve making difficult judgments, for example, about the *net* values of technical and product innovations financed by the profits from the higher prices concentrated industries can charge. These economic benefits must be netted out against judgmental conclusions about entry barriers, which reduce competition, and the disincentives to managers of a too comfortable market position. Closely related to questions of market concentration are those associated with the degree to which the leaders of large firms are members of a national industrial elite whose close and socially relevant associations with each other are facilitated by their overlapping memberships on each others corporate boards of directors, a relationship referred to as interlocking directorships, a matter to which we turn next.

Interlocking Directorates

Few business practices have been as vulnerable to liberal and radical criticisms as those of the so-called money trust. Recent evidence suggests that the "old" money trust began to decline in significance as an interlocked apparatus after the famous Pujo Hearings in 1912, after the deaths of many of the early moguls, after the profitability of trust activities began to decline, after public relations campaigns were directed against the members, and after the money trust members, themselves, grew sensitive to the legal attacks and criticisms, otherwise, that were directed at them.

The most thorough recent assessment of interlocking, direct and indirect, of corporate directors in the years 1912, 1935, 1964, 1969, and 1974 involving 100 industrial, 25 transportation, 20 banks, 10 insurance companies, and 12 large investment houses, i.e., "big business," has been conducted by Bunting. He shows that interlocking practices in general have increased overall since 1912, but that "heavy" interlocking (the number of companies in which 25 or more directors interlock with directors of other corporations) has declined overall.[31] The bulk of the increase, he notes from a careful intersectoral analysis, is at-

---

31. David Bunting, "Corporate Interlocking, Part I—The Money Trust," *Directors and Boards: The Journal of Corporate Action*, 1 (1976), 6-15.

tributable to developments occurring among industrial corporations, though financial organizations became the dominant source of concentrated economic power in big business. By 1974, 100 percent of the companies in the "new" money trust were banks or insurance companies.[32]

These facts do not, by themselves, tell us what is the significance of the developments under examination, however. Thus Bunting was not able to identify any clear implications, for example, of interlocking directorships for competition. He does report, however, that "between 10 and 30 percent of the variation in returns on investment is 'explained' [in regression analysis] by . . . company interlocking, with the greatest percentage explained in banking than in any other sector (sic.)."[33] Bunting recognizes that economic factors (e.g. industry type, concentration, relative company size, relative industry standing, industry classification) among others may influence the relationship between return and interlocking. But the study of some of these is not easy, as we saw in connection with concentration above. It is also difficult to study firms' behavior in a world of conglomerated firms, a matter to which we will turn in the next section. Bunting also recognizes, apropos of measuring the performance of firms for example, that there are difficulties in measuring return on investment accurately from corporate data from which advertising and certain other investment-like expenditures are excluded. We have no readily available method, in short, for determining whether interlocked firms can earn higher returns by virtue of their interlocked character than otherwise would be the case.

Results paralleling those obtained by Bunting have been reported by Sonquist and Koenig in a study of 401 central corporations linked to each other by two or more common directors in 1969.[34] Sonquist and Koenig's criteria of interlocking were thus a good deal looser than Bunting's and they therefore recorded more interlocking than Bunting. But they were faced with the same difficulties as Bunting in measuring differences in the performances of the more and less interlocked firms; their conclusions, like Bunting's, do not add weight, therefore, to what is rather compelling circumstantial evidence of a community of well developed interests among a relatively small number of top corporate leaders.

Conglomeration in Enterprise

The great wave of corporate mergers in the 1960s and the apparent renewal of acquisitive urges among managers in the late 1970s have distracted social

---

32. David Bunting, "Corporate Interlocking, Part II—The Modern Money Trust," *Directors and Boards: The Journal of Corporate Action,* 1 (1976), 27-37.

33. David Bunting, "Corporate Interlocking, Part III—Interlocks and Return on Investment," *Directors and Boards: The Journal of Corporate Action,* 1 (1976), 7.

34. John A. Sonquist and Thomas Koenig, "Interlocking Directorates in the Top U.S. Corporations: A Graph Theory Approach," *The Insurgent Sociologist,* 5, 3 (1975), 196-225.

scientists and policy makers from traditional and now less urgent questions about concentration and interlocking directorships. The newest wave of mergers is especially interesting in that there is some evidence that they are entered into more selectively by the more reputable, big corporations than was the case in the 1960s. Many of these acquisitions appear simply, meanwhile, to be alternatives to actual corporate expansions, by the acquiring firms, into areas in which they would be competing with the acquired firms anyway.[35]

Some policy makers and social science investigators regard conglomerates as having greater implications for the structure of industrial society because mergers along conglomerate lines lead to consolidated data in disclosures, consolidations that make performance tests of managers of particular subsidiaries more difficult to apply. Conglomerated mergers, for example, (1) permit more subtle evasions of market forces because the "parents" can "cross-subsidize" (i.e., support) their marginally performing subsidiaries, (2) can arrange mutually supporting procurement and sales agreements (called reciprocity), and (3) can facilitate cost-reducing intramural (and non-competitively determined) transfer prices for the exchange of goods and services within conglomerates. That the movement has been a significant one in numerical terms is shown clearly in statistical data: The share of total assets held by the top 200 industrials jumped four points, from 57 to 61 percent, from 1966 to 1968. This development resulted largely and essentially from conglomerates. "Indeed, by 1968, the top 100 held a larger share than had been held by the top 200 in 1950, an increase attributable primarily to mergers."[36] As Mueller, a long-time student of economic structure, sees it, the important point is not whether the share of assets held by the top 200 or even the top 100 increases. Rather, he argues, that "The most relevant measure of conglomerate business is the share held by *all* very large corporations." On this point, Mueller notes that ". . . one such index is the share held by industrial corporations with assets of $1 billion or more. Whereas in 1929 there were only three corporations of this size, by 1973 there were 136 . . . [whose] share of manufacturing assets grew from 8 percent in 1939 to 53 percent in 1973. Even allowing for inflation of asset values, the crucial fact is that, in 1973, so few corporations controlled more than half of all manufacturing assets. Moreover, another 24 percent of the assets were held by corporations [many of which are also conglomerated] with assets between $100 million and $1 billion."[37]

The conglomerate merger movements of recent times partly represent responses to what corporate leaders conceive to be overly rigid readings of antitrust law by Justice Department antitrusters. They note that their corporations

---

35. See "The Great Takeover Binge," *Business Week* (November 14, 1977), pp. 176-84.

36. Willard F. Mueller, "Conglomerates: A 'Non-Industry'" in Adams (ed.), *The Structure of American Industry,* p. 443.

37. Ibid., pp. 445.

have thereby suffered in the marketplace against foreign competitors who are subject, back home, to fewer restrictions on their efforts to enjoy economies of scale through expansion and diversification along traditional lines. The result, says Mueller, has been:

> to enhance further the absolute and relative size of many already large corporations, as well as to create many new ones. . . . Many [of the 100 largest industrials in 1974] were substantial firms in 1960, when ten ranked among the top 100 industrials and 22 ranked among the top 500. Whereas sales of all corporations engaged primarily in manufacturing grew by 135 per cent from 1960-1974, these corporations grew by 772 per cent. All but two of these 25 corporations grew by more than 500 per cent and 11 grew by more than 1,000 per cent during the period. All had annual sales of more than $2 billion in 1974, and all but one increased its rank among the top industrial corporations.[38]

The figures are frightening ones. Or so one is encouraged to believe; and perhaps one ought to heed warnings of the resulting threats to democracy and, potentially to efficiency as well. But no investigators have been able to delineate and specify the actual consequences for market processes of firms that, from a theoretical point of view, enjoy so many organizational-economic advantages.[39] The most demonstrable advantages to the managers of conglomerates inhere in the difficulty their putative bosses, the stockholders, and other interested parties have in gauging the performance of conglomerates' *component companies* from disclosure of consolidated data.[40] Some will see the resulting difficulties for obtaining traditional "market tests" of managers' performance to be exaggerated by the shift over from the sale of shares to investors to borrowed funds in the financing of corporate activities and undertakings.[41] In theory it would be preferable for investors generally to decide which firms deserve support, not the managers of financial institutions with basic interests linked all too often to those of their corporate debtors!

The older problems, attending concentration through vertical and horizontal integration, still attract some public policy makers and researchers, but as with interlocking directorates and conglomerates, the data do not conclusively show that the advantages to top managers of dominant companies in highly concentrated industries are not offset, in some measure, by advantages to con-

---

38. Ibid., pp. 455-57.

39. Peter O. Steiner, *Mergers: Motives, Effects, Policies* (Ann Arbor: University of Michigan Press, 1975).

40. Stanley E. Boyle and Philip W. Jaynes, *Conglomerate Merger Performance: An Empirical Analysis of Nine Corporations* (Washington, D.C.: Government Printing Office, 1972).

41. "The Debt Economy," *Business Week* (October 12, 1974), pp. 45-116.

sumers. Thus, livelier versions of competition often imply what may be unacceptable sacrifices of economies attributable to scale, to large size, and reductions thereby in the risk capital available for technical and product innovations. There may also be related net benefits, in industrial development terms, of the outcomes of long planning periods and of research and development investments. One widely respected authority regards these investments and planning efforts to be well balanced against the risks that "dominants" will act in a predatory fashion.[42]

The best evidence that dominant firms in concentrated industries can serve themselves, without any necessary (and ideal) regard for social interests, pertains to the auto and steel industries. Thus, Eckstein and Fromm have concluded from detailed studies that the wholesale price index would have risen 40 percent less than in fact it did, in the period 1947-1958, had the prices for steel and autos risen at the same lower rates of other wholesale prices in more competitive markets, i.e., in markets in which "dominants" could not administer prices in accordance with noncompetitive standards. And Markham, in comparisons of the secular and cyclical price behavior of nine "concentrated" and four "atomistically structured" industries, from 1953 to 1959, reported that the steel and auto industries "exhibited pricing patterns patently inconsistent with supply and demand movements...."[43]

The evidence in this and the previous section bears upon questions about the powers of dominant corporations in concentrated industries. Questions can also be asked about the powers that have accrued to the managers of these and other large corporations as a result of the fact that the relationship between many of them and the large technical and managerial staffs they direct to their stockholder-employers have become increasingly tenuous. This separation of ownership from control has indeed become a conspicuous—almost an identifying characteristic of modern business, the cause and consequences of which have interested policy makers and social scientists especially since the appearance of a pathbreaking empirical study of the trends by Berle and Means.[44] The facts pertaining to recent times show that individual stockholders are certainly no more in direct control of their corporate properties now than they were in the days of Berle and Means' investigation. Thus, in the revised version of the 1932 assessment, the investigators report that "While in 1929 only 88 of the 200 largest corporations were classed as management controlled, by 1963 196 or 84.5 percent, were so classed. And in 1929, 22 corporations were classed as

42. Scherer, *Industrial Market Structure,* pp. 9-38, 518-42.

43. Eckstein and Fromm's and Markhaus' results are summarized in Scherer, *Industrial Market Structure,* pp. 298-99.

44. Adolph A. Berle and Gardner C. Means, *The Corporation and Private Property* (New York: Macmillan, 1968). This is a recent edition, containing more current data in a new appendix, of a volume first published in 1932. The issues involved were treated in a general fashion in many places in the writings of Karl Marx, Thorstein Veblen, and Max Weber.

privately owned or controlled by the owners through majority ownership, while only 5 were so classed in 1963.... The corporate revolution," the authors write, "marches on."[45] Using slightly different criteria, Larner reports that 84 percent of the 200 largest, and 70 percent of the next 300 nonfinancial organizations, are controlled by managers rather than by owners.[46] The patterns in the United Kingdom, derived in a thoughtful comparative analysis, are not appreciably different.[47]

Not all stockholders are small investors, of course; large blocs of equities are held by institutional investors some of whom, like pension funds and other large financial institutions, have obvious concerns about the performance of managers of the companies in which they invest, companies whose growth and profits are a matter of basic economic interest. And these interests make some scholars anxious over the degree to which managers are responsive to ordinary, "small" stockholders' interests. Berle, himself, had been concerned about the potential power of pension funds and, more recently, Drucker is concerned about a potential hue and cry among inflation-suffering pensioners for greater dividends from the corporations in their funds' portfolios.[48] Additional concern is also expressed, in and out of business circles as we have noted, about the drift away from equity (stock) sales in favor of corporate borrowing. Taken together, the concerns are much like those expressed in other eras: Are owners left out of the economic play and are managers thus responsible only to themselves and to a relatively small number of like-minded large investors? Does the growing use of retained (undistributed earnings), depreciation allowances (afforded in tax laws as incentives) and borrowed funds spare the professional manager the obligation to face different and putatively more demanding, critical tests in the traditional financial marketplace?

The relevant data are not altogether reassuring. The evidence suggests that economic decisions in the large pace-setting corporations—decisions about production levels, prices, labor requirements, technological changes, layoffs and labor relations, decisions affecting the well-being of communities, the operations of labor markets, and the operation of large sectors of the larger economy—are made by a relatively small segment of the American population. Thus stockholders do still earn dividends from corporations, but "dividends

---

45. Ibid., p. xx.

46. Robert J. Larner, *Management Control and the Large Corporation* (Cambridge, Mass.: Harvard University Press, 1970).

47. Sargent Florence, *The Logic of British and American Industry,* 3rd ed. (London: Routledge and Kegan Paul, 1972), pp. 203-58.

48. Adolph A. Berle, *Economic Power and the Free Society* (Santa Barbara, California: Center for the Study of Democratic Institutions, 1957); and Peter F. Drucker, *The Unseen Revolution: How Pension Fund Socialism Came to America* (New York: Harper & Row, 1976). The concerns of large institutional investors are more likely to be expressed in their buying and selling of shares than in month-to-month efforts targeted at managers' behavior.

from public corporate stocks were the most concentrated type of income. . . . The richest one-fifth of American households . . . accounted [in 1962] for 82 percent of all dividend income."[49] Linkages between a small number of wealthy stockholders and upper-level managers, it is feared, are sufficiently well developed to reduce the prospects that the former will control and discipline the latter. Jacoby suggests, however, that the membership composition of the wealthy business-related members of this group changes constantly, that its members often sell their own closely held companies, or the stocks they hold in publicly held and often larger companies, and that their heirs, not infrequently, "slip downward" in wealth ranking, thus becoming impotent instruments of control, even as new entrepreneurs-investors are successful.[50]

Others are not so sanguine. Thus Zeitlin has shown that "As of 1964, the 100 largest commercial banks in the U.S. held 46 percent of all the deposits in 13,775 commercial banks in the country . . ." while "the largest banks surveyed in 10 major cities, not including the West Coast, hold 5 percent or more of the common stock in 147 (29 percent of the 500 largest industrial corporations,)" and that banks, in turn, have also become management-controlled—perhaps as many as 75 percent of the large banks.[51] Once again, the fact that these banks make loans to corporations whose other sources of funds are cash flow (retained earnings plus tax-afforded depreciation allowances) means that a growing number of corporations are once-removed from investment decisions by the putatively return-maximizing individual investors favored in neoclassical economic theory. These concerns have led a number of policy makers and social scientists to focus upon the managers themselves. Again, the issues we continue to join bear upon the relations among different interest groups and among different role incumbents in industrial society.

MANAGERS

In studies of managers the emphases are upon (1) their relative performance patterns in owner-controlled and manager-controlled firms; (2) the technical and organizational (or bureaucratic) forces that have led to "managerialism" in America; and (3) the ideology of business leaders. Selected materials from these three bodies of research will be considered in the three remaining sections of this chapter.

---

49. Neil H. Jacoby, *Corporate Power and Social Responsibility: A Blueprint for the Future* (New York: Macmillan, 1973), p. 39.

50. Ibid., p. 39.

51. See Maurice Zeitlin, ed., *American Society, Inc.,* pp. 259-60.

Managers and Owners

Basic to the controversy over the separation of ownership from control is the question of whether managers in owner-controlled companies, compared with other managers, march to a different drummer. It needs to be noted first, though, that top level professional managers are not without equity interests in their firms. Thus, Burck has considered data on 500 heads of industrial and 700 heads of nonindustrial firms, and reports that while most managers do not come from stockholders' ranks, three of four managers nowadays, hold from $100,000 to $1,000,000 in equity interests in the firms by which they are employed.[52] Such data do not prove much about managers' behavior, as such; nor is it clear that stockholders are interested only in dividends, and not stock-appreciating corporate growth. Available measures of the performance of owners and managers are selective in character and are only a little bit more helpful in disposing of the main issues. Thus Wildsmith investigated diverse management actions in a 1973 study and reports that it is difficult to make comparisons of owner and "managers" firms that are operationally useful:

> Managerial theories are . . . more realistic in their assumptions and as a consequence they predict responses which in most cases are different from those of profit maximisers and closer to those found in reality. *However, the managerial models are no more operational than entrepreneurial models: they are analytic rather than descriptive or prescriptive.* . . .[53]

Wildsmith goes on to point out that evidence about differences in the behavior of the two types of managers in a variety of decision-making areas are either inconclusive or contradictory. "Managers identify to an unagreed extent with stockholders," he writes, and "in a situation in which conflict arises, managers are constrained to a disputed degree by the capital market."[54] Capital market controls, Wildsmith writes, operate (1) through stockholders; (2) the market-depressing sales of shares; and (3) through the fears of managers that their circumstances will be affected by their firms' being taken over in acquisition movements. Wildsmith emphasizes that the relative importance of these control mechanisms to managers' actions varies. Baumol offers relevant evidence that professional managers have opportunities to act rationally on bases other than those given in profit-maximizing rules, in favor of long-term growth, for example,[55] but stockholders may often also have interests in such growth rather than in dividend receipts.

52. Charles C. Burck, "A Group Profile of the *Fortune* 500 Chief Executives," *Fortune,* 93, 5 (1976), 173-77, 308-12.

53. J. R. Wildsmith, *Managerial Theories of the Firm* (New York: Dunnellen, 1973).

54. Ibid., pp. 125-26.

55. Ibid., pp. 125-26.

Stano, an economist, assumes that stockholders' immediate concerns are with the rate of return on their investments and concludes from a study of the (1965) "Fortune 500" firms that the managers of management-controlled firms during 1963-1972 used their own discretion while those in owner-controlled firms were responsive to the interests of the controlling stockholder group.[56] These results confirmed earlier ones by Baumol that professional managers are less averse to risk than the others. Stano reports that one of the clearest manifestations of the differences between owner-controlled managers' and others is the formers' hesitancies about financial and market risks and their greater reluctance to undertake corporate expansion efforts by mergers and acquisitions.

In all, the evidence that the separation of ownership and control has produced remarkable effects on the economic actions of firms is like the evidence pertaining to the effects of this process of differentiation on community power structures. We simply cannot point to this differentiation or separation process with confident expectations that it explains, by itself, much of the variance that has been observable in communities or firms.[57] Managers may well differ in their ways as corporate and community leaders, but the differences are more likely to be attributable to differences in circumstances, especially market conditions, and to differences in their abilities to cope with challenges and to act on their opportunities. Such differences in managers' ways are thus apparently not patterned along the theoretical lines staked out by those concerned with the evolution of proprietary arrangements and changes in ownership patterns per se.

Managers, Careers, Backgrounds, and Beliefs

Paralleling interests in the accumulation of capital by the larger corporations through decades-long policies of plowing back earnings and the emergence of a managerial cadre have been interests in (1) the impact of corporate growth, (2) the intensification of investments in technological aids to production, and (3) the routinization of the activities organic to a firm's operations.[58] These three developments have generally been seen by industrial sociologists to contrib-

---

56. Miron Stano, "Monopoly Power, Ownership Control, and Corporate Performance," *Bell Journal of Economics*, 7, 2A (1976), 672-79.

57. See Rolf Dahrendorf, *Class and Class Conflict in Modern Society* (London: Routledge and Kegan Paul, 1959); John Child, *The Business Enterprise in Modern Industrial Society* (London: Collier-Macmillan, 1969), pp. 34-58; and Frederic L. Pryor, *Property and Industrial Organization in Communist and Capitalist Nations* (Bloomington: Indiana University Press, 1973), pp. 114-31.

58. For useful detailed treatments of these developments, see Amitai Etzioni, *Modern Organizations* (Englewood Cliffs, N.J.: Prentice-Hall, 1964); Charles Perrow, *Complex Organizations: A Critical Essay* (Glenview, Ill.: Scott, Foresman, 1972); and Peter M. Blau and Marshall W. Meyer, *Bureaucracy in Modern Society*, 2nd ed. (New York: Random House, 1971).

ute to the characteristics of organization we identified in other sections of this book with the concept of bureaucratization.[58] Critical questions have been raised, especially, about the managers of these enterprises, about whether the routes to corporate and economic influence have changed and about whether business leaders' perspectives—their ideologies—have come to reflect their positions as technocrats, bureaucrats, or "organization men."

The first of these questions about businessmen's backgrounds and careers has been addressed by students with diverse interests in the subject but they tend to be cut from the same cloth.[59] Thus whether investigators have a general concern with social mobility or a particular concern with the structure and functioning of the business sector of the American economy, the emphasis has been upon social and organizational career experiences—sometimes only one of these—of the very top-most groups of business leaders: corporate presidents, board chairman, and executive vice presidents—the names are generally selected from among the leaders of largest corporations in each of the time periods that have excited the interests of a particular investigator. The results of these studies, when taken together, show that America's business leaders have rarely come from the ranks of lower blue-collar parents, though recent top leaders are less frequently from the ranks of the wealthiest of Americans than they were in earlier periods. These studies also show that, while they come from the "outside," as "professionals," and not typically from the ranks of stockholders, three of four top executives nowadays hold considerable equity interests as we saw above.

Several of the authors of the earliest studies used the term "bureaucratic" to characterize the career progressions of nonowners or nonentrepreneurs/founders, i.e. the careers of "professional" managers. The term is not an es-

---

59. The earliest of these were by F. W. Taussig and S. C. Joslyn, *American Business Leaders* (New York: Macmillan, 1932); Robert A. Gordon, *Business Leadership in the Large Corporations* (Washington, D.C.: Brookings Institution, 1945); and C. Wright Mills, "The American Business Elite: A Collective Portrait," *The Journal of Economic History,* 5, Supplement 5 (December 1945), 42. The more recent studies include William Miller, "The Business Elite in Business Bureaucracies," in William Miller (ed.), *Men in Business* (Cambridge, Mass.: Harvard University Press, 1952), pp. 286–307; Suzanne Keller, "The Social Origins and Career Lives of Three Generations of American Business Leaders" (Ph.D. dissertation, Columbia University, 1953); Mable Newcomer, *The Big Business Executive: The Factors That Made Him: 1900–1950* (New York: Columbia University Press, 1955); W. Lloyd Warner and James C. Abegglen, *Occupational Mobility* (Minneapolis: University of Minnesota Press, 1955), and *Big Business Leaders in America* (New York: Harper & Row, 1955); Editors of *FORTUNE, The Executive Life* (Garden City, N.Y.: Doubleday, 1956); Seymour Martin Lipset and Reinhard Bendix, *Social Mobility in Industrial Society* (Berkeley and Los Angeles: University of California Press, 1959); William P. Dommermuth, *The Road to the Top: A Study of the Careers of Corporation Presidents* (Austin: University of Texas Bureau of Business Research, 1965); *The Big Business Executive, 1964* (New York: Scientific American, 1965); Jay M. Gould, *The Technical Elite* (New York: Augustus M. Kelley, 1966); Burck, "A Group Profile of the Fortune 500 Chief Executives" (includes heads of 500 "industrials" and 300 men who run nonindustrials).

pecially apt one: When we think of bureaucracy we think in organizational terms, terms most readily identified, as we have seen, with the ideas of Max Weber. The data in the early studies of business careers, however, typically reveal a great deal of interindustry mobility, in general, and of intraindustry transfers, especially.[60] The conceptual leap involved in moving from organizations as bureaucracies to entire industries conceived as bureaucracies is a considerable one.

More recent evidence does point somewhat more clearly to the coupling of corporate size with the bureaucratization of business leaders' careers, i.e., with protracted periods of service within one large organization. Thus a 1976 survey of chief executive officers by *Fortune* magazine indicates that the managers of the 100 largest firms have moved about less frequently than those heading the firms ranked from 401 to 500 in size. The first groups' members have worked on the average for 1.8 companies; the figure for the other is 2.8. About 30 percent of the first group worked their way up from the lower rungs of their corporate ladders, an experience shared by barely 12 percent of the second group. Their differential service records are reflected further in the fact that the heads of the bottom fifth of our largest corporations worked for their companies about half as long as those in the top fifth before becoming chief executive officers.[61] The investigator suggests that the concept of career bureaucratization is far more applicable to managers' careers in the very largest of the very large firms in our economy than to managers as a general rule.

This conclusion does not support another widely held belief that the bureaucratization of business leaders' careers results from factors rooted in technological developments, since the association observed of career length is with company size, a variable that tells us little precisely about executive careers, or about the effects of technological differences among the top 500 firms in shaping leaders' careers. Although the term bureaucratization may be very usefully applied to the careers of specialists, as such, it is a mite less revealing or suggestive of implications when it is applied to modern top level managers. As Burck points out, 62 percent of his respondents have served in many rather than few of their companies' departments or divisions; this stands in marked contrast to the experiences of earlier generations of managers who were far less broadly grounded in management practices and less knowledgeable about sophisticated theories relevant to an enterprise's complex operations. The modern manager is far more likely to be a "generalist" than a specialist.[62]

That highly competent persons may have very different career experiences within differentially "bureaucratized" elements within the same organizations

---

60. See, particularly, Reinhard Bendix, *Work and Authority in Industry: Ideologies of Management in the Course of Industrialization* (New York: John Wiley, 1956), pp. 234-35.

61. Burck, "A Group Profile," pp. 177, 308.

62. Ibid., p. 308.

has, of course, long been recognized by sociologists. Thus the careers of air corps and military police officers in the U.S. Army in World War II were very different, and led to differences in the attitudes of the more bureaucratized experiences of MPs and the less bureaucratized experiences of air corpsmen. Indeed, the original analyses of these differences helped give substance to social psychological concepts of "relative deprivation";[63] The more "bureaucratized" MPs were more contented than air corpsmen, though the latter required many more promotions.

It may also be pointed out that Weber and others have regarded the extensive use of modernized double-entry bookkeeping methods as one of the most significant indicators of the bureaucratization of large organizations. The fact is, however, that there is a stormy debate in the U.S. over the specific accounting rules that should govern "a myriad of individual situations. Such rules . . . are necessary for consistent performance of [the jobs of lawyers, accountants and company executives] . . . and also for defense against charges for malpractice."[64] Thus, managers have been obliged, in a period of inflation, to become inventive entrepreneurs in their disclosure of financial information, an obligation induced by lively arguments in business, in the Securities and Exchange Commission, and in the accounting profession about such questions as whether inventory and equipment should be valued at their purchase or their replacement costs. Accounting procedures, in short, are by *no* means as crystalized and routinized as popular wisdom would have us believe. Whether by the "career" or "accounting" standards in the theory of bureaucracy available to us, modern corporations "fail" the test in a few critical respects. We suggest that parts of the test in received organizational theory, like many tests bearing on social life in recent years, need some revision if it is to give us finer readings than available from the crude litmus paper model currently available to industrial sociologists.

Not only may it be somewhat misleading to view managerial career exposures in accordance with an unrevealing model of organization but it may be misleading, as well, as the accounting issue may suggest, as an aid to our scientific understanding of what business leaders do in their positions of bureaucratic leadership,[65] a matter to which we turn in the next section.

63. For discussions and reviews of differences in the organizational careers of officers in different segments of the U.S. Army in World War II see Edward A. Shils, "Primary Groups in the American Army," and Hans Speier, "The American Soldier and the Sociology of Military Organization," in Robert K. Merton and Paul F. Lazarsfeld (eds.), *Continuities in Social Research: Studies in the Scope and Method of "The American Soldier"* (New York: Free Press, 1950), pp. 106-32, 169ff.

64. "Washington and Business," *New York Times,* July 12, 1976, p. 2.

65. For an exposition of an alternative view of top managers as leaders who embody an organization's purposes rather than as bureaucrats, see the seminal work by Phillip Selznick, *Leadership in Administration—A Sociological Interpretation* (New York: Harper & Row, 1957). The conceptions of top level managers as social leaders and human relationists will be reviewed in chapter 7.

Managers as Decision Makers

It is clear from the discussion so far that the routes to corporate leadership have changed with the separation of control from ownership. The paths in the early periods of businessmens' careers are represented by the main (and separate) speciality occupations in business organizations—marketing, production, finance. While these skills are separated at the lower managerial levels, they are later subsumed in the "general management" skills of the officers who finally gain access to chief executives' suites.

It is the case that some careers in business organizations or government bureaus are bureaucratic in that they involve highly specialized jobs in hierarchically ordered divisions or bureaus, jobs for which there are clear standards and job requirements.[66] Managers at upper levels, however, typically operate in very ambiguous circumstances. These managers, even in machine-paced manufacturing, rarely perform tasks whose character is essentially delineated by the graphs, charts, computers, rules, and regulations that surround corporate staff personnel. Rather, they negotiate with government regulators and lenders, dicker in general terms with suppliers, and spend considerable time managing lateral relationships among key groups within the corporation in a most ad hoc fashion.[67]

Indeed, there is evidence to suggest that some managers—including successful ones—do not approximate the model presented by economists any more than the one proffered by social scientists who emphasize the bureaucratic quality of business enterprise. Thus Kaplan and his colleagues report, in a study of pricing policies, that

> It was evident that most of the executives with whom the interviews were conducted did not ordinarily concern themselves with pricing details; instances appeared in which they were not intimately aware of how their products were priced. Even those who were quite familiar with company policy in the pricing area were among those who could not illustrate the policy by a detailed follow-through of particular price decisions. . . . Even where the people doing the pricing tended to have certain staff information placed before them into consideration often remained obscure. . . .

---

66. We may note in connection with public servants, that a powerful predictor of the mobility experiences of higher level civil service workers is the number of different *agencies* in which they have worked. See Ivar Berg, *Education and Jobs: The Great Training Robbery* (New York: Praeger, 1970), pp. 169-79.

67. See Albert Shapero's review of a book of *Harvard Business Review Articles on Management* (New York: Harper & Row, 1976) in "What Management Says and What Managers Do," *Fortune*, 93, 5 (May 1976), 275-76. For a discussion of the real, as compared with the stereotyped view of top and middle managers' jobs, see Leonard Sayles, *Managerial Behavior: Administration in Complex Organizations* (New York: McGraw-Hill, 1964).

Repeatedly, reference was made to the "art" or "feel" of pricing rather than observance of a formula.[68]

In an equally revealing study given the effects on an organization's employees involved, Sayles and Chandler looked at make-or-buy, or subcontracting decisions, and reported that

> ... complex cost calculations were not employed universally [in determining whether it is cheaper to contract-out or to do the work inside] but rather were limited to about three-fifths of the group. Of the remaining 40 percent, about 30 percent made absolutely no cost calculations. Surprisingly, the character of the computing system had no relationship to conclusions regarding relative cost. ...
> Size of plant *seemed* to have *some* relationship to estimates of the relative cost of contracting-out versus in-plant operations. A significant majority of the larger plants *considered* contracting-out cheaper than inside work.[69]

Similarly ad hoc, essentially nonbureaucratic, and "noneconomic" behavior has been reported in separate studies of corporate manpower practices. (These studies, by H. G. Heneman, Jr. and George Seltzer, and by Daniel E. Diamond and Hrach Bedrosian, will be discussed in chapter 6.)

Our discussion should not be taken to mean that firms have not become larger and more complex; we are simply saying that the term bureaucratization as we have come to define it in sociological terms can be almost as much of a confusing label as the "red tape" label in popular associations attached to the term. Thus it is clear that while modern technology may compel managers to work in complex organizations, it does not compel them to (1) build their organizations to particular sizes; or (2) divide the labors and skills in their organizations in accordance with readily apprehended rules, rules that may be virtually given by the technologies they adopt. Thus the extensive concentration of industry—another version of bureaucracy in the economy—results from the open choices of managers in dominant firms, not from limited and specifically bureaucratic-type choices imposed by efficiency considerations immanent in technology. Bain, for example, has shown that in 11 out of 20 industry cases, the most efficient (i.e. lowest cost) plant accounted for less than 2.5 percent of the national sales of the industry. The figure was 7.5 percent in 15 of the 20 cases. He also reports that the cost advantages of multiplant firms were "either

---

68. Abraham D. H. Kaplan, Joel B. Dirlam, and Robert Lanzilotti, *Pricing in Big Business: A Case Approach* (Washington, D.C.: Brookings Institution, 1958), p. 5.

69. Leonard R. Sayles and Margaret K. Chandler, *Contracting-Out: A Study of Management Decision Making* (New York: Columbia University Graduate School of Business, 1959), p. 36. Emphases added.

negligible or totally absent" in 6 of 20 industries; they were fairly small or negligible in 6; no adequate data were available for estimating purposes in the other 8.[70] As Adams concludes, in a review of Bain's and others' data, "These findings hardly support the contention that existing concentration [i.e., the dominant sales figures achieved by a relatively few very large firms] in American industry can be explained in terms of technological imperatives."[71] Adams goes on to point out that, in a number of relevant cases, "it seems that . . . medium-sized and small firms outperform their giant rivals. Moreover, a breaking down of huge firms does not necessarily have fatal effects on efficiency or profitability."[72]

Bendix has identified the bureaucratization of industry, and the resulting development of managerialism with the growing proportion of administrative personnel relative to production personnel in five industrial nations. Specifically, he links the rise in the numbers of administrators to the subdivision of entrepreneural functions "such that each phase, such as recruitment, pay, administration, etc., becomes the task of a separate administrative staff consisting of technical and administrative specialists as well as a number of salaried employees performing routine work."[73]

Increasing size, meantime, does entail increased administrative problems of delegation, of decision making, of monitoring, and of intramural coordination within enterprises. In the process of growth, organizations face the challenges inherent in both rationalizing and routinizing tasks; in codifying procedures; in designing effective spans of control; in developing information, personnel, and other "systems"; in ordering both hierarchical and lateral relationships; and in providing staff work and staff support to persons and groups nominally said to be incumbents of "line" roles.[74] But, while the sizes of firms themselves help to account for the expansion of their administration cadres, it by no means accounts for all of it. Thus, in Bendix's data the numbers of *technicians* increase

---

70. Joe S. Bain, *Barriers to New Competition* (Cambridge, Mass.: Harvard University Press, 1956), pp. 73, 85–88ff.

71. Walter Adams (ed.), *The Structure of American Industry,* 4th ed. (New York: Macmillan, 1971), p. 486.

72. Ibid., p. 487.

73. Reinhard Bendix, *Work and Authority: Ideologies of Management in the Course of Industrialization* (New York: John Wiley, 1965), p. 216. This study was among those undertaken under the aegis of the Inter-University Consortium upon whose works we drew in chapter 3.

74. For an early discussion of the longitudinal process, see Ernest Dale, *Planning and Developing the Company Organization Structure,* Research Report no. 20 (New York: American Management Association, 1952). For a helpful and brief discussion of more recent data, see Charles Perrow, *Complex Organizations: A Critical Essay* (Glenview, Ill.: Scott, Foresman, 1972). For a discussion of intramanagerial level tasks and roles, see Leonard Sayles, *Managerial Behavior: Administration in Complex Organizations* (New York: McGraw-Hill, 1964).

but those of *administrative employees* do not necessarily increase with size; white-collar expansion, in general, appears to vary somewhat with the type of industry:

> Thus, a high proportion of administrative *and* technical employees will be found in most capital intensive industries . . . This is also true of industries which require much supervision and technical work. . . .[75]

The data considered in the chapter up to this point suggest that business leaders are less constrained by market and technological functions in building the large corporation, and that these corporate giants appear to exercise some, but necessarily all, of their options to exploit their market positions and thereby to reap "excess" profits, to dominate community life, or to control political institutions. This power—both in potential and kinetic terms—cannot so readily be attributed to technical factors. Nor can it be so readily legitimized as the essentially unintended consequence of the actions of property holders simply pursuing the freedoms given affirmative sanction in law and in tradition.

It is a fact, furthermore, that this power cannot be readily linked in pragmatic terms to economic efficiency either. The upshot is that there are tensions in society among powerful business groups, incomplete though their use of power may be, and other groups concerned with the society's interests in the disposition of its human and other resources. And partisans on the businessman's side cannot seek to allay the tensions by appealing to efficiency, to business necessity, or to the play of technical imperatives.

On one side we therefore see efforts by business leaders to defend their roles and, on the other, by other groups to regulate them. Space does not permit us to explore these tensions between business and society in great detail. The literature on the subject would oblige us to look under and around a number of sizable boulders on what is a very rocky institutional landscape: It would involve our examining the main developments involving hundreds of laws, many regulatory agencies, and innumerable technical arguments, especially in the literature in economics and political science, over whether regulations are effective and reasonable.[76] It is to the point, however, to suggest that businessmen

---

75. Bendix, *Work and Authority*, 223-24. Emphasis added. Note the parallels, here, between the developments in forms with those discussed earlier in communities and in occupational structures.

76. For helpful summaries, representing different perspectives, see George J. Sigler, *The Citizen and the State: Essays on Regulation* (Chicago: University of Chicago Press, 1975); Theodore J. Lowi, *The End of Liberalism: Ideology, Policy and the Crisis of Public Authority* (New York: Norton, 1969); James W. McKie, *Social Responsibility and the Business Predicament: Studies in the Regulation of Economic Activity* (Washington, D.C.: Brookings Institution, 1974); Scherer, Industrial Market Strategy; James Q. Wilson, "The Dead Hand of Regulation," *The Public Interest*, 46 (1971), 3-14; Richard A. Posner, "Theories of Economic Regulation," *The Bell Journal of Economics and Management Science*, 5, 2, (Autumn 1974), 325-58.

either are disposed both to deny that they are powerful and to seek to ground their admittedly significant roles in society in terms that will clothe them with legitimacy.

Managers and Ideology

On the one hand, business leaders generally tend to downgrade their capacities to shape the environments in which they operate. In the language of scientists, they more often see themselves as "intervening" than as "independent" variables in the conventional but key calculations according to which the structure and functioning of national economies are assessed. They tend to see themselves as rational economic decision makers, at once bounded and guided by (1) the best information they can mobilize on prices, interest rates, tax policies, government expenditures, labor markets, the practices of corporations and the fickle moods of investors, clients, other "constituencies," and so forth; (2) straightfoward (general) accounting criteria according to which costs and returns may be toted up; and (3) their individual ethical commitments. Business leaders argue that governments' functions, in all this, are to prescribe a minimum orderliness, to facilitate predictability in commercial transactions and to punish violations and perversions of law and decency, respectively. Inefficiency, they argue, is a crime against economic rationality punishable by what are matter of factly taken to be the cruel and usual actions of competitors and customers in the marketplace.

In this view of the businessman, "monopoly power" is not viewed with alarm. The most important fact about exploitative monopoly power in industry (as contrasted with monopoly in labor and governmentally produced monopoly) as Milton Friedman puts the matter, is "its relative unimportance from the point of view of the economy as a whole."[77]

This perspective, according to which businessmen are construed as a more passive than active force, in which they are far more often reactors to than initiators in economic affairs is shared by some of the world's ranking economic theoreticians. Arthur Burns, former Columbia University economist and president of the influential National Bureau of Economic Research, chairman of President Dwight Eisenhower's Council of Economic Advisors, counsellor in President Richard Nixon's official Cabinet, and former chairman of the board of the Federal Reserve Bank, specifically sees business as an "intervening" variable between the causes of economic events and the events themselves. In his and many like-minded colleagues views about and appraisals of the growth, level of activity, and utilization of manpower in the U.S. in the period 1946-1966, for example, the key determinants were public policies, union demands, and presi-

---

77. *Capitalism and Freedom* (Chicago: University of Chicago Press, 1962), p. 119. For a larger treatment of these several points, see Berg, "The Impact of Business on America," and "Business Ideology and American Society" in Berg, *The Business of America*, pp. 3-33 and 146-66.

dential speeches. In his accounting for the waxing and waning of business prosperity, Burns would be joined by most business leaders in attaching relatively little importance to the initiatives of business. Business leaders, in this view, are either confident—in which case they invest, create jobs, and make socially rewarding judgments regarding all-important inventory choices, for example—or they are the unconfident and therefore understandably reluctant actors who are falsely blamed for recessions. Confidence, this view continues, is undermined by federal budget deficits, union-wrought inflation, new taxes and either direct or indirect price controls, and by payments imbalances in international accounts.

Critics on the left and in liberals' ranks, meantime, would likely see elements of a confidence game in Burns' and his followers' views of the necessary conditions for promoting business optimism. Following are the "constructive actions" by Presidents Kennedy and Johnson that, according to Burns, restored the business community's confidence after President Kennedy's climactic and confidence shattering confrontation over price increases with the big companies in the steel industry in 1962; Burns' list tells us a good deal about the substance of which business confidence is generated:

1. The granting of liberalized, "more realistic" depreciation allowances in corporate tax provisions.
2. An investment tax credit formulated in line with business wishes.
3. A sweeping tax reduction for corporations and individuals, otherwise.
4. President Kennedy's "firmness in handling the Cuban missile crisis in the fall of 1962 [that] made Americans feel better about themselves and their country...."
5. The rejection of larger federal spending, while favoring tax reduction, as a fiscal stimulant for the economy.
6. President Johnson's "judicious handling" of the office he inherited after the tragic assassination of Mr. Kennedy.
7. President Johnson's first budget, which "supplied new and more tangible evidence that our nation's fiscal policy was really changing."
8. President Johnson's proof of the "new mood of frugality . . . by announcing cuts in expenditures or by indicating that the new policy of tax reduction [would] be continued."
9. President Johnson's "business-like manner."
10. President Johnson's new appointments from which businessmen "drew encouragement."[78]

The events mentioned by Burns are no longer newsworthy—we have had both booms and busts since the nation's resources were held hostage to confidence in 1966—but the perspective is not "dated" by any means as Burns'

---

78. The list is paraphrased from the discussion in Arthur F. Burns, *The Management of Prosperity, The 1965 Fairless Lectures* (New York: Columbia University and Carnegie Presses, 1966), pp. 20–23. Though a decade old, the list of basic issues is rarely presented so pithily. The underlying logic informs assertions of the "confidence" perspective no less today than in 1966.

arguments in 1977 with President Carter have made unmistakably clear. Nor are the principles, held to be fundamental by those large numbers for whom Burns speaks, much threatened by what some take to be the paradoxical qualities if not the internally inconsistent quality of the principles at stake.

There are, of course, other views of the modern businessman than the widely held one outlined by Burns. Thus some view modern managers as living heirs to much (though not all) of the legacy of the so-called Robber Barons of earlier days.[79] Others view them as powerful heads of massive enterprises whose long-term planning requirements force them into efforts to reduce if not simply to subvert the volatile, disruptive effects of highly competitive markets. In the second of these two views, businessmen are rational, applied economists faced with economic imperatives the responses to which are subversive of *society*—especially middle- and working-class interests—but subversive neither of the *corporations* nor of capitalism.[80]

Finally, managers have been seen by some as victims of strains in their roles as businessmen. This last group sees businessmen driven to articulate an "official" ideology along the lines Burns stakes out in his assessment, but to pursue, in practice, a series of policies that require what the ideology rejects: supportive government actions of the precise types Burns applauds in his explanation of the businessman's restored confidence.

The effort to explain contradictions between business belief and business practice in social psychological terms received its fullest documentation in a book by Francis Sutton, a sociologist, in collaboration with three distinguished and policy-wise economists.[81] Their analysis of role strains and the resulting

---

79. The innumerable books and releases by Ralph Nader and many of his collaborators who seek to heighten competition while augmenting market forces, through a variety of modernized regulatory measures, are cases in point. See Ralph Nader, Mark Green, and Joel Seligman, *Taming the Giant Corporation* (New York: Norton, 1976).

80. For a cogent presentation of a neo-Marxist version of growing concentration and exploitation and their ultimate corollary, imperialism, see Paul A. Baran and Paul M. Sweezy, *Monopoly Capital: An Essay on the American Economic and Social Order* (New York: Monthly Review Press, 1966). For a non-Marxist assessment, together with a discussion of the prospects for socialism see Joseph A. Schumpeter, *Capitalism, Socialism and Democracy* (New York: Harper & Row, 1942).

81. Francis X. Sutton, Seymour E. Harris, Carl Kaysen, and James Tobin, *The American Business Creed* (Cambridge, Mass.: Harvard University Press, 1956). Similar data have been examined, on what he terms "an ill-defined constituency," by Robert Heilbroner, "The View from the Top," in Earl Cheit (ed.), *The Business Establishment* (New York: John Wiley, 1964), p. 3. For discussions see Louis Schneider, *Industrial Sociology: The Social Relations of Industry and the Community*, 2nd ed. (New York: McGraw-Hill, 1969), pp. 146-51; and David Rogers and Ivar Berg, "Occupation and Ideology: The Case of the Small Businessman," in *Human Organization*, 20 (Fall 1961), 103-11. As Schneider points out, the classic treatment of ideology as justificatory behavior is by Karl Mannheim, *Ideology and Utopia: An Introduction to the Sociology of Knowledge* (New York: Harcourt Brace Jovanovich 1946), ch. 11.

inconsistencies of businessmen may in fact be correct, overall; a difficulty arises, however, from the fact that imputations of beliefs about economic processes, the nature of business, and much more, are made to businessmen as a class while the documentation refers to the productions of business trade association writers, to business spokesman, in short to the ideological productions of paid, professional ideologues, not business practitioners.

A parallel approach, in its social-psychological definition of the problem, emphasizes their disconcernment with what businessmen take to be the hostility of regulators. The resulting problems of effective regulation are, as a psychological approach would intimate, amenable to treatment. Thus Lane suggests that because businessmen's attitudes toward society's efforts to control them are "anchored in . . . group relationships" an effort to educate businessmen individually would be a waste. Regulators should be sympathetic, strive to remove deprivations and, by working with businessmen in groups, prepare the way to a "salubrious reconstruction of attitudes."[82]

CONCLUSION

We may conclude by suggesting that as older claims to legitimacy rooted in private property concepts have been subverted by events, businessmen strive to locate new claims. In stating these claims about their widergoing roles as leaders in society, they are disposed to (1) point accusing fingers at governments' and government regulators' fetters on their freedoms to maximize economic utilities; and (2) locate their ideology in a loose framework of ideas like those used by the leaders of social movements, ideas that emphasize their sense of responsibility. In chapter 6 we will see that managers have sought to legitimate their narrower roles, as employers, by identifying their leadership techniques with those propounded by a number of social scientists who have studied human relations in the workplace.

---

82. Robert E. Lane, *The Regulation of Businessmen: Social Conditions of Government Economic Control* (New Haven: Yale University Press, 1954), pp. 126-27. The less psychological approach, an approach that emphasizes interests of "pressure groupings," among which there are *different clusters* of businessmen with *different* interests in *diverse* matters, including tariffs, e.g., is described in Robin Williams, *American Society: A Sociological Interpretation,* 3rd ed. (New York: Knopf, 1970), pp. 292-300. The earlier psychological approach has a larger following in respect of intramural problems in business organizations than in respect of macrosocial problems involving business firms, as we shall see below.

CHAPTER 5
UNIONS
AND
UNION LEADERS

INTRODUCTION

Just as informed corporate apologists and knowledgeable critics have engaged each other in heated debates about the relative vulnerabilities and powers of corporations, so there have been arguments among antagonists about the consequential impacts of unions on the structure and functioning of industrial society. Although it is difficult to balance the evidence, it is possible to join a number of issues related to unions' roles, issues that in many respects parallel those broached in the preceding chapter. Three themes, the social role of property, the social impacts of physical technology, and the social consequences of expansion in the service sectors of industrial societies, are of particular relevance once again.

Consider that unions had their origins in European guilds which, as we have noted, operated under public charters guaranteeing a number of the interests of members. In this important respect, guilds—and later unions—shared interests with publicly chartered corporations in changing the character of relationships rooted in earlier and much simpler concepts of property. Indeed, union members in modern America have gained property rights in their occupational skills, in their jobs, in some of their fringe benefits, and sometimes in their occasional controls over the accesses to jobs. Employees have also gained property rights in numerous strands in the "web of rules."[1]

1. For a discussion of property-creating initiatives undertaken by the U.S. government on behalf of a multitude of interest groups, see Charles Reich, "The New Property," *Yale Law Journal*, 73, 5 (April 1974), 733-87.

It is something of an irony, in fact, that union members and the (larger number of) beneficiaries of the spill-over effects of unionists' efforts have gained these claims and rights even as modern managers have become increasingly separated from the stockholders who nowadays are the owners of corporations only in the most nominal sense of the term.

The point is that while these two developments do not add up to anything like a complete reversal of institutional arrangements, over the relatively short history of America's industrialization, they helpfully direct one's attentions away from conventional ideas about unions as embodiments of the interests of propertyless workers engaged in a kind of nascent class warfare with capitalist owners. The facts that workers in the industrial nations became separated from the ownership of the means of production and that the owners of capital became separated from the control of their corporate properties are important (1) to an understanding of the differentiations of their social structures that have accompanied industrialization, and (2) to an understanding of contending groups' efforts to develop ideologies that legitimate their activities; they are not so obviously important to an understanding of their members' actions.[2] Once again, property ownership turns out to be a problematical variable in social analysis; its use as a "predictor" in social scientific analysis produces no clear results.

Consider, in connection with the second of our themes, that while unions as we know them in modern western Europe and the U.S. are clearly among the byproducts of the industrialization process, their essential ways and even the perspectives and attitudes of their members are not readily understood in terms of the physical technologies we identify with that process. Indeed, unions—their structures, their operations, and their members' orientations—are more easily identified with (1) democratic impulses; (2) loosely egalitarian conceptions of the role of the state; and (3) the occupational and hierarchical characters of industries and employer organizations, respectively, than with tools, machines, assembly lines, and factory methods otherwise. As in our earlier conceptions of industrialism per se, of occupational structures, of industry structures, of the development of managerialism, and of managers' roles, it is judicious to avoid assessments anchored essentially in technological determinism. Just as business leaders, political leaders, government regulators, competitors, customers, and workers (collectively representing many different interests) have contributed to the emergent patterns of corporate and government structures and practices in an evolving network of social relations, so unions have come to reflect myriad social interests in their ways, their means and their effects on industrial systems.

The third and final theme is closely related to the second: Among the most noteworthy of the more remarkable features of unionism in the U.S.,

---

2. For a discussion of the process of structural differentiation in economic systems, of the role of ideologies in these systems and of the development of unions in terms matching those in this exposition, see Neil J. Smelser, *The Sociology of Economic Life*, 2nd ed. (Englewood Cliffs, N.J.: Prentice-Hall, 1976), pp. 46-53, 59-71, and 148-63.

especially, are those linked to the fact that union growth in recent decades has taken place outside of union organizers' haunts of other days—in the service, not in the manufacturing, sector; this growth has been especially great among the ranks of government workers, while unionization in traditional areas of union strength has actually declined.

UNIONS AND SOCIETY

In the following sections we will consider unions' agendas of concern and the public's and theorists' conceptions of unions.

Unions' Agendas

Like corporations and governments, unions play important parts in shaping occupational structures and in spinning the "web of rules" in accordance with which the system functions. The following specific interests are high on the agendas of union leaders and their members:

1. Public policies targeted on low levels of unemployment the better to assure favorable conditions in labor markets.
2. Public policies calculated to reduce the threat of product imports from low wage economies.
3. The election of political leaders favorably disposed to organized labors' ends and to the various components of collective bargaining practice including the use of the strike weapon, peaceful picketing, and popular boycotts directed against "recalcitrant" employers.
4. (In western Europe) the support of national labor parties and the election of their leaders to national and local legislative bodies.
5. Low interest rates, the better to help stimulate demand for an economy's output, especially its output of houses and so-called durable consumer goods.
6. The passage of laws that (1) facilitate union organizing drives; (2) raise expenditures for health, occupational safety, education, and some welfare programs; and (3) are both aimed at reducing the depth of cyclical economic downswings and at tempering the employment and income-related effects of downswings.

In the U.S. collective bargaining agreements often augment unemployment compensation laws by their provisions for benefits supplementing those guaranteed in public programs. One basic difference between western European and American unionism inheres in the fact that American unions are only loosely identified with national political parties and, in the absence of western European nations' highly developed national health and welfare schemes, much preoccupied with expansions in the nonwage benefit programs included in bargaining agreements. The Japanese case, as we saw in chapter 1, falls somewhere between the western European and American systems in these respects: Corporations, not public programs, provide comprehensive "fringe benefits" to nearly half of all Japanese workers, but largely on their own initiative rather than as a byproduct of collective bargaining. While many managers dislike fringe benefit demands, their existence multiplies the number of negotiable issues in collective bargaining and thus increases the margins for trade-offs in contract negotiations.

Mention of trade-offs and labor management agreements calls to mind the agenda of unionists' interests in their more immediate working conditions, especially among American unionists. In western Europe, national unions have little to say about labor and management relations at the plant, office, or shop level; in the U.S. collective bargaining is far more decentralized. In western Europe, labor-management relations typically involve officers of national unions and representatives of all the firms in an industry, in what are termed industry-wide bargaining agreements. In the U.S. some general issues are formally joined and resolved by national or international leaders and the officers drawn from a single firm while other parts of a labor agreement are hammered out in bargaining at the plant level. In this so-called local level bargaining, workers' own locally elected representatives meet with leaders from the firm who, in cases involving the subsidiary units, are joined by leaders from their parent firms.

In local-level bargaining, interests in wages and benefits are literally joined with interests in contract language having to do with managers' and employees' rights, privileges, and immunities. The resulting local agreements can run to many pages and provide a fairly detailed framework for a day-to-day relationship in which there are likely to be recurring questions, both procedural and substantive, about how fast is fast, how reasonable is reasonable, and how fair is fair in connection with job demands, work jurisdictions, task assignments, discipline (an all-important matter!), crew sizes, and, typically, the roles of seniority considerations. Since disagreements can occur over the precise meanings of contract language, most contracts provide for procedures, including grievance machinery and sometimes arbitration, for resolving differences. The machinery thus provided serves to help the parties avoid strikes and lockouts but it may also become part and parcel of the bargaining process as both parties seek to win advantages in the grievance process that they were unable to win in the formal and informal discussions that result in the formal agreement.[3]

The reader will note that the word "contract" has been used sparingly in this outline. The courts in America have been increasingly unwilling to entangle themselves in collective bargaining agreements. Indeed, the courts have given considerable sanction to the idea that collective bargaining agreements constitute a body of "industrial common law." In doing so the courts have essentially extended logic, associated with the passage of basic federal labor laws, that the parties to labor agreements should solve their own specific problems

---

3. James W. Kuhn, *Bargaining in Grievance Settlements* (New York: Columbia University Press, 1961).

within a broader framework of evolving public policies and regulatory provisions.[4] Unions in the U.S. are thus enabled by law to play a part in fixing the rules and standards by which the conditions of work are established and modified. On each of two sides, corporate and governmental units, each with their own stewardships over large segments of a society's human and physical resources, seek to impose their definitions of efficiency, equity, justice, and opportunity in accordance with what their leaders take to be the best balances of public and private interests. On a third side, unions seek to influence the "web of rules" in accordance with which the overall quality of life is determined, with which goods and services are produced and distributed, with which opportunities are defined and allocated, and with which the economic and organizational circumstances that govern their lives as income earners and workers, respectively, are defined.

Unions and the Public

Bok and Dunlop have suggested that one can identify the problematical aspects of such an agenda of well-articulated interests by examining the attitudes of union and nonunion members toward unions and union interests. After comparing survey data for the years 1950, 1956, and 1964, these investigators report that Americans believe strongly in the right of employees to belong to unions, in order to secure adequate wages and working conditions from management, but that large proportions of the population are critical, nonetheless, of union activities and union leaders.[5] The views are widely held, for example, that unions bring on unnecessary strikes, are often the scenes of corruption, and are led by persons who are "more unreliable, self-interested and insensitive to the general welfare than other highly influential figures in the society."[6] Though union members are consistently more favorably disposed toward unions, the differences in attitudes between them and their unorganized peers are moderate. In general, Americans believe that workers should be allowed to join unions, that unions are chiefly responsible for workers' gains, but that unions have grown enough, that they should be closely regulated, that courts should resolve disputes leading to strikes in excess of three weeks and that, while unions should urge their members to vote, they should not collect funds for political campaigns or campaign, as unions, for candidates. The most critical attitudes, meanwhile, occur among intellectuals and business executives. The former believe that unions have lost their moral drive and, depreciatingly, that the movement has become more and more given to "pork chop," to "business unionism," and to bread and butter rather than larger issues. Business

---

4. *United Steelworkers vs. Warrior and Gulf Navigation Co.,* 363 U.S. 574 (1960).

5. Derek C. Bok and John T. Dunlop, *Labor and the American Community* (New York: Simon & Schuster, 1970), pp. 1–41.

6. Ibid., p. 19.

executives generally see unions as obstacles to productivity gains, to effective management control, to managers' capacities to respond to market forces, and to their unilateral effort to deal harmoniously with employees.

Unions and Theorists

The brief review of popular concerns about unionism in America reveals a set of basic issues that in many ways parallel those identified by social and economic theorists, over the past 50 years, who have sought to account for unions. Thus Dunlop and a number of his followers view unions as the functional equivalent of firms: Union leaders are assumed to understand labor market processes, and to maximize their members' economic returns in accord, so to speak, with what the traffic will bear.[7] For Dunlop's thesis to hold, it would have to be shown, among other things, that unions perceive a trade-off between wage and other benefits. When market forces make wage gains difficult, in this view, unions seek to take wages out of competition. Wage demands would thus have to be inversely related to unemployment rates. Dunlop, himself, has demonstrated the first of these conditions in studies of the clothing workers, the hosiery workers, and the hatters, among others.[8] The other condition is met if it can be shown that union wage gains are statistically linked, over time, to unemployment rates. This linkage can be observed in the data only if the unemployment rates are so calculated as to include estimates of "discouraged" workers, i.e., "reserve workers" who are in fact not at work but who do not report to U.S. Labor Department interviewers that they are looking for jobs. The linkage is not observable between conventional unemployment rates and wage gains.[9] Thus, while the relevant evidence is less than compelling, it is highly supportive of the view of unions as businesses.

In a contrasting view, held by the late Arthur Ross and others, unionists do not appear to perceive that there is any trade-off in labor markets between wages and employment,[10] and that they therefore overlook the employment

---

7. John T. Dunlop, *Wage Determination under Trade Unions* (New York: Augustus M. Kelley, 1950).

8. For a recent discussion of Dunlop's "model," see Daniel J. B. Mitchell, "Union Wage Policies: The Ross-Dunlop Debate Reopened," *Industrial Relations* (February 1972), pp. 46-61.

9. See Vroman, "Manufacturing Wage Behavior with Special Reference to the Period 1967-1966, *Review of Economies and Statistics,* 52 (May 1970), 160-67; and "The Labor Force Reserve: A Re-estimate," *Industrial Relations,* 60 (October 1970), 379-93; and Mitchell, "Union Wage Policies," pp. 135-36. "Unemployed workers" are survey respondents without jobs who have actively sought jobs during a given period.

10. Arthur M. Ross was a labor economist who served for a time as director of the Bureau of Labor Statistics. His basic conceptions are spelled out in *Trade Union Wage Policy* (Berkeley: University of California Press, 1948), and, with Paul T. Hartman, in *Changing Patterns of Industrial Conflict* (New York: John Wiley, 1960).

implications of wage demands for a fixed quantity of labor in efforts to achieve the highest wage. Union leaders, in this view, are essentially the political leaders of complex institutions whose members have diverse interests. Adherents to this view urge that single minded attention to a union's wage policies leads to misconceptions of unions as institutions. The "economic" and "political" views of Dunlop and Ross, respectively, have not been reconciled, but the prospects for their reconciliation will be adumbrated, later, in a discussion of unions and inflation.

A third view, while allowing for unions' wage interests, emphasizes their concerns with job security and with the rules governing work processes mentioned above.[11] Again, neither wage interests nor the political complexities of unions are denied by those taking this view, but they are recognized as being secondary to workers' preoccupations with the protection of their longer-term occupational claims and the protection, day by day, from the potentially arbitrary ways of those in authority.

In a fourth view, one that will concern us in the next chapter, unionization represents the failure of employers in recognizing the psychological and social psychological needs of workers. Among the perceived failures of managers are those incident to their view of workers as rational economic agents who are indifferent, as such, to work place social relationships and to the demonstrably impersonal character of efficient bureaucratic organizational arrangements. In this view, associated with a school of thought called human relations, managers can either avoid unions or temper their multiple effects on the firm by applying techniques derived from social science theory and research. These techniques are designed to make work less tedious, communications more egalitarian, and otherwise more satisfying, and work group relationships more gratifying.[12]

Even a brief consideration of these views will suggest the possibility that barring the last, there are no necessary conflicts among these different logics unless they are individually pushed to the extreme. Unions can be many things at the same time and, indeed, be different things to different members, or classes of members, at the same time. Union leaders, after all, can gauge what the market will bear by observing managers' resistance to their demands,[13] even as they seek politically to balance the interests of younger workers' interests in wages, older workers' interests in pension benefits and the interests of women and

---

11. See Selig Perlman, *A Theory of the Labor Movement* (New York: Macmillan, 1928).

12. For a brief but classic statement of this view by an adherent, see Elton Mayo, *The Human Problems of an Industrial Civilization* (New York: Macmillan, 1933). For a classic statement of unions' capacities to provide for these very needs, see Frank Tannenbaum, *The Labor Movement: Its Conservative Functions and Social Consequences* (New York: G. P. Putnam's, 1921); and "The Social Functions of Trade Unionism," *Political Science Quarterly*, 62 (1947), 161-82.

13. We may note in passing, however, that there is in fact not much better evidence that managers study labor market developments, in the short run, any more assiduously than do their union counterparts. See chapter 6.

blacks in reducing discriminatory obstacles to their mobility. Similarly, unions can represent workers' interests in job security, in job classification systems, in work rules, and in grievance procedures that assure due process. And, we may add, labor leaders either discover how to use these multiple interests effectively, as bargaining chips, or they will fail of reelection to their posts.

In the next three sections we will consider materials bearing upon union efforts and activities in areas of concern suggested to be critical in the unions' agendas, in the public's responses to surveys, and in the assessments of unions by authoritative scholars reviewed above. The discussion will begin with materials having to do with unions' overall impacts on society, then with unions and communities and, finally, with unions, employer organizations, and members. The materials are thus organized, in line with our alpine metaphor, from macroscopic to more or less microscopic levels of analysis.

UNIONS AND THE SOCIAL SYSTEM

The discussion in the preceding section directs attention to the fact that unions have interests in the nation's political and economic structure. It also suggested that the character of unions' efforts to serve their interests and the outcomes of these efforts will awaken the interests of other groups in society. Among recurrent topics are (1) unions' political effectiveness; (2) their impacts on prices; (3) their effects on productivity and technological change; (4) their impacts on income distribution; (5) their impacts on the allocation of opportunity; (6) their impacts on national economic policies; (7) their impacts on public policies generally; and (8) their impact on the degree of conflict in society. We turn to these topics separately, though it is well to recognize that most of the detailed issues are closely interwoven in the world of affairs.

Labor and the Political System

Although several of America's early labor groups sought to form political parties, most of organized labor's modern-day political efforts have been conducted from outside political parties. Indeed, the American Federation of Labor's leaders were determined, earlier on, to stand apart even from the established parties, to be politically independent, to be essentially nonpartisan in their actions, to pursue only very narrow if self-serving goals (thus avoiding broader efforts to reform society), and to enjoy the apparent advantages of acting as a special interest group.

To say that the old AF of L's leaders were "determined" is not to deny the difficulties of an alternative path. The obstacles to more coherent union political program were—and are—considerable.

> The multiple jurisdictional character of our Federal system makes party organization very difficult. The fact that the U.S. had been relatively free

of class-based politics and the related fact of the heterogeneity of the labor ranks has made it difficult to facilitate political consensus.[14]

The resistance, in America, to class conscious politics, the widely shared belief in social mobility, the divisions in a society of emigrant groups with different traditions, loyalties, and even languages, and the self-protective impulses of differentially skilled job and occupational incumbents long obliged union leaders to avoid triggering dissent within unions by urging actions that would be resented by interest-groups-within-an-interest-group. There was, in addition, the apprehension among leaders that unions' welfare-like programs in collective bargaining would be displaced by public policies targeted on similar objectives. Such positions made less sense to the unionists emerging later in the mass production industries whose shared experiences nearer the bottom of the occupational structure helped to overcome the internal divisions that fragmented their predecessors; the experience of large-scale unemployment, during the great depression, sharpened the differences between skilled craftsmen and so-called industrial workers, and left the latter critical of the Federation's misgivings about unemployment benefits.

The advent of industrial unionism thus changed the composition of the labor movement, increased its size and redirected its politics. The initial drift of the trade union movement toward the democratic party was much encouraged by the passage of the Wagner Act which removed most of the legal barriers to effective collective bargaining and made a number of highly effective employers' anti-union tactics illegal. The passage, under New Deal sponsorship, of social security, a system of unemployment insurance, and minimum wage legislation, as Bok and Dunlop note, "gave organized labor a much greater stake in the activities of government . . . [they] . . . brought a taste of gain to be achieved through political action. They also made union members dependent upon a series of statutory safeguards and benefits."[15]

Both the AFL and CIO were obliged to battle, after World War II, against popularly supported legislation targeted on the containment of what was widely perceived to be excessive union power and unacceptable levels of corruption in labor management relations—the so-called Taft-Hartley and Landrum-Griffin Acts in 1947 and 1959. Organized labor's politics have thus reflected their circumstances: When the public thought workers should enjoy the right to organize, unions were able to enjoy public support without a well-developed political action program; as they acted upon their options they lost public support and were obliged to fight organized but losing campaigns against legislation designed to contain them. They have, since then, become actively involved

---

14. This discussion is based upon one of very few available brief and even-handed summaries of materials bearing upon labor in national and state politics in Bok and Dunlop, *Labor and the American Community,* pp. 384–426.

15. Ibid., p. 391.

in efforts to affect the economic and social policies of an industrial society by conventional political means.

It may be said of union political efforts more concretely that they have reflected the positions of a relatively small number of politically conscious liberal-reform leaders, on one side, and to some degree, the "have not" character of the major of their rank and file members. The facts, moreover, that unions were not and are not now made up of a homogeneous population of interests, and that most unionists guarded their decentralized local organizations' interests have detracted greatly from a sustained and disciplined brand of partisan politics. As we noted at the outset, unionists were and are only slightly different from the vast majority of nonunion workers in the complexity of their interests and preoccupations. The additional fact that political actions are costly has contributed to the essentially problematical situation facing union leaders who are obliged to remain responsive to dues-paying voters in local unions.

Unions can of course try to act as "swing vote" entities that seek to mobilize their members quickly to throw their weight to a favored and sympathetic candidate in close elections, or to capture urban or statewide political machines, or to support a particular party through thick and thin. They can also seek to increase voter registrations, ring doorbells, and distribute campaign information. They must contend with the reality that political party leaders often and readily take labor support for granted, however.

The net effects of unions' political efforts are not readily measured but it is fair to say that they have little effect on the judiciary, only occasional successes with legislators and some limited influence on executive branches of government. Even if the 23 percent of the work force that belongs to unions, together with all the eligible voters in their families, could be mobilized in support of even specific actions having to do with narrow workers' interests—and they cannot be thus consistently mobilized—unionists regularly face traditions, regulations, and competition that act as bars to easy victories.

Even in their efforts to help shape the Department of Labor's leadership and its policies, unionists must face the political facts of life in a pluralistic society: Presidential and other high level appointments must be made with an eye to other groups' interests, to the need for the confidence of other constituencies in elected leaders' independence, and to the need for trade-offs with other groups as the organized parties gain and then lose in elections involving key political appointment makers. The potentially most frightening effects of union politics are those that could materialize when employers and unions band together in support of tariffs, and against emerging strike regulations, or environmental protection efforts, or in favor of special subsidies to particular industries. The fact that these prospective allies have as many potentially conflicting as collaborative interests makes for a shaky alliance. The fact that unions make innumerable tactical errors in their dealings with both Congress and state legislatures further tempers labor's popularly feared political power. Thus unions may correctly be charged with making too many threats, with ignoring politically helpful republicans in their lobbying efforts, with being slow to compromise, and with preparing unimpressively superficial and overly doctrinaire memoranda in support of their legislative proposals and endorsements.[16]

The sum and substance of unions' influence on the nation's political life, while not exactly trivial, nevertheless, is much too easily exaggerated. Unions engage in essentially the same types of efforts used by other interest groups but are substantially more vulnerable to public misgivings and, in part as a corollary, much weakened as a political force by divisions built around regional, ethnic, occupational, sectoral, and age differences and, in recent years, by differences in sex. The differences in attitudes, for example, between union-organized federal employees' and those of union taxpayers in the private sector toward public sector wage scales and work benefits are sharpening year by year.

We may conclude by suggesting that organized labor succeeds in shaping the politics of America's industrial order to the extent that its efforts embody principles of procedure and substance that are in line with those endorsed by the larger nonunion majority. Its failures reflect the difficulties of a movement that suffers the suspicions of many and, like the larger society, houses a most heterogeneous collection of contrasting and sometimes competing interest groupings.

Unions and the Economy

One might expect that questions about unions' economic power might be addressed with a good deal less equivocation than those pertaining to their political impacts. These questions are not more readily answered in dispositive fashion, however, than those about political power. The fact is that the scientific study of wage determination is increasingly hampered by challenges borne of the increasing complexities in an economy shot through with what economists call "market imperfections," an economy that is also enmeshed in a world of interdependent economies each of which are individually hosts to their own "market imperfections."

In general, economists doubt whether unions could, even if they wanted to, "play any generally beneficial role [vis-à-vis members] in the setting of wages."[17] Indeed, economists have taken a variety of specific positions on the

---

16. Ibid., p. 411; Sar Levitan, "Union Lobbyists' Contributions to Tough Labor Legislation," *Labor Law Journal,* (October 1959), pp. 677-78; Alan K. McAdams, *Power and Politics in Labor Legislation* (New York: Columbia University Press, 1964); Frank Bonilla, "When Is Petition 'Pressure'?" *Public Opinion Quarterly* (Spring 1956), pp. 39, 46; Raymond A. Bauer, Ithiel de Sola Pool, and Lewis Anthony Dexter, *American Business and Public Policy* (New York: Atherton Press, 1963), p. 324.

17. Neil W. Chamberlain and James W. Kuhn, *Collective Bargaining* (New York: McGraw-Hill, 1965), pp. 311-12. One of the values of this volume, on which our discussion is based, is that the authors view the economy in institutional rather than atomistic terms.

subject ranging from a view of unions as ingenuous reformers, to the view of unions as egregiously exploitative monopolies. Economists, since Adam Smith, have organized their theoretical conceptions of economies about individualistic values, a conception that attributes essentially rational economic motives to persons and to collectivities. Both are regarded as being ultimately submissive to competitive processes. While *unions appear* to economists to be the collectivities that they are, however, most *corporate acts* are *conceived* by economists, as by the courts, as those of legal persons. The effect is to exempt all but a handful of corporate practices from the analytical treatment accorded unions; only the markedly anticompetitive acts of corporations are treated in the same framework as that employed in the examination of unions. The resulting theory, widely accepted in lay circles, is that union-won wages are compared abstractly with those that would be paid were there no unions representing the workers in labor markets under scrutiny. Employers would, in that event, pay a "normal equilibrium wage," a wage established by the economic cross-pressures, over time, of the demand for and supply of labor. Such a model is substantially flawed however when it is enlisted in support of explanation for either the reality or desirability of a given wage policy. In particular, the classic market model virtually misrepresents relevant decision-making processes because these occur in a society that is composed, to a very significant degree, not of *unions* and *corporate persons* but of highly interdependent *groups* and *collectivities, most* of whose leaders have considerably wide margins for discretion.[18]

As Chamberlain and Kuhn, among others, point out, if the model does not adequately take account of the institutional facts of life then it will misdirect our attention from the complicated sets of forces that (1) determine prices for labor or other factor inputs in an industrial society; (2) determine employment levels, skill utilization patterns, employment hiring standards; and (3) determine even inflation rates. Chamberlain and Kuhn outline the consequences of taking the more realistic view:

> If we cannot rely on automatic market forces to provide those guides and hold the bargainers to them, we must establish other guides and compulsions of a kind compatible with a democratic society. . . . Economic variables do not relate to one another in unambiguous ways. . . . Market research suggests that job availability rather than wage differentials is more effective in distributing labor. Although obviously prices and wages remain as important forces in our society, the price *system* as a comprehensive synthetic means of economic control and economic integration is being recognized as a theoretical abstraction of questionable reliability. We are discovering that in our evolving culture many economic relationships come into existence and are perpetuated or allowed to disintegrate for

---

18. We may remind ourselves of the discussion, earlier, of questions pertaining to corporate ownership and control. See also ibid., pp. 311-12.

reasons other than price. The forces operating in our economy are many; they are not all traceable to the market....[19]

Chamberlain and Kuhn add that important questions about which forces involved in the distribution of economic (and therefore other) goods are to be publicly encouraged and which sublimated, and how best to direct or channel and monitor these forces are major ones nowadays. We may add that the questions are not more sensibly addressed by conceiving of corporations as innocent individual persons, and unions as large aggregations of individuals. And not only unions contribute to market imperfections by their united behavior. Corporations are not persons, after all, but collectivities; economic motives are not the only motives among social actions, furthermore, and society is not, by many means, ordered essentially by market forces either as these are contemplated in theory or as they exist in the real world.

To put it another way, economies are important *sub*sets of societies. Men and women join unions for pecuniary *and* other reasons, and society tolerates a number of institutional arrangements other than unions that snarl the fine lines of abstract economic analyses. It is clearly easier to *postulate* pecuniary motives, perfect competition, marginal productivity pricing, free labor mobility, and all the rest, than to demonstrate the degree of their validity in the world of people, including the people summed up in the term "corporation," whose lives are tangled skeins. As Chamberlain and Kuhn point out in regard to pecuniary motives, for example, such motives have never been viewed by economists "as an exclusive force . . . [but the assumption] . . . has nevertheless been employed in economic theory as *though* it operated unalloyed. The justification [being] that it permits a more precise and conclusive system of deductive and, at the same time, can be supported as a reasonably close approximation to reality."[20] The fact is that the approximation is not a bad one, especially over the long run. But as Keynes, the English economist, pointed out, the long run can be a person's whole lifetime. In successions of short runs, institutional arrangements created for other-than-just-economic purposes do get between economic

---

19. Chamberlain and Kuhn, *Collective Bargaining*, pp. 326-27. See also Richard Lester and Joseph Shuster (eds.), *Insights in Labor Issues* (New York: Macmillan, 1948), pp. 197ff; John T. Dunlop, "The Task of Contemporary Wage Theory," in George W. Taylor and Frank C. Pierson (eds.), *New Concepts in Wage Determination*, (New York: McGraw-Hill, 1957), pp. 117-39; E. Robert Livernash, "The Internal Wage Structure," in Taylor and Pierson (eds.) *New Concepts in Wage Determination*, pp. 140-72; Fritz Machlup, "Theories of the Firm: Marginalist, Behavioral, Managerial," *American Economic Review*, 57 (1967), 1-33; Dennis H. Robertson, "Wage Grumbles," in William Fellner and Bernard F. Haley (eds.), *Readings in the Theory of Income Distribution* (London: Allen & Unwin, 1954), pp. 221-36. For a more sociologically inspired discussion, see Ivar Berg, *Education and Jobs: The Great Training Robbery* (New York: Praeger, 1970), pp. 19-37.

20. Chamberlain and Kuhn, *Collective Bargaining*, pp. 329-30.

analysts' theories and the numerous price, wage, cost, and other parameters widely used in measuring a society's economic health.

One of the most familiar arguments about unions' economic effects, of course, is the two-phased one that links union wages to inflation and inflation to the "skewing" of income distribution among more productive and less productive members of a population. According to this argument, unionists and employers are favored by the ability of the latter to pass on the unproductive portion of wage increases, (that not "justified" by productivity gains) negotiated at the collective bargaining table. Thoughtful readers are invited to fish out the many assumptions about pricing, wage determination, and market processes underlying that compound proposition. Kerr, a labor economist with "institutionalist" credentials that make him an especially agreeable party to sociological discourse, has termed the debate among economists about unions, income distribution, and inflation, "the confusion of tongues."[21] After sorting out the main views of economists who, at the extremes, see unions as the principal agents or the principal victims of inflation and skewed income distribution, Kerr suggests that all of them are right and all of them are wrong, concluding that all are right

> to the extent that they suggest that some kinds of unions could have the suggested effects under some kinds of circumstances. All of them are wrong, to the extent they suggest (and some do not) that their conclusions are the universal rules. The only universal rule is that there are all kinds of unions operating under all kinds of circumstances and they can have all kinds of effects. . . . Truth is more likely to emerge from studying the *impacts of the unions* than *"the impact of the union."*[22]

Kerr goes on to divide unions into five general types according to their approach to price stability. In the descending order of their impact on price stability, the types of unions and their "natural habitats" are:

1. "Agent of the state," found in authoritarian societies.
2. "Social partners," found in social democratic contexts.
3. "Sectional bargainers," found in free enterprise systems.
4. "Class bargainers," found in a semiclass or semifeudal societies.
5. "Enemies of the system," found in semiclass or semifeudal societies in the course of their "decay."

Next, Kerr relates the potential impacts of unions on money wage levels

---

21. Clark Kerr, "The Impact of Unions on the Level of Wages," in E. Wight Bakke, Clark Kerr, and Charles W. Arnold (eds.), *Unions, Management and the Public*, 3rd ed. (New York: Harcourt Brace Jovanovich, 1967), p. 609.

22. Ibid, p. 611 (emphases added).

(1) to the policies of other insitutions (government and employers); (2) to employment conditions; (3) and to labor market conditions.[23] Kerr cross-tabulates the "types," "conditions," and "policies" in Table 5-1. Although the methodological problems in connection with each assessment are not small ones, dates on unions and price levels from the UK, the USSR, Norway, Sweden, Holland, Germany, and Italy are in conformity with patterns predicted in the model's cells. As Kerr notes,

> Putting together the variety of types of unions and the variety of environmental settings results in a variety of potential effects. Unions raise the general level of money wages greatly; or perhaps only a little. Unions reduce the general level of money wages substantially; or perhaps only a little. Or perhaps they have no effect at all. It all depends. And it all depends on type and circumstances, as the summary . . . suggests.[24]

The foregoing discussion helps us to pinpoint issues that make for difficulties in assessing *any* of the macroscopic social questions pertaining to unions' affects, not just wage questions. Second, the analyses help to make it clear that unions, especially in Japan, the U.S., and western Europe are of a piece with their larger systems; to the extent they are potent at all, unions are not *unilaterally* potent. Third, as the discussion of unions' status in the U.S. has indicated, wage "demands" are part and parcel of the quests of persons and groups in the U.S. for equity, efficiency, equality, and for practicable ways to make a system made up of groups with differentiated and changing interests, work, day by day as well as fiscal year by fiscal year.

These concerns, meanwhile, lead us to seek answers "to the perennial but immediate problem of the rights of individuals and groups in our society; [in the past as now] we use the courts as a principal instrument for providing us with at least provisional answers."[25] If we add to the role of the courts only the laws the courts interpret, and the growing role of arbitrators, we see quickly the truncated role of market forces. (See the discussion of the roles of the courts, the Congress, and of parties to agreements in connection with arbitration in chapter 4.) To the extent that people in society seek to maintain slowly shifting balances among competing groups' and persons' values and claims, to that extent the threads of economists' analyses permit them to weave a coarse fabric, at best. For the industrial sociologist the problems are only slightly different from those of economists, as we have seen in looking at the problem area of labor markets

---

23. Kerr's focus is on wages, not "benefits." We may remind ourselves that, in some countries, and in some U.S. collective bargaining cases, employers are spared obligations to bargain over "nonwage" issues. Health insurance arrangements in the UK and Scandinavia, e.g., are subjects for national political adjudication, not for collective bargaining.

24. Kerr, "The Impact of Unions," p. 613.

25. Chamberlain and Kuhn, *Collective Bargaining*, p. 276.

Table 5-1 Factors Relating to Union Impact on General Level of Money Wages

	TYPE OF UNION	POLICIES OF OTHER INSTITUTIONS	EMPLOYMENT CONDITIONS	LABOR MARKET CONDITIONS
Raise Level	"Enemy of the System"	"Guaranteed" Full Employment	Depression	
	"Class Bargainer"		Downswing	New Recruits
(As Compared with What Would Otherwise Prevail)		Administered Prices		
	"Sectional Bargainer"		Stable Full Employment	
	a. State of Excitement	Government Settlements to Avoid Strikes		
	b. State of Normality		Upswing	
	"Partners in Social Control"	Government Review of Wage Settlements		
Reduce Level	"Agent of the State"	Government Wage Control	"Overly Full" Employment	Immobile Labor Force

Source: Clark Kerr, "The Impact of Unions on the Level of Wages," in E. Wight Bakke, Clark Kerr, and Charles W. Arnold, Unions, Management and the Public, 3rd ed. (New York: Harcourt Brace Jovanovich, 1967), p. 614.

and unions. In this problem area, the skills organic to the two disciplines usefully complement each other.

Unions, Technology, and Productivity

Unions are among the strategic institutional agencies involved in spinning the "web of rules" in industrial societies of which we spoke in chapter 2. As such they play an important codeterminate part in designing the social technology some aspects of which we also stressed when we viewed industrial systems from higher altitudes. Among the critical contributions that unions make to a society's social technology are those that grow out of their efforts to minimize what might well otherwise be the overridingly determinate effects on workers' lives of physical technology. Their contributions also grow out of workers' efforts to balance the frequent preoccupations of managers with the maximization of the output of physical technology. (Managers are, of course, not always bent upon maximizing output. As we saw in the preceding chapters, managers sometimes avail themselves of favorable market positions that are made even more advantageous by restricting output for longer or shorter periods.) These contributions became more visible, and more visibly controversial, as we survey the institutional terrain from positions nearer ground level.

The issues involved are closely bound up with those that appear in connection with general questions about the wage and income effects of unions. The specific questions have to do with whether unions' slow technological change tie managers' hands by restrictive work rules and otherwise set limits on efficiency and productivity. As readers might expect, from exposure to popular treatments of the subject, the issues are more than a little vexed.

Though unions have sometimes fought specifically against the employment of new production processes, they have generally sought instead to bargain over changes and by attaching conditions to them, to gain a share for their members of the productivity gains borne of new methods and machines. What appear, as in the case of the Luddites discussed in chapter 1, to be the psychological reactions of men and women who are fearful of change per se turn out, most typically, to be the businesslike reactions of investors who seek to protect the proprietary returns on their skills, their loyalties, and their imaginations. Like employers who purchase others' new patents on methods that would otherwise accelerate the inevitable obsolescence of their *own* plant and equipment, organized workers have sometimes successfully sought to husband *their* capital, including their human capital investments in training;[26] they have also sought to capitalize on their own best estimates of economic and related developments, as in the case of railroad firemen, described in chapter 2, who secured seats on diesel engines. Only in accordance with a readily controvertible two-valued logic may one regard managers as being judicious when they correctly anticipate long-term trends, and workers as being exploitatively antisocial when they do the same. Unions thus do affect the ways in which tools and machines are used. On one side, the short-run implications of the bargains that shape these 'ways' may sometimes be different from the long run implications, as the railroad case well illustrates. On another side, both parties to agreements about work methods may be the beneficiaries of businesslike quid pro quo exchanges.

Unions can affect the operation of a company in six identifiably different ways.[27] First, they can bargain for and seek to establish rules that fix machine

26. For a view of employees as skill acquirers who bid for jobs and thus receive training in addition to wages and salaries as components of their returns in a particular job, see Lester Thurow, *Generating Inequality: Mechanisms of Distribution in the U.S. Economy* (New York: Basic Books, 1975).

27. We emphasize that the resulting effects may be positive *or* negative, from a management perspective. It should also be stressed that some of the effects noted

speeds, crew sizes, rules that can also have the very important "essential characteristic of regulating the proportion of labor to capital ... ,"[28] an arrangement that makes it more difficult for managers to substitute machinery or new work procedures compared with arrangements that merely add production costs. A second set of arrangements involves payments to workers in excess of their actual output. Such rules can require that workers be paid for all of a day or week only a part of which they have been "called in" to work; extra hours of work required by safety rules, work standards below those deemed sensible by engineering standards; the performance of unnecessary work or the retention of redundant tasks.

The costs of such rules can be offset, in some instances, by "pass throughs" of costs to consumers, by the energetic pursuit of new methods and by energetic bargaining designed to use, more effectively, the "excess" labor generated by a rule. On the face of it and by managers' standards these rules are inefficient. One should be cautious, however, about defining efficiency too narrowly or one-sidedly. It is thus hazardous to single out one "inefficient" rule from the whole complex of rules hammered out in bargains between unions and managers; by scrutinizing such rules in isolation from others one can fail to see the tradeoffs in which unions engage in their pursuit of those rules that so readily offend uncritical observers.[29]

Third, unions can affect the rate at which technological changes are introduced by their effect on the wage differentials employers are obliged to pay. Rules of this sort are sometimes designed to dampen managers' enthusiasm for changes that unions interpret to require higher skills, for example. In other instances wage differentials will encourage employers to mechanize further in order to reduce their needs for higher skilled help.

Fourth, unions bargain over a host of personnel policies having to do with worker morale, training, supervision, and performance. It is a sign of the utility of some of the unions' involvements in programs targeted on improving the

---

can occur in unorganized settings, as well as those in which unions have become significantly involved in decisions related to business operations. Employees may bargain effectively, for example, on the basis of the perceived values of services and skills, to be exempted from certain tasks, procedures, or personnel rules. Students and professors are thus familiar with differences in class size, teaching schedules, and academic leaves among different groups of unorganized faculty and research staff members of a university. Many of the differences are protected by traditions that operate as iron laws of "adhocracy."

28. Bok and Dunlop, *Labor and the American Community*, p. 264.

29. For a detailed discussion of rules in which no unions were involved, see Fritz J. Roethlisberger and William J. Dickson, *Management and the Worker* (Cambridge, Mass.: Harvard University Press, 1939); and Stanley Mathewson, *Restriction of Output Among Unorganized Workers* (New York: Viking Press, 1931). For evenhanded discussions of work rules, see Sumner H. Slichter, *Union Policies and Industrial Management* (Washington, D.C.: Brookings Institution, 1941); and Sumner H. Slichter, James J. Healy, and Robert E. Livernash, *The Impact of Collective Bargaining on Management* (Washington, D.C.: Brookings Institution, 1960).

quality of a labor force that some of their preferences—for seniority, and principles in assignments and promotions, for example—are adopted in firms that have no dealings with unions. Ultimately, employees seek equity, procedural fairness, and effective and equitable supervision, sensible safety arrangements, and some degree of participation in the design of their working conditions. Unions pursue these and related issues as a matter of course and, in so doing, can often augment or reinforce the efforts of progressive managers to improve performance.

Fifth, unions and managers have worked together in the interest of protecting their firms' competitive positions; they have invested their own funds in development-type activities, as in the case of the lithographers in packaging and printing techniques. And they have collaborated in the development of efficient methods, as in on the west coast docks, discussed in chapter 2;[30] they have even provided technical assistance to managers, as in the case of the textile industry with its myriad of small firms.

Finally, Bok and Dunlop speak for many observers in pointing out that the challenges laid before managers in collective bargaining, "if viewed broadly," have "created superior and better balanced management, even though some exceptions must be recognized."[31] Viewed thus broadly: (1) work rules occurred before unions enjoyed much influence—as we noted above, these restrictions by workers can be usefully compared with their own restrictions on production by managers who are alert to markets;[32] (2) their negative effects are easily overstated and their contributions to stability in organizational settings easily overlooked; (3) some even contribute to efficiency; (4) the price paid in bargaining by unions in return for restrictive rules is often of considerable value to the managers who agreed to their implementation; (5) work rules covering work place, crew sizes, and job requirements are among the most negotiable coins in the bargaining realm; they thus have long-term values to both parties to labor agreements, parties who must frequently seek to avoid hard and fast win or lose, so-called zero-sum situations, and who need continually to discover bargainable "quids" for negotiable "quos."[33]

It is also the case, as blue-collar unions have begun to decline, as they are criticized in the public press, in periods of low unemployment, as job jurisdictions become progressively less distinct, and as managers become more alert to

---

30. See Charles Killingsworth, "The Modernization of West Coast Longshore Work Rules," *Industrial and Labor Relations Review* (April 1962), pp. 295–306.

31. Bok and Dunlop, *Labor and the American Community*, p. 267. See also Slichter, Healy, and Livernash, *The Impact of Collective Bargaining*, pp. 950ff.

32. See Stanley B. Mathewson, *Restriction of Output Among Unorganized Workers* (New York: Viking Press, 1931); and Donald Roy, "Work Satisfactions and Social Rewards in Quota Achievement," *American Sociological Review,* 18, 5 (October 1953).

33. For a series of brief illustrative cases see James W. Kuhn and Ivar Berg, "Bargaining and Work Rules Disputes," in *Social Research,* (1900), pp. 466–81.

the bargains struck by first line supervisors, that restrictive work rules become more vulnerable.[34]

In the next section we consider the matter of strikes and industrial conflict, a matter like work rules that has concerned policy makers, scholars, and laymen.

Industrial Conflict and Industrial Relations

One of the main bones of contention in post-World War II sociological discussions has been over the social role of conflict. As we have emphasized in the preceding chapter, a version of arguments about "class" conflict has almost necessarily appeared in the pages of industrial sociological discussions about the causes of strikes, and over methods for dealing with such industrial conflicts.

The subject is a broad one and could (and has) consumed many pages;[35] it lends itself not at all to a brief review, especially because of controversies among academics about the meaning of strike behavior. In particular, human relationists have focused upon the prospects for *avoiding* if not gainsaying conflict. Human relationists have tended not to see strikes as the occasionally necessary methods for dealing with matters over which legitimately conflicting economic or democratic interests are at stake. Industrial relationists, on the other hand, are struck by the patterns in accordance with which grievances and strikes occur. There is no evidence, as industrial relationists see it, that psychological traits, needs or dispositions are distributed among workers and managers in ways that correspond to the distributions of data on strikes. In appraising the human and industrial relationists views, finally, it needs to be kept clearly in mind that strikes are rare. In the U.S., for example, man-days idle as a proportion of "available" worktime have been less, usually much less, than one percent—in every year since World War II but 1964.[36]

Two major approaches to the explanation of strikes' causes may be discerned in the industrial relations literature. One seeks to locate the causes in the bargaining process; the other in the differential capacities of various work groups to take collective actions.[37] In view of the fact that most lost time due to strikes

---

34. This was the conclusion of a Brookings Institution study as long ago as 1960. See Slichter, Healy, and Livernash, *The Impact of Collective Bargaining*, pp. 333-34, 947.

35. For a most helpful overview of the subject, see the essays in Arthur Kornhauser, Robert Dubin, and Arthur Ross (eds.), *Industrial Conflict* (New York: McGraw-Hill, 1954).

36. The figure for 1964 was 1.04. Bureau of Labor Statistics, *Analysis of Work Stoppages, 1973,* Bulletin 1877 (Washington, D.C.: Government Printing Office, 1975), Table A-1, p. 4.

37. David Snyder, "Institutional Setting and Industrial Conflict: Comparative Analyses of France, Italy and the United States," *American Sociological Review,* 40 (June 1975), 259-78.

in the U.S. is associated with the negotiation or renegotiation of labor agreements, the focus of American research has been on contract-related disputes. Industrial relationists, finally, tend to view strikes as exercises in worker participation, exercises that are not likely to be displaced by human relations reforms, calling for *more* worker participation but *less* conflict.

The following propositions may be adduced from the best available research on industrial conflict, in general, and on strikes, in particular.[38]

> 1. "Generally, as investment per worker grows, management becomes more concerned with the consent of the employees who work with this investment . . . [and is] . . . less inclined to dismiss their welfare thoughtlessly than if these employees wielded picks and shovels."[39] The result is that fewer conflicts over dismissals occur.
>
> 2. " . . . a man is, to an extent, his job; and the employer, to the worker is the job the employer makes available . . . a 'good job' consists, of course, of more than the totality of tasks performed and the concept includes good supervision and good working conditions. Satisfaction or dissatisfaction with jobs *per se,* however, affects worker attitudes toward the employer, the volume of grievances, and the propensity to strike."[40]
>
> 3. Efficiency and favorable costs situation is related to higher wages and what Kerr calls "a standard of administered prices." In addition, industrial peace is enhanced by the close attachment of a plant to a particular location. The implication is that the company has to get along with the union since it is not mobile by reason of its investment.[41]
>
> 4. Union instability, including instability borne of "democratic factionalism" in national and/or local unions, as well as rural unionism, are closely linked to grievance and strike patterns. A reduction in workers' independence is often accompanied by an increase in labor-management "peace."[42] As Kerr puts it, this is not infrequently " . . . a triumph of union-management fraternity over worker liberty."[43]
>
> 5. Industrial conflicts are more difficult to organize (and, when organized

---

38. These propositions have been abstracted from a careful review of source materials by Dr. Marcia K. Freedman of the Columbia University Conservation of Human Resources Project in connection with I. Berg, M. Freedman, and M. Freeman, *Managers and Work Reform: A Limited Engagement* (New York: Free Press, 1978) pp. 124-52.

39. Clark Kerr, "Industrial Peace and the Collective Bargaining Environment," *Labor and Management in Industrial Society* (Garden City, N.Y.: Doubleday, 1964), p. 152.

40. Ibid, p. 153.

41. Ibid., passim.

42. See the author's "the nice kind of union democracy", in *Columbia University Forum,* 5, 2 (Spring 1965), 18-23.

43. Kerr, *Labor and Industrial Conflict.*

and mounted, to end) in work settings characterized by complex occupational structures.[44]

6. As union-management relations become institutionalized and "sufficiently integrated" the "system-state" persists, i.e. industrial conflict rates become stable.[45]

7. The relationships between strike activity and economic conditions are not terribly clear, despite research stretching back to 1921 by Hansen, then by Rees (in 1952); by Levitt (1953), Goldner (1953); by Blitz (1954); and, more recently by Weintraub, Ashenfelter, and Johnson; Britt and Galle; Stern and Flannagan; Strauss and Ulman. The most recent effort suggests that while managers must have the wherewithal to pay demanded pay increases, workers will convert demands into strikes either when they fear losses in "real" earnings (as in recent years) or when prosperity continues long enough for workers to expect increases in real earnings. In general, otherwise, there is a negative correlation between strike activity, in aggregate terms, and the unemployment rate.[46]

8. U.S. strike analyses are more sensitively explained when they are distinguished, first off, by length and when considered, second, industry-by-industry.

The last point invites attention to an analytical position somewhere between the most dedicated anticonflict organizational reformers among human relations enthusiasts, on one side, and the conflict-conscious industrial relationists, on the other. Thus the evidence from studies by Kuhn (on international

---

44. For a discussion in theoretical terms anchored in Durkheim's notions that offered as a hypothesis in 1953 by Robert Dubin, see his "Industrial Conflict: "Occupational Structure and Industrial Conflict," in Kornhauser et al., *Industrial Conflict*, pp. 221-31.

45. For a reassessment of data and confirmation of the proposition, which was offered as an hypothesis in 1953 by Robert Dubin, see his "Industrial Conflict: The Power of Prediction," in *Industrial and Labor Relations Review*, 18 (April 1965), 357-63. For an exchange, regarding Dubin's methods, see Orley Ashenfelter, William S. Pierce, and Robert Dubin, *Industrial and Labor Relations Review*, 19 (1966), 92-95.

46. Alvin Hansen, "Cycles of Strikes," *American Economic Review*, 11 (December 1921), 616-21; Albert Rees "Industrial Conflict and Business Fluctuations," *Journal of Political Economy*, 60 (October 1952) 371-82; Theodore Levitt, "Prosperity versus Strikes," *Industrial and Labor Relations Review*, 6 (January 1953), 220-26; William Goldner, "Strikes and Prosperity," *Industrial Labor Relations Review*, 6 (July 1953), 580-85; Rudolf C. Blitz, "Prosperity versus Strikes Reconsidered," *Industrial and Labor Relations Review*, 7 (April 1954), 449-56; Orley Ashenfelter and George E. Johnson, "Bargaining Theory, Trade Unions and Industrial Strike Activity," *American Economic Review*, 59 (March 1969), 35-49; David Britt and Omer R. Galle, "Industrial Conflict and Unionization," *American Sociological Review*, 37 (1972), 46-57; Robert N. Stern, "Intermetropolitan Patterns of Strike Frequency," *Industrial and Labor Relations Review*, 29 (January 1976), 218-35; Robert J. Flanagan, George Strauss, and Lloyd Ulman, "Worker Discontent and Work Place Behavior," *Industrial Relations* (May 1974), pp. 101-23.

data), and by Britt and Galle (of American data)[47] underscores the fact that patterns inferred from aggregated data on strikes, in general, do not fit data on "short" strikes. Kuhn's analysis, for example, highlights the (local) role of effective grievance procedures in reducing "short" strikes in the U.S. and the (more distant) role of labor parties in reducing the numbers of long strikes in other nations.

Studies of strikes-by-industry,[48] meantime, clearly show that industry-specific variables cannot be ignored. Analyses by Berg, Freedman, and Freeman showed, in addition to the role of industry-specific economic and structural conditions,[49] the role of "local," non-economic issues in industrial conflicts:[50] To gain a sense of these issues and thus of the character of worker discontents that are almost never captured in surveys of worker morale, one can peruse the specific information generated from their field studies by the U.S. Bureau of Labor Statistics of major strikes. The following picture may be drawn from such a perusal of data on short strikes:[51]

1. In four out of the five years, there were five railroad strikes on crew-size issues, involving firemen, trainmen, and switchmen.
2. The Communications Workers carried on three short major strikes in 1970 alone, two over work-classification assignments and one over protection against crime in the areas of particular work assignments.
3. There were two longshore strikes in New York-New Jersey, both over the issue of hiring new men.
4. Each year there were strikes in coal—over health and safety, payment of disability benefits, arrest of pickets, welfare fund administration, the

---

47. James Kuhn, "Grievance Machinery and Strikes in Australia," *Industrial and Labor Relations Review,* vol. 8, no. 2 (January 1955); and David W. Britt and Omer Galle, "Structural Antecedents of the Shape of Strikes: A Comparative Analysis," *American Sociological Review,* 39 (October 1974), 642-51.

48. See Clerk Kerr and Abraham Siegel, "The Interindustry Propensity to Strike—An International Comparison," in Arthur Kornhauser, Robert Dubin, and Arthur Ross, *Industrial Conflict* (New York: McGraw-Hill, 1954); Britt and Galle, "Industrial Conflict and Unionization"; Robert N. Stern, "Intermetropolitan Patterns of Strike Frequency," *Industrial and Labor Relations Review,* 29 (January 1976), 218-35; and Berg, Freedman, and Freeman, *Managers and Work Reforms,* ch. 11.

49. This development was anticipated by Hoxie in 1928. See Robert F. Hoxie, *Trade Unionism in the United States* (New York: Appleton-Century-Crofts, 1928), in which it is argued that bargaining patterns will vary by industry as a function of differences, for example, in industry structures.

50. Summarized from Ivar Berg, Marcia Freedman, and Michael Freeman, *Managers and Work Reforms: A Limited Engagement* (New York: Free Press, 1978), ch. 6.

51. U.S. Bureau of Labor Statistics, *Analysis of Work Stoppages,* Bulletins 1646, 1687, 1727, 1777, and 1877 (Washington, D.C.: Government Printing Office, 1970-1975). "Major" strikes are those involving 10,000 workers or more during a contract period for the years 1968-1972.

discharge of union officials and intraunion matters connected with the criminal conduct of union officers.

5. There were four major strikes at one General Electric location in Louisville, Kentucky alone—over a disciplinary action, over work assignments and back pay, and over the wage scale of 16 floor-sweepers. These four strikes lasted a total of 25 days (two less than 6 days and two more than 6 days).

6. In 1968, 1969, and 1972, there were major auto industry strikes (all at General Motors) over job classification, production standards, and unresolved grievances. In 1968, there were two strikes in Flint, Michigan over local unresolved issues. In 1969, over a period of 87 days there were stoppages staggered over various plants in six states "in protest of merger of GM's Chevrolet and Fisher Body divisions . . . [which] created some different pay scales for similar jobs. . . ." And in 1972, there was a series of short stoppages (in the course of 59 days), nationwide, concerning production standards, which came to an end when "grievances and other issues were settled according to conditions at the various plants."

7. In 1968 and 1969, there were five major one-day teachers' strikes directed toward influencing state legislatures. An additional long strike occurred in New York City in the showdown between the union and a decentralized school district over teacher dismissals.

These vignettes help to illustrate a number of workers' concerns about which organized workers, at least, can and do take concerted action. More importantly they serve to drive home the point that workers' concerns reflect developments that are ultimately rooted in larger social and economic processes as well as in the intraorganizational processes upon which human relationists center attention.

UNIONS, COMMUNITIES, AND MEMBERS

Although the burden of social science attention has been on corporate rather than union impacts, there need be no doubt that unions, too, have interests in community life. Unions have thus been long concerned with the impact of strikes on community well-being and often defend efforts to secure or enlarge "SUB" payments (Supplemental Unemployment Benefits), even during strikes (as in New York and Rhode Island), but especially during layoffs, as supportive of community no less than member interests. Druggists, grocers, landlords, and local mortgage holders, obviously, are highly vulnerable (in relatively smaller communities, especially) to the effects of labor market processes and of labor-management relations. Even the most cold-hearted of bankers, for example, will view repossessed homes and automobiles with considerable alarm.

In addition, union assets, including pension funds, are more often invested in school and municipal bonds, government securities, and housing developments than in common stocks, though a few sizable investments—the Teamsters in Montgomery Ward Company and in Las Vegas casinos, the United Mine Workers in banks and coal companies, the Amalgamated Clothing Workers in banks—are made in private-sector undertakings that may nourish communities, regions, or the economy, overall.[52]

Theoretical and empirical efforts to comprehend more direct union-community relations, meantime, are scarce. When corporations relocate from a community, local unions are not infrequently reduced to vestiges of their former selves and their leaders left without the sustenance to even assist members in locating new jobs; even more rarely do the marooned workers and leaders manage to follow the corporate flag to its new staff.

There has, however, been one comprehensive effort to delineate a large number of business and labor impacts on communities. Thus, though studies of the larger problems of community power have been numerous, as noted in our discussion of corporations, only one seminal volume (by Form and Miller) has self-consciously focused a great deal of attention on unions, per se.[53] Among other valuable typologies and constructs introduced by these investigators is one that helps to order data at the institutional level on the power of business, labor, and the family. According to these investigations, variations among communities, like the ones in Figure 5-1, "arise from differences in the economic structure of various communities or plants,"[54] as follows:

In the first model (A):[55]

> Business dictates all phases of work schedules without much concern for their effects on home life. It considers this to be a management prerogative. Workers must accommodate family life to industrial operations. The conditions for the appearance of Model A are: one-industry town with limited labor market or an industry-dominated town where there is no labor union or where labor unions are very weak.

In the second model (B):

> Management is generally in control of production and scheduling of work time. It is conscious of the family needs of workers, but considers them to be secondary to the attainment of economic goals. Management works out rules with the union concerning seniority, rights of workers to be on certain shifts and to have access to desirable jobs, and related matters, but the specific authority over work assignments and scheduling is reserved as appearance of Model B are: strong management authority, fairly strong union, and available surplus labor.

---

52. See for example H. Robert Bartell, Jr., "National Union Assets, 1959-1961," *Industrial and Labor Relations Review,* 19 (October 1965), 81ff.

53. William H. Form and Delbert C. Miller, *Industry, Labor and Community* (New York: Harper & Row, 1960).

54. Ibid., p. 394.

55. These descriptions are taken from ibid., pp. 395-96.

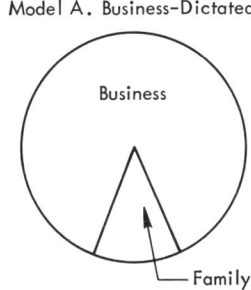
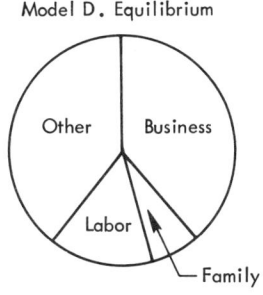
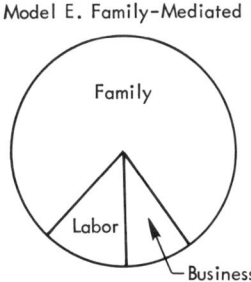

Figure 5-1. Five Power Complex Models of Management, Labor, and Family Relations.

Source: William H. Form and Delbert C. Miller, *Industry, Labor, and Community* (New York: Harper & Row, 1960), p. 396

Unions, in model C:

> attempt to share management's "right" to determine work schedules and other things which might affect family life. They demand codification of procedures to guard seniority and other rights of the workers. The Unions work for annual wages and greater welfare benefits, to be administered by labor-management councils. The conditions for the appearance of Model C

are: strong labor unions in an industry which depends on the local labor force entirely because it is highly skilled and great costs would be incurred in training new workers.

In the "equilibrium model" (D):

> Unions are strong and so are other segments in the community such as civic associations. Management's decisions have to be considered in the light of their possible repercussions on their local reputations. A balance is struck between the desires of management, labor, and community and home pressures. Industry councils plans may be established. The conditions for the appearance of Model D are: a highly integrated community responsibility shared by all citizens. Labor is highly organized, highly skilled, and actively interested in community life. Family values may become increasingly powerful if a general manpower shortage develops. A reduced work week and a higher standard of living could give the family greater choice and power over working conditions.

Finally, in the "Family-Mediated Model (E):

> Family values are dominant and take precedence in the determination of work conditions. The conditions for the appearance of Model E are: family ownership of an enterprise or high economic security, in which the family becomes a more powerful determiner of its own activities. This is especially likely in certain religious or cooperative communities dominated by familistic norms."

The typology derived by these industrial sociologists is especially valuable in that it highlights the interdependency of the two important "industrial" agencies, corporations, and unions, with *other* agencies in society.

In the final section of this chapter we consider the relationships between unions as organizations and their constituents.

UNIONS AND MEMBERS

Blue collar unionism in the private sector, we have noted, has declined in recent years even as it has become increasingly difficult to delineate and measure the impacts of these "classical" unions on the body politic, on the economy, on managers as conceived in textbooks, or on communities.

Unions and union-like associations have grown outside blue-collar ranks in the manufacturing sector, in services and among white collarites to be sure. But differences in the backgrounds, especially the educational backgrounds and the interests of these new recruits to organized labor's colors suggest that they will not simply emulate their predecessors. Legal and other pressures on organized public servants to eschew the strike weapon, for example, will likely lead to the increasing use of arbitration. Such a development will undoubtedly add to popular displeasure over blue-collar strikes, and therefore to popular and legal endorsements of arbitration proceedings in the profit sector.

Reductions in the scope of traditional union leaders' powers to exercise militant leadership, meanwhile, were discernible well before blue collarites were the surprised witnesses to the emergence of new and refined collective bargaining modes among such unlikely comrades as airline pilots, musicians in symphony orchestras, police officers, school teachers, and medical interns and residents. Indeed, the leaders of unions in the blue collar world have long known the difficulties in harnessing the different interests of older and younger workers, of workers of different skills, of workers in different regions, in different companies of the same industry, and the interests of different workers in the different locations of multiplant companies. These union leaders have also come to learn that the public is both charmed and outraged by these internal divisions, and the strains generated thereby, and that the public's confusions about its interests and the interests of different unionists has not stopped legislators from adding requirements for union democracy to the already considerable complexities that attend collective bargaining as a result of internal divisions.

Membership Control of Unions

Indeed, the matter of union democracy provides a case in point. Americans have not insisted that all private associations be democratic in their operations, but we have been quite insistent that unions are the agents of their members and that it is in their and thus in the public's interest that (1) they be responsive to their members, and (2) they promote their members' welfare within the society's "web of rules." As Bok and Dunlop point out we seek to enable union members (1) "to exert pressure on their leaders to pay attention to the needs and desires of the rank and file in formulating policies and programs . . ."; (2) to enjoy "the sense of participation they derive from helping to select union officials and influence important policy decisions"; and (3) by their democratic experience to have unionists help us multiply the stakes Americans otherwise have in democratic governance in the Republic.[56]

The national commitment to union democracy, like the commitment to collective bargaining, does of course involve some trade-offs of social and private benefits against social and private costs. Thus, we cannot assume that voters in unions will always support persons or positions that consistently reflect the interests of a majority of the larger population. Nor can we be any more certain of the best balance in any democratic system as between very high or very low voter participation rates either over long periods of time in particular elections. Finally, it is not equally evident to all who might legitimately argue about it what the best balance is between direct and representative democracy, between

---

56. Bok and Dunlop, *Labor and the American Community*, pp. 71-72.

workers and union counsels, in the conduct of a generally democratic systems' business.

Labor and closely related civil and criminal laws do not speak to these questions in specific ways; union leaders and union members are left to their own devices, for the most part, in constructing the specific structures and procedures of democratic union governance. While a relatively small number of variations may be observed in the detailed characters of the relationships between international or national unions and their locals[57] and of the specific types of democratic arrangements occurring among locals, there are considerable differences in the outcomes; some democratic unions are corrupt while some are models of purity; some are self-servingly insensitive to community or national interests while others are concerned with the commonwealth while serving themselves; some are able to attract large turnouts for meetings and elections and are regularly the scenes of lively debates over issues both substantive and procedural around which shifting coalitions of interests among worker groups are accommodated one to another; others can attract little participation in meetings whose workings are dominated by one or two very small groups of activists.

The public's wishes can complicate matters further. We sometimes like it when the democratic voters in a local vote to revoke their affiliation with an unpopular national or international union, as in Cincinnati, Ohio when milk drivers there voted to disaffiliate with James R. Hoffa's Teamsters in 1961. But many citizens in New York were unsettled by local journalists' reports, in the same year however, that local cement truck drivers had voted to cut off deliveries to the Verrazano Bridge construction site, just after cavernous holes for the anchor pilings had been excavated and as a rainy fall season began: The local drivers had acted in contravention of James R. Hoffa's urge that the drivers ratify a settlement on which he and other national officers had worked assiduously with employers.[58]

Of particular interest is the question of member participation in the formal governance of unions. Relevant data on the subject will suggest to some that union democracy, as such, does not and will not likely work very well; to others the data will suggest that members enjoy, all things considered, about as much democracy as they want, and that most unionists are satisfied that those

---

57. For brief discussions of these variations, see Edward B. Harvey, *Industrial Society: Structures, Roles and Relations* (Homewood, Ill.: Dorsey Press, 1975), pp. 257-67; Seymour M. Lipset, Martin Trow, and James S. Coleman, *Union Democracy: The Internal Politics of the International Typographical Union* (New York: Free Press, 1956); Jack Barbash, *Labor's Grass Roots* (New York: Harper & Row, 1961); and Daisey L. Tagliacozzo, "Trade Union Government: A Bibliographical Review," *The American Journal of Sociology*, 6, 6 (May 1956), 554-81.

58. There are no systematic statistical studies of the outcomes of democratic union votes or of the public's reactions to most strikes, settlements, or to the intraunion developments that follow therefrom. For an illustrative discussion of a number of specific cases and the reactions of the popular press to them, see Ivar Berg, "The Nice Kind of Union Democracy," *Columbia University Forum*, 5, 2 (1962), 18-24.

of their interests that a union can serve are indeed satisfactorily served. Thus Sayles and Strauss reported in 1958 that member participation in major votes, like those to arm their representatives with the strike weapon, or those involved in contract negotiations, ranged from 40 to 80 percent; at regular meetings such participation ranged from 2 to 8 percent. Participation rates go up in proportion to the ease with which votes may be cast. Thus, as few as 20 percent of a local's members will participate in officer elections unless voting is made easy, as when ballot boxes are placed at exit gates. In the latter case participation can reach 90 percent.[59]

Harvey, in a recent summary of the evidence gathered by a number of investigators on the participation of union members in the political life of their locals reports as follows:[60]

> 1. Participation is higher among members who are socially oriented toward the union than those who are oriented to the community or neighborhood.
> 2. Participation is higher in the various separate departments of local unions whose members derive economic, political, or social satisfaction from their unions when satisfaction is measured by the number of satisfactory grievance settlements.
> 3. The more homogeneous members are in respect of job tasks, pay, ethnicity, and related social and economic attributes, the more they are likely to view their locals favorably.
> 4. Workers are more involved in local union decision making when their work brings them into close contact and when these contacts extend beyond the workplace.[61]
> 5. Participation is higher among better paid workers in more prestigeful jobs and among workers in craft than in industrial locals.
> 6. Finally, participation increases with job importance and, perhaps for that reason, with job satisfaction.

It should be stressed that the facts of members' participation do not predict the *outcomes* of participation. Thus Sayles, in a study of auto workers, reports that the highest rates of participation in grievance procedures and in union activities occur among what he calls "strategic groups" whose successful members usually work independently in jobs near but not at the top of the plant's occupational ladder.[62] In a similar vein, the security of union officers

---

59. Leonard R. Sayles and George Strauss, "What the Worker Really Thinks of His Union," *Harvard Business Review*, 31 (May-June 1958), 94-102; and Leonard R. Sayles and George Strauss, *Human Behavior in Organizations* (Englewood Cliffs, N.J.: Prentice-Hall, 1966), pp. 118-19.

60. Edward B. Harvey, *Industrial Society: Structures, Roles and Relations* (Homewood, Ill.: Dorsey Press, 1975), pp. 268-70.

61. See especially Lipset, Trow, and Coleman, *Union Democracy*.

62. Leonard R. Sayles, *Behavior of Industrial Work Groups* (New York: John Wiley, 1958).

has decreased as the law has facilitated more rank and file participation. Thus, "Between five successive two-year periods, 1961-1971, the number of national unions changing presidents reached between 20 to 30 percent of the total. For the period 1969-1971, 49 unions or 28 percent changed presidents."[63] While no longitudinal studies of local union elections over very long periods are available, Henle reports that, during 1963-1966, changes in leadership occurred in more than half of the locals in Milwaukee; two or more such changes occurred in 17 percent of the locals.[64] Because most of the changes in national leadership followed upon the death, retirement, or resignation of incumbent presidents, the statistics are not readily interpretable: The changes in leadership may or may not, otherwise, represent member dissatisfactions with their leaders. And, it must be emphasized, changes in leadership may or may not contribute to "improvements" in a union's behavior from members', managers', or the public's point of view.

Union democracy does of course facilitate members' opportunities to reject contract offers or to reject their unions' services outright. The evidence on these points shows a sharp increase in contract rejections in those situations, specifically, that have been handled by Federal Mediation and Conciliation Service mediators, from 1964 to 1967, from 8.7 to 14.2 percent of some 7,000 cases. There has been a gradual decline since 1967.[65] These findings do not tell us whether the decline results from more satisfactory agreements, from sharper contract-"selling" efforts by leaders to the rank and file, or from less critical attitudes among worker constituents.

Petitions to the NLRB by members asking that their unions be decertified, meanwhile, have never been very numerous but, in recent years, there has been some increase, from 600 to 700 in the early 1960s, to over 1,000 in 1972. There were 451 NLRB-sponsored elections held, pursuant to workers' petitions in this period, with the unions retaining their certifications in between 30 and 35 percent of the elections in which membership participation rates averaged 50 percent.[66]

CONCLUSION

A review of pertinent materials about unions and their leaders, their places in the minds and among the institutions of Americans, and about their internal problems reveals a picture not radically different from that of corporations.

63. Peter Henle, "Economic Effects: Reviewing the Evidence," in Jerome M. Rosow (ed.), *The Worker and the Job: Coping with Change* (Englewood Cliffs, N.J.:Prentice-Hall, 1974), p. 138.

64. Ibid., p. 139.

65. Ibid., p. 137.

66. Ibid., pp. 139-40.

Their leaders are obliged to be responsive to a number of constituencies, a fact that tempers in a number of pointed ways their capacity to act unilaterally in the service of global ideologies. Like large corporations, the larger unions have some economic impacts but they are not, despite apparent monopolistic controls, by any means the sovereign dictators of economic conditions even in the sectors of the economy in which they are most visible. A more accurate if somewhat unpopular judgment, in many circles, would hold that unions have become important but not dominant component constituencies in a pluralistic system; their presence most assuredly adds credibility to Berle's notion that the U.S. is an "economic republic."

The presence of unions does not, however, offer a convenient explanation for even a majority of the critical parameters descriptive of wage contours among industries, and therefore of the patterns of income distribution in the U.S. Their interests in the shape and content of the occupational structure, of skill hierarchies within the structures and segments, and of working conditions among and within industries, firms, and public agencies have not been accompanied by economic or political "clout" sufficient to make them the *preponent* forces pictured by their angriest critics. There is not doubt, however, that their presence presents both demands and opportunities, among others in their worlds, to which regular and systematic attention and energy must be allocated by managers. Not infrequently, it is the unions' internal *divisions* along lines of age, sex, and skill differences, rather than their capacities for *united* actions, that contribute most to some managers' and many thoughtful critics' apprehensions.

Finally, it is notable that corporations and unions, despite a number of common problems and features, are assessed within intellectual, ideological, and legal frameworks that are rooted in a two-valued logic. The evaluations that result from the application of what are essentially differential standards do not contribute as much to one's understanding of the industrial system and its "webs of rules" as would evaluations that are anchored in somewhat less disjoint modes of discourse.

CHAPTER 6
MANAGERS, WORKERS, AND ORGANIZATIONS

INTRODUCTION

Although our emphases in the earliest chapters were upon macroscopic forces in industrial systems, we have regularly referred to arrangements that are more plainly visible, after our metaphor, from ground level. The fact is that while many of the institutional arrangements of social systems are not perfectly articulated, as noted in chapter 2, they are sufficiently of a piece to impinge upon each other in a variety of ways. Up to this point these "systemic" qualities of industrial societies have caused us few analytical problems; but the differences among analysts regarding the weight of explanatory factors are quite noticeably linked, in most instances, to differences in their political-philosophical perspectives.

When we move to a consideration of workers and managers in their actual work settings, however, we confront a very large body of relevant studies by investigators whose efforts are more subtly informed by concerns that are ideologically tinged. Most of these investigators would agree, in principle, that social relationships in the workplace are influenced by "outside" forces and developments, but a substantial number emphasize intra-organizational processes, proximal working conditions, and local developments almost to the exclusion of extra organizational or wider forces, conditions, and developments. Those who stress intraorganizational phenomena thus tend to borrow more from the first than the second of two main approaches to the study of the workaday world, an approach in which work settings are seen in isolation from the larger society. In this chapter we will consider the intellectual roots, the assumptions, and the main lines of the findings of investigators, in and out of business,[1] whose work falls within the loose boundaries of each of these evolving approaches. Among our specific concerns will be the rather different prescriptions for improving the quality of working life that have followed from studies by the two schools' adherents.[2]

One of these traditions or schools has evolved around a series of perceptions, findings, and prescriptions that have, almost from the school's founding in the 1930s, been referred to as "human relations." The second approach, which we may call "industrial relations and human resources," is a little less a school than a loose confederation of denominations, several of whose intellectual origins go back to the period of the French Revolution, to the writings of Henri St. Simon, and to Karl Marxs' and Frederich Engles' critiques of capitalism. The industrial relations approach also has roots in the work of "institutional economists" in the period 1900-1950. These economists were interested in norms, the rules of conduct, and in established ways of thinking as well as in more conventional economic variables. We will refer to the second approach simply as the industrial relations approach.

Among the major differences between the two approaches are those stemming from the differences in the weights they assign to (1) workers' and managers' psychologies; (2) the causes of and the place of conflict in society; (3) workers' immediate work tasks, their immediate associations with each other, and their relationships with those immediately in authority over them; (4) different definitions of the economic and noneconomic interests of employees; and, finally, (5) macroscopic public and microscopic private policies regarding work reform efforts. The two approaches have been well represented in recent debates over worker dissatisfaction in Congress and in print and picture tube.[3]

---

1. A growing number of corporations have recently added highly accomplished social scientists to their boards of directors while a larger number have long hired social scientists as well as social science graduates to their staffs or as part time consultants to personnel, industrial relations, marketing, and corporate research departments. In addition, many corporations have opened their doors to social science data gatherers, especially from the faculty ranks of the nation's leading schools of business. Indeed, one of the schools of thought considered here was born in collaborative efforts between businessmen and Harvard Business School professors in the 1930s.

2. See, for example, *Work in America,* Report of a Special Task Force to the Secretary of Health, Education and Welfare (Cambridge, Mass.: MIT Press, 1973).

3. See "Hearings on Worker Alienation" before the Subcommittee on Employment, Manpower and Poverty of the Senate Committee on Labor and Public Welfare, 92nd Congress, 2nd Session (1972). For an overview of the various perspectives on and prospects for reforms targeted on the "quality of work" in America, see Ivar Berg, Marcia Freedman, and Michael Freeman, *Managers and Work Reform: A Limited Engagement* (New York: Free Press, 1978).

INDUSTRIAL RELATIONS

Though expressions of outrage against "capitalist" employers are widely sprinkled throughout *Capital,* his most famous work, Marx made it clear that he absolved capitalists of any personal blame for "exploiting" workers.[4] Employers, in his analysis, were "personification(s) of economic categories, embodiments of particular class relations and class interests." As such, employers are simply driven, by the logics of their roles as economic agents rather than by psychological needs, to act exploitatively toward employees. "My standpoint," Marx wrote in a prefatory description of his quest for the "law of motion" governing capitalism, "from which the evolution of the economic formation of society is viewed as a process of natural history, can less than any other make the individual responsible for relations whose creation he socially remains, however much he may subjectively raise himself above them." Marx went on to identify workers' true interests to lie in the revolutionary dissolution of the ties between capitalists and the political and legal system that protected the private ownership of capital. Separated from ownership of the means of production, the worker became a commodity; he would recognize that he was estranged from the product of his labor and from his work, and therefore alienated from himself, but for the (transient) distractions of his consciousness by essentially inconsequential "reform" and labor movements and by conventional ideologies. These distractions and ideologies, Marx held, were designed by property owners and their allies to legitimate the status quo and, otherwise, to make radical political and economic changes appear irreligious, unpatriotic, or unnatural.[5]

Relatively few students of work have adhered to the prescriptive side of the Marxian critique but the conception that economic roles and their demands on incumbents are defined by their particular places in social, political, and economic structures is one that has found wide favor among those we here link to the loose confederation identified as industrial relationists. For these students, workers, managers, and the incumbents of other economic and social roles have fundamentally different interests and perceptions, differences that lead to conflicts that lead them, ultimately, in turn, either to fight or to bargain over the ways in which the interests—including the claims, rights, privileges, and im-

---

4. See the author's preface to the first edition, Karl Marx, *Capital,* vol. 1, translated by Samuel Moore (New York: Modern Library Edition, undated), p. 15.

5. For an evenhanded discussion of the numerous shadings of meaning imputed to the concepts of "alienation," "estrangement," and what Marx termed "false consciousness," see Richard Schacht, *Alienation* (Garden City, N.Y.: Doubleday, 1971), and the introductory essay therein by Walter Kaufman. For a discussion of social scientists' use of "alienation," see Melvin Seeman, "Alienation Studies," in Alex Inkeles (ed.), *Annual Review of Sociology,* vol. 2 (Palo Alto, Calif.: Annual Review, 1975), pp. 91-123. For an empirical application of the essentially Marxian conception of alienation to work place experience, see Melvin L. Kohn and Carmi Schooler, "Occupational Experience and Psychological Functioning: An Assessment of Reciprocal Effects," *American Sociological Review,* 38 (February 1973), 97-118.

munities of differentially situated groups—will be served in societies, in communities, and in organizational settings. Individual industrial relationists will differ over the width of the gap in the interests of different individuals and groups in the political economic play, and over the margins for the relatively peaceful accommodation of interests.[6] They are generally inclined, however, to start from the assumption that there *are* conflicts, and from there to move to investigations designed to identify the methods by which conflicts may be resolved and to study the institutional-organizational arrangements employed by interest groups' members and their leaders in efforts to defend or extend their claims and rights.[7]

While industrial relationists attend to organizational studies by the human relations school, they are far more attentive to extraorganizational circumstances in shaping the attitudes and behavior of managers and employees. The tend to be especially sensitive to the effects of business conditions, business cycles in particular, upon such basic organizational matters as turnover, absenteeism, and collective bargaining demands, and they tend to view unions, where they occur, as the outcomes of essentially rational employee efforts to influence their economic and organizational destinies. They tend, finally, to assign higher priority to the specific ways in which managers strive to divide and allocate labor and labor skills, to organize skill hierarchies and to set crew sizes, the work pace, the spatial locations, and the speeds of machines, than they do to technology, as such, in shaping working conditions. Industrial relationists thus stress what we have, throughout our discussion, called social technology as the most critical determinate of experiences in the workaday world. We will return to industrial relations studies after a somewhat more detailed review, in the next section, of the human relations school.

HUMAN RELATIONS

Although there were a few more or less modern social science-type efforts to examine management methods and work experiences prior to the late 1920s, most earlier efforts concentrated on efforts to make large and growing organizations more rational. On one side, students of management focused on managers' roles as the designers of corporate hierarchies. These students focused upon managements' separable functional activities—production, marketing, finance—activities which could be readily coordinated and about which effective long

---

6. For some of the differences among contemporary critics of capitalism by members of what the editor calls left and liberal groups, see Maurice Zeitlin (ed.), *American Society, Inc.: Studies of the Social Structure and Political Economy of the United States,* 2nd ed. (Chicago: Rand McNally, 1977).

7. For a detailed assessment of the differential treatments accorded conflict in studies of organizations, see Sherman Krupp, *Pattern in Organizational Analysis* (New York: Holt, Rinehart and Winston, 1961).

range planning could be undertaken.[8] On another side, heavily influenced by the writings and preachments of F. W. Taylor, students of production focused on the details of work tasks, the better to identify the most economically efficient work procedures. These two streams of concern fed a common concern with making industry more efficient and the nation's economic pie larger.[9] Some business leaders saw these emphases on science and empiricism to be a threat to private property in that they played down property ownership in favor of professional expertise in the legitimation of managers' authority. Many of the themes in these two strands, with their stresses on the application of science to production and to organizational design, meanwhile, may be found in the writings by Henri St. Simon, after the French Revolution and, later, in the classic studies of bureaucratic structures by Max Weber.[10]

The human relations school, meanwhile, had its origin in collaborative studies of work groups by Harvard Business School professors and business leaders. Basic to these studies in the late 1930s and beyond, were a series of experiments and studies at Western Electric's Hawthorne works, the original purposes of which were to better understand industrial fatigue. As it developed, the investigators reported, after a six-year-long series of experiments and studies ending in 1933, that worker output was far more discernibly related to changes in supervisory practices, to the work groups' own prescriptive and proscriptive norms and to the social psychological factors bearing upon group formation and group membership than to variations in physical working conditions, or to the number and duration of rest pauses.

Since the results of these investigations[11] there have appeared hundreds of plant-, office-, and shop-level studies of workers' attitudes and personalities, and

---

8. See Henri Fayol, *General and Industrial Administration* (London: Sir Isaac Pitman, 1949); J. D. Mooney and A. C. Reiley, *The Principles of Organization* (New York: Harper & Row, 1939); and Mary Parker Follett, *Dynamic Administration* (New York: Harper & Row, 1940).

9. Frederick W. Tayler, *The Principles of Scientific Management* (New York: Harper & Row, 1911).

10. For a brief comparison of St. Simon's and Weber's conceptions of rationality in administration and organization with those organic to human relations, see Alvin Gouldner, "Organizational Analysis," in Robert K. Merton, Leonard Broom, and Leonard S. Cottrell, Jr. (eds.), *Sociology Today* (New York: Basic Books, 1959), pp. 423-428. For other comparisons of managerial and scientific management treatments with Weber's ideas and those in human relations, see Amitai Etzioni, *Modern Organizations* (Englewood Cliffs, N.J.: Prentice-Hall, 1964); Charles Perrow, *Complex Organizations: A Critical Essay* (Glenview, Ill.: Scott, Foresman, 1972), pp. 61-204; and Peter Blau and Marshall W. Meyer, *Bureaucracy in Modern Society*, 2nd ed. (New York: Random House, 1971).

11. For a brief summary of the so-called Western Electric Hawthorne experiments, see George C. Homans, *The Fatigue of Workers* (New York: Reinhold, 1941), pp. 56-65. Detailed descriptions may be found in Elton Mayo, *The Human Problems of an Industrial Civilization* (New York: Macmillan, 1933); T. N. Whitehead, *The Industrial Worker,* 2 vols. (Cambridge, Mass.: Harvard University Press, 1930); Fritz J. Roethlisberger and William J. Dickson, *Management and the Worker* (Cambridge, Mass.: Harvard University Press, 1939).

of workers' differential dispositions and responses toward group memberships, group norms, and compliance; toward supervisory practices and incentive systems; and toward rules and procedures. In addition, there have been innumerable studies of the behavioral and attitudinal correlates of the size of the organizational subunits in which employees find themselves, and of the different task requirements, production methods, work flow arrangements and skill hierarchies that immediately confront employees in their worksettings. In most of these studies, investigators have sought to discover both the conditions and the ordering of the conditions that contribute to satisfactions of workers as measured in attitude surveys and in studies of workers' compliance with orders and rules, their absenteeism and turnover rates, and their grievances. The materials in the next several subsections are illustrative of human relations studies. The piecemeal topics will then be drawn together in a brief critique of human relations studies and of the prescriptions most often inferred therefrom.

Workers and Work Groups

It is one of the staple findings in human relations studies that workers are more satisfied, in general, to the extent to which their jobs permit them to interact with others, a finding that squares well with findings about individuals and groups outside of conventional work settings,[12] under clinical-experimental conditions, and sometimes even in other than American cultural settings.[13] All things being equal, the status, ethnic diversity, skills, ages, and modal personality of a group's members held constant, groups provide their members with companionship; a sense of identification; friendly understanding; guides to acceptable behavior; oportunities for the expression of initiative and creativity—though sometimes at what managers may deem is at their expense; and protection from outside pressures, management demands, and the unilateral imposition of what are seen to be unacceptable and unfair changes in working conditions, work pace, or rules regarding tools. While work groups do not consistently dominate their members, least of all the more "individualistic" personalities among them, they can be and often are demonstrably potent in shaping their perceptions and cognitions, and their behavior.[14]

12. See, for example, Kurt Lewin, "Group Decision and Social Change," and R. Lippett and R. White, "An Experimental Study of Leadership and Group Life," in Eleanor E. Maccoby, Theordore E. Newcomb, and E. L. Hartley (eds.), *Readings in Social Psychology* (New York: Holt, Rinehart and Winston, 1958), pp. 197-212 and 496-511; Edward A. Shils, "Primary Groups in the American Army [in World War II]" in Robert K. Merton and Paul F. Lazarsfeld (eds.), *Continuities in Social Research: Studies in the Scope and Method of the American Soldier* (New York: Free Press, 1950), pp. 16-39; Edgar H. Schein and Warren G. Bennis, *Personal and Organizational Change* (New York: John Wiley, 1965).

13. See George C. Homans, *The Human Group* (New York: Harcourt Brace Jovanovich, 1950).

14. These are discussed in detail in Leonard R. Sayles and George Strauss, *Human Behavior in Organizations* (Englewood Cliffs, N.J.: Prentice-Hall, 1966), pp. 83-87.

Workers and Supervisors

Closely akin to studies of workers and groups are studies of workers and supervisory patterns which have been reviewed and assessed by Sayles and Strauss; Dubin, Homans, Mann, and Miller; Porter, Lawlor, and Hackman; Hunt; Yukl; and Ritchie.[15] The last of these investigators points out that research on supervision has shifted from early emphases on leadership traits to later emphases on supervisory "styles" and then, most recently, to a "systems" approach according to which supervisors roles are best understood as segments of larger configurations of roles rather than in isolation. Among the difficulties attending research on supervision, Ritchie notes, are (1) those always attached to cross-sectional research which, by definition, neglects the lag, over time, between shifts in supervisory practices, shifts in the climate of organization, and employee reactions to these shifts; (2) those generally attaching to survey research, of distinguishing "between real attitudes, socially desirable answers . . . climate, and [actual vs. reported] supervisory behavior"; (3) those attaching to measuring effectiveness; (4) those attached to establishing direction of causality as between supervisory behavior and workers' performance; and, finally (5) those attaching to the apparent increase in resistance of respondents to being research subjects.[16] Despite these difficulties, a few well-founded generalizations have emerged.

The work of Lewin, Lippet, and White in the late 1930s pointed to the relevance of a distinction between "people"- and "production-centered" supervisors;[17] by the early 1960s the evidence suggested that employee-centered supervisors lead to both higher productivity and higher worker satisfaction.[18] To these orientations, Mann added: the importance to both production and satis-

---

15. Sayles and Strauss, *Human Behavior,* pp. 155-228; Robert Dubin, George C. Homans, Floyd C. Mann, and Delbert C. Miller, *Leadership and Productivity* (San Francisco: Chandler, 1965), especially pp. 46-50, 66-67, and 102-3; Lyman W. Porter, Edward E. Lawlor III, and J. Richard Hackman, *Behavior in Organizations* (New York: McGraw-Hill, 1975), pp. 184-86; 119-20; 422-34; J. G. Hunt, "Organizational Leadership: Some Theoretical and Empirical Considerations" in Karl O. Magnusen, *Organizational Design, Development and Behavior: A Situational View* (Glenview, Ill.: Scott, Foresman, 1977), pp. 281-96; Gary Yukl, "Toward a Behavioral Theory of Leadership," *Organizational Behavior and Human Performance,* 6, 4 (July 1971), 414-40; J. B. Ritchie, "Supervision," in George Strauss, Raymond E. Miles, Charles C. Snow, and Arnold S. Tannenbaum, *Organizational Behavior: Research and Issues* (Madison, Wisc.: Industrial Relations Research Association, 1974), pp. 51-76.

16. Ritchie, "Supervision," pp. 56-57.

17. Kurt Lewin, Ronald Lippit, and Robert K. White, "Patterns of Aggressive Behavior in Experimentally Created Social Climates," *Journal of Social Psychology,* 10 (1939), 271-99. For a detailed review, from which the propositions in this and the next several paragraphs are drawn, see Ritchie, "Supervision," pp. 58-70.

18. Likert, 1969.

faction of technical and administrative skills.[19] Thereafter Bauer and Seashore showed that, in addition to communicating these orientations and possessing these skills, supervisors need to stress the achievement of group goals, provide the resources needed to accomplish work tasks, and facilitate interaction among workers to be successful.[20] In most recent times, investigators who have pursued the "trait" approach to supervision have borrowed and elaborated upon a "contingency model," first proposed by Fiedler,[21] which states that the appropriate leadership style *in a given situation* is a function of (1) leader-member relations, (2) task structure, and (3) position power. The combination of these variables, according to Ritchie, determines the "favorableness of the situation" in which the supervisor must lead.[22]

Though these conclusions are well supported by evidence, they do embody some confusion, as Ritchie has noted, between supervisors' attitudes and supervisors' behavior.[23] Thus Ritchie and Miles have showed that "attitude may be more important than strategy in subordinate satisfaction," but both need to be accounted for in performance.[24] Increasingly, researchers focus on the situational circumstances within which supervisors are obliged to operate that facilitate or constrain their efforts—the so-called supervisory context[25]—and upon wider organizational factors that condition both supervisors' and workers' attitudes and behavior.[26] In the latter case, emphases are placed on the capacities of top level managers to deal with *their* problems and the effects, on supervisors and workers, of higher level managers' overall capacities to manage.[27] Assertions in the literature on supervision about organizational arrangements that transcend the proximal or immediate situation of workers and supervisors are not typically followed up, however, with systematic studies of managers as the entrepreneurs, marketers or investors whose decisions set, fix and change the larger

19. Mann '65.

20. B & S '66

21. Fiedler 61, Fiedler/Chems 74. Emphases added.

22. Ritchie, "Supervision," p. 60. See also Dubin et al., *Leadership and Productivity,* pp. 46-50.

23. Ritchie, "Supervision."

24. J. B. Ritchie and Raymond E. Miles, "An Analysis of Quantity and Quality of Participation as Mediating Variables," *Personnel Psychology,* 23 (Autumn, 1900), 355.

25. See Ritchie, "Supervision," pp. 65-71.

26. George C. Homans, "Effort, Supervision and Productivity," in Dubin et al., *Leadership and Productivity,* pp. 51-67.

27. Ibid.; and Ivar Berg, Marcia Freedman, and Michael Freeman, *Managers and Work Reform: A Limited Engagement* (New York: Free Press, 1978), pp. 115-123.

organizational contexts and situations stressed in contemporary human relations studies of supervision. Human relations studies on the impact of technology and technological arrangements, as we will see next, are also conducted as though these arrangements may be separated from higher level management decision-making processes.

Technology, Size, Satisfaction, and Productivity[28]

The following questions have been among the most essential of those that have guided the research on workers by human relationists.[29] It will be well to keep these research agenda items in mind as we continue our journey:

1. To what extent are the satisfaction and dissatisfactions of workers related to their performance, in general, and their productivity, in particular?
2. To what extent can the sources and determinates of workers' satisfactions and dissatisfactions be pinpointed, whatever their implications for worker performance?
3. To what extent can the sources of satisfaction and dissatisfaction be ordered, in respect of their importance, as "explanations" of observed variations in worker reactions to the world of occupational experiences generally, and concrete work experiences in particular?[30]
4. To what extent are the forces, circumstances, and events that appear, in statistical and analytical terms, to reduce dissatisfactions and heighten satisfactions amenable to influence and intervention?
5. To what extent are employers, particularly, and worker representatives, to a lesser degree, concerned about and capable of acting upon options suggested in answers to the previous questions?

It is possible that we will discover, some day, that the performance patterns and productivity of Americans are related in complicated but in systematic ways to the measurable satisfactions and dissatisfactions of these citizens, a possibility suggested by the research agenda. The fact is that if indeed there is a matrix of relationships like the one implied in the questions, it is an exceedingly hard one to construct: The answer to the first question must be an essentially

---

28. The bulk of the materials in this section have been abstracted from a study by Berg et al., *Managers and Work Reform*, ch. 3; and from a most helpful mimeographed report, "The Personal, Corporate, and Societal Implications of Employment" (Ann Arbor, Mich.: Survey Research Center, 1975) by Robert P. Quinn and Stanley Seashore.

29. Robert J. Flanagan, George Strauss, and Lloyd Ulman, "Worker Discontent and Workplace Behavior," *Industrial Relations,* 13 (May 1974), 101–23, for a confrontation of these questions with data on the types that interest industrial relationists.

30. For book-length reviews of research and bibliography, see Porter et al., *Behavior in Organizations,* especially part 3, pp. 221–310.

negative one, however, for conceptual and methodological among other reasons. In the first place, as Quinn and his colleagues have pointed out, it may be doubted " . . . whether there is any empirical justification for assuming a unidimensional construct representing 'overall job performance.'" . . . Among the reasons for doubting the validity of such a construct are logical ones arising in part "from the common findings that some elements of performance may be *negatively* correlated, that the elements interact, and that the resulting single measure does not reflect well the values implied by the initial choice of elemental measures."[31] The discussion by Quinn and his associates is of special interest because it reflects not only an appreciation for innumerable studies by others but their own experiences, in the meticulous exploitation of the most current of available data on the satisfactions and dissatisfactions of national probability samples of employed Americans in 1969 and 1973.[32]

Raymond K. Katzell, Daniel Yankelovich, and a panel of advisors appointed by the National Science Foundation, meanwhile, have recently reviewed nine studies of selected worker behavior patterns, worker performance, and the satisfactions of workers exposed to a variety of different job designs. They conclude that while job design, job challenges, and other intrinsic job characteristics are often correlated with satisfaction they are not consistently related to productivity or with "manifestations of avoidance"—absenteeism or turnover.[33] Quinn and his colleagues are probably correct in their judgment that, at best, the relationship between workers' satisfactions and their performance are concomitant in nature, which is to say that the two are related when high levels of performance are valued as means to workers' other aims and ends.[34]

In addition to the problematical quality of the conceptualization of worker performance are problems in defining and measuring satisfaction. As Quinn, Staines, and McCullough point out, different job satisfaction survey measures have different points at which discontent begins to register. Thus, in the 1969 Working Conditions and the 1973 Quality of Working Life Surveys, the most recent of many surveys, six different items were employed to measure "overall" job satisfaction. The percentage of dissatisfied workers varied from 14

31. Quinn and Seashore, "Implications of Employment," pp. 23-24 (emphasis in original). These authors cite reviews by Victor Vroom and Frederick Herzberg of studies in 27 organizational settings in which the aggregated results are highly ambiguous.

32. For another helpful discussion of the policy implications of productivity-performance-attitude materials, see Robert P. Quinn, Graham L. Staines, and Margaret R. McCullough, *Job Satisfaction: Is There a Trend?* Manpower Research Monograph no. 30 (Washington, D.C.: Government Printing Office, 1974).

33. Raymond A. Katzell, Daniel Yankelovich, et al., *Work, Productivity and Job Satisfaction: An Evaluation of Policy-Related Research* (New York: The Psychological Corporation, 1975), pp. 151-52 (emphasis added).

34. Quinn and Seashore, "Implications of Employment," p. 30.

to 51 on the six items suggesting that different questions tap different "thresholds of discontent":

> More dissatisfaction is reported when workers are asked whether they enjoy their jobs ... than when "satisfaction" with the job is asked about specifically.
> More dissatisfaction is reported when the question concerns another—even a hypothetical—worker than when the question focuses on the respondent.
> More dissatisfaction is reported when the question raises the (hypothetical) issue of the worker's reliving his or her life than when it directs attention to the worker's present reaction to the job.
> More dissatisfaction is reported when workers are invited to consider attractive alternatives to the present jobs than when they are asked for their reactions to their present jobs on a noncomparative basis.
> More dissatisfaction is reported when permissible answers to a question include several degrees of dissatisfaction (and especially a response alternative reflecting ambivalence or indifference).[35]

In addition, it is far easier to determine the *relative* satisfactions of different workers than to determine absolute levels of dissatisfaction.[36] The conclusions are thus well founded in the best available and most recent evidence that:

> Except for recent and anticipated improvements of measures, there is no reason to expect that future investigations will be any more consistent in identifying substantial positive relationships between job satisfaction and performance than other investigations have been hitherto.
> There is no compelling theoretical reason for expecting any sort of across-the-board relationship between satisfaction and performance.
> Even when such relationships *are* identified they cannot automatically be interpreted as indicating that high satisfaction is a cause of good performance. There are two competing interpretations.
>
>   1. it is actually the good performance that is creating the high satisfaction;
>   2. there is no causal association between satisfaction and importance but both are in fact the product of some third factor.[37]

In the absence of evidence sufficient to test these interpretations it is hazardous to imply, as many consulting social scientists do, that managers will

---

35. Quinn, Staines, and McCullough, *Job Satisfaction*, p. 51.

36. Ibid. p. 53. We may gainsay, in concerns with *relative* dissatisfactions, the question raised by Mayer Zald of whether these are not "cerebral correlations," resulting from a general "yay-saying" tendency among American workers.

37. Quinn and Seashore, "Implications of Employment," pp. 31-32.

earn returns, in terms of employee performance, on investments in interventions designed to improve workers' morale.[38] The fact that we are in no position to account directly and to any significant degree for variations in worker performance through examinations of the distributions of their satisfaction and dissatisfactions is not to reject the hypothesis that workers' attitudes and feelings about work are related to their work experiences or to the local or proximal conditions that shape these experiences. Neither do anomalous relationships between satisfaction and performance necessarily mean that scholars or others should for that reason be unconcerned with pinpointing and reducing the discontents of employees.

As one might expect, there are discernible relationships between work exposures and the responses to surveys among employed Americans; the second of the research issues, regarding the sources of discontent thus deserves a somewhat less ambiguous, less negative answers than those addressed to the first question. Once again, Quinn and his associates can report from the 1969 Working Conditions Survey that:

> 1. In spite of public speculation to the contrary, there is no conclusive evidence of a widespread, dramatic decline in job satisfaction. Reanalysis of 15 national surveys conducted since 1958 indicates that there has not been any significant decrease in overall levels of job satisfaction over the last decade.
> 2. Job satisfaction among blacks and other minority groups has been consistently lower than that of whites, but has fluctuated as much as 13 percent in the past 11 years. These changes do not correspond to any consistent pattern and are most probably due to sampling error.
> 3. Younger workers are less satisfied with their jobs than older workers, but this had been true for the past 15 years. Therefore, the much-discussed large decline in job satisfaction of younger workers has not been substantiated.
> 4. Among occupational categories, professional-technical workers, managers, officials, and proprietors register the highest levels of job satisfaction, while operatives and nonfarm laborers register the lowest. Nondomestic service workers and clerical workers are also among the relatively dissatisfied, a factor of potential importance since these workers represent a growing sector of the labor force.
> 5. Women workers, by and large, are about as contented with their jobs as are men. But it appears that women workers with one or more children under six years of age in their households are significantly less satisfied than are either women without preschoolers in the household or male workers in general.
> 6. Among workers without a college degree, there is little relationship between educational level and job satisfaction. Those with college degrees, however, have high levels of job satisfaction. Surprisingly low levels of satisfaction are registered by workers with some education but no degree.

---

38. For a discussion of consultants' urgings, see Berg et al., *Managers and Work Reform.*

7. When asked to identify the individual facets of the job which were of greatest importance to them, most workers in a national sample gave high ratings to the availability of the resources needed to perform well and to the challenge of their jobs and lower ratings to financial rewards and "comfort" factors. Blue-collar workers, however, tended to consider pay more significant than the challenge of the job, while women workers were somewhat more interested in "comfort" than were men. Because the "average" American worker appears to seek many things simultaneously (e.g., good pay, interesting work) from each job, there may be no one way to increase job satisfaction.

8. A long list of job-related stresses have been implicated in various types of physical and mental illnesses, indicating that expressions of job dissatisfaction may be viewed as an important early warning system to both employees and employers.[39]

It is of interest, given the findings reported in the preceding section, to elaborate on item seven in the conclusions by Quinn et al. Thus, a large and representative sample of employed Americans made a great deal of the issues raised in the Working Conditions and Quality of Employment Life Surveys that bear upon their sense of the quality of their employers as managers. When single questions that appear to bear somewhat less directly upon the matter, like questions about supervisors, have been raised in surveys they have not generally been interpreted in the human relations tradition as casting light on the quality, the competence, and therefore, ultimately, the very legitimacy of upper-level managers in American society.

In the 1969 and 1973 surveys, workers were afforded several such opportunities, and from 61 to more than 68 percent reported the subjects as being "very important" to them. The items used by Quinn and his colleagues in the construction of an index they called "resources," and the percentages for all workers reporting that the issues were *important* to them were as follows: "I receive enough help and equipment to get the job done," 68.4 percent; "I have enough information to get the job done," 68.1 percent; "My responsibilities are clearly defined," 61.2 percent; "my supervisor is competent in doing his job," 61.1 percent.[40]

We may note, too, the sixth item in Quinn's list, dealing with relevant correlates of the formal educational achievements of employed Americans, and the observation that 36 percent of American workers had more education than they thought they needed to do their jobs.[41] Less subjective comparisons of the uses employers make of workers' educational achievements indicate that managers under-utilize the formal educational achievements of perhaps as much

---

39. Quinn, Staines and McCullough, *Job Satisfaction,* pp. 1-2.

40. For a tabular comparison of the importance of 23 facets grouped under five indices, see ibid., p. 16.

41. Ibid., p. 27.

as one-third of the work force.[42] The much mourned passing of the "work ethic" among employed Americans may, indeed, be matched by the failure of managers to exercise rationally and fully the "rights to manage," rights about whose threatened status managers have expressed much concern in recent years.

The matters of managers' performance and legitimacy are raised here simply to underscore the tentativeness of the reply that may be offered to the question of whether it is possible to pinpoint the determinants of worker satisfactions and dissatisfactions. The newer facts, regarding managers' mobilization of "resources" and the related issues of manpower utilization, suggest that much is yet to be done before we cay say that all of the sources of worker content and discontent have been delineated in available research.

In general, although there are exceptions, workers are demonstrably more satisfied (depending, as Quinn reminds us, on the type and wording of questions put to survey respondents) to the extent that they feel secure and adequately rewarded; to the extent to which they enjoy psychologically (and often economically) supportive relationships with coworkers; to the extent to which their supervisors are both able and civilized; to the extent to which their jobs are not overridingly dangerous to life and limb; to the degree to which their jobs utilize more, rather than fewer, of their skills, aptitudes, intelligence, and formal educational achievements; and to the degree to which they have opportunities to shape or, more likely, to enjoy some "codeterminative" rights (or powers) in establishing their conditions of work. The general principles here allow, of course for variations. Thus, there are, in the vast literature on work, cases of workers who favor opportunities for daydreaming over challenges in their work; who are ruggedly individualistic and therefore offended by the pressures of coworkers' norms; of workers who enjoy coping with occupational hazards; and of workers who thrive upon and self-servingly exploit ambiguities in organizational demands.[43]

It has been argued that whatever else operates on workers—work group

---

42. Berg et al., *Managers and Work Reform,* ch. 6 and 3.

43. For an earlier overview, see Chris Argyris, *Personality and Organization: The Conflict Between System and Individual* (New York: Harper & Row, 1957). For views about some of the variations around the principle, see, for example, the following studies whose very titles will suggest the variations around the means: Melville Dalton, *Men Who Manage* (New York: John Wiley, 1959); Donald Roy, "Quota Restriction and Goldbricking in a Machine Shop," *American Journal of Sociology* 57 (March 1952), 427–42; "Work Satisfaction and Social Reward in Quota Achievement: An Analysis of Piecework Incentive," *American Sociological Review,* 18 (October 1953), 507–14; "Efficiency and 'the Fix': Informal Intergroup Relations in a Piecework Shop," *American Journal of Sociology,* 60 (November 1954), 225–66. See also Melville Dalton, "The Industrial Rate-buster: A Characterization," *Applied Anthropology,* 7 (1948), 5–18. Finally, see Leonard Sayles and George Strauss, *The Local Union* (New York: Harcourt Brace Jovanovich, 1967); James W. Kuhn, *Bargaining in the Grievance Process* (New York: Columbia University Press, 1961); and Ivar Berg and James W. Kuhn, "The Assumptions of Featherbedding," *Labor Law Journal,* 13 (April 1962), 277–83.

experiences; managers' styles; wage, salary, and benefit programs; supervisory practices; and other social and organizational policy arrangements—the most critical factors affecting the nature of work experiences are those deriving from the size of organizations and the technology used in the production process. The effects of these features on workers are not, however, more readily predictable in work settings than were the effects of technology discussed in other chapters. Thus, in a summary of studies conducted prior to 1961, the emphasis by human relations writers on size is supported in varying degrees in two-thirds of the 39 studies reviewed. It should be pointed out, however, that these studies (which investigated the effects of size on satisfaction, absenteeism, turnover, accidents, labor disputes, and productivity) were conducted in diverse organizational settings—factories and mines (15); stores (2); divisions and departments (11); work groups (7); and "other" (4),[44] making it virtually impossible to conclude much about *which* type of size is at issue, that of the *parent* organization or of the *subsystem* of an organization from which subjects are sampled.

The literature dealing with organizational size, meanwhile, is not exactly scarce. In addition to the review by Porter et al., 100 primary studies were carefully briefed by Ingham, of the United Kingdom, in the course of a study on work orientations, expectations, rewards, deprivation, absenteeism, and turnover among the skilled and semiskilled employees in two departments of one large British firm and the skilled and semiskilled workers in each of eight small firms. Ingham concludes, from his review, and from his investigation (in which technology was held constant) that there is no consistent relationship between size and various measures of worker performance and that this is the case because workers are, themselves, of different orientations—"economizers-instrumentalists" and "identifiers"—in *both* large and small organizations:

> . . . [In] *both* large and small organizations there was a high level of congruence between the workers' wants and expectations (orientations) and the organizational rewards structure. This kind of approach went some considerable way towards explaining why there was no significant difference between the labour turnover rates of the small and large organizations.[45]

Ingham's explanation leans on the observed distributions of "congruent" and "incongruent orientations," and on workers' "definitions of situation," the latter among employees in organizations that afford relatively more or fewer "economic-instrumental" versus "noninstrumental" rewards. Larger organizations, he sensibly suggests, offer relatively more "instrumental" (economic) rewards and tend to retain workers with complementary "orientations"; smaller

---

44. Porter et al., *Behavior in Organizations*, p. 251.

45. Geoffrey K. Ingham, *Size of Industrial Organization and Worker Behavior* (Cambridge, England: Cambridge University Press, 1970), p. 143 (emphasis in the original).

organizations offer greater noneconomic, more "expressive" opportunities and rewards, and tend to retain workers for whom wages, per se, are relatively less important than the social-psychological "expressive" rewards.

Closely related (and, as noted, held constant in Ingham's studies) is the matter of "technology," an old chestnut among social science problems, as we have repeatedly seen, since Marx, especially, shredded the factory system out from the capitalist system for special commentary. It is the case that a kind of neo-Marxist model of technology's global impact on work and therefore on workers' satisfactions has attracted a significant number of social scientists over the years; it is as if one retains his radical political-economic critique of capitalism while essentially substituting for it an assessment of the independent effects of technology. A great deal has been made, for example, of a series of case studies in the printing, textile, automobile, and chemical industries by an investigator who augmented his observations by a selective examination of blue-collar survey data that were originally collected by the Roper Organization in 1947.[46] Blauner's main thesis is a questionable one in terms of the available evidence, however.

Thus, we may some day have the data to show, as he claims, that "the industrial system distributes alienation unevenly among its blue-collar force, just as our economic system distributes income unevenly," and that among the key differentiating factors that give an industry its distinctively alienating capacities is its technology, defined as ". . . the complex of physical objects and technical operations (both manual and machine) regularly employed in turning out the goods and services produced by an industry."[47] A detailed analysis of the responses of the factory workers among 16 industries included in the Roper survey on which the popular thesis has come essentially to rest does not support the conclusion that "powerlessness," "meaninglessness," "isolation," and "self-estrangement"—four dimensions of alienation identified in Blauner's study—vary systematically "in form and intensity" in accordance with differences in technology. Evidence of a clinical nature from four case studies conducted by Blauner are supportive of such a conclusion. But there are both ambiguities and anomalies in the Roper survey data and in Blauner's analysis that leave one dubious of clear conclusions about the relationship between "technology," work experience, and work attitudes. Consider that there were 18 questions in the Roper survey dealing with work experience; when these data are examined systematically rather than selectively, as by Blauner, the results on 9 of the 18 items were unabiguously consistent with Blauner's technology hypotheses; 4 yield anomalous results; and 5 actually contradict it.

Parallel studies are productive of the same equivocal results. Thus, Wedderburn and Compton report, from a systematic study of over 400 employees in

---

46. Robert Blauner, *Alienation and Freedom: The Factory Worker and His Industry* (Chicago: University of Chicago Press, 1964).

47. Ibid., pp. 5, 6.

a British chemical complex, that while some differences in the attitudes and behavior of workers vary with the technologically determined differences in their work obligations, others are more clearly correlated with differences in workers' personal backgrounds, personal attitudes, previous work experiences and expectations, and in work task differences that could not readily be linked to technology in Blauner's sense. Among the reasons: while some technologies are "pure," others are not so easily classified. Though some workers' shops were using "the same dominant technology, in accordance with a relatively crude classification, [they] were revealed on further investigation to be different in important respects."[48] The implication of this finding is that investigators run even larger risks of oversimplification in analysis when, as in the Roper data, workers are members of different *firms* and subfirm work units, as well as of different industries.

There are two studies of the impact of technology, conceived somewhat differently in which the results do support more determinate conclusions about technology. Thus Sayles and Kuhn, in parallel studies in the auto and rubber industries conducted in the late 1950s, found that there were marked differences in the numbers and types of grievances of workers differentially situated at different points in the "workflows" in the two industrial settings. The investigators reported that some workers—those with higher-level skills and in work locations that permitted them considerable overall control over work processes—used grievances, generally concerning their working conditions, as highly effective adjuncts to their bargaining strategies. Less opportunely situated workers, with more modest skills, had somewhat similar dissatisfactions but were either apathetic toward or much more undisciplined—less "strategic"—in their uses of the grievance machinery provided in their union agreements.[49]

It should be emphasized that while technology influenced the viability of the unionists' strategies and tactics observed by Sayles and by Kuhn, the actual data on technology refer to *units* of *work flows*. Sayles' and Kuhn's notions about technology thus could be and have effectively, and readily, been applied even to essentially machineless situations of white-collar workers in which the explanatory powers of diverse work processes, and what we earlier discussed as social technology, in generating dissatisfaction could be examined.[50] The

---

48. Dorothy Wedderburn and Rosemary Compton, *Workers' Attitudes and Technology* (Cambridge, England: Cambridge University Press, 1972). One subset of findings, those pertaining specifically to workers whose jobs most precisely parallel those of the chemical industry workers in the Roper survey, are, however, entirely consistent with those urged by Blauner.

49. Leonard R. Sayles, *Behavior in Industrial Work Groups: Prediction and Control* (New York: John Wiley, 1958); and James Kuhn, *Bargaining in the Grievance Settlement* (New York: Comumbia University Press, 1961).

50. See E. C. Wegner and Leonard R. Sayles, *Cases in Organizational and Administrative Behavior* (Englewood Cliffs, N.J.: Prentice-Hall, 1974); Leonard R. Sayles, *Managerial Behavior* (New York: McGraw Hill, 1964); and Eliot Chapple and Leonard Sayles, *The Measure of Management* (New York: Macmillan, 1961).

observed results closely parallel those reported by Sayles and by Kuhn in their rubber and auto industry investigations.

Critiques of Human Relations

It was one of the main legacies of the Renaissance, and the modernization process thereafter, that the superordination of a few men, and of selective ideas, over vastly larger numbers of people and over competing ideas, respectively, would not go forever unchallenged in western societies. The subordination of the many by the few may generally be enforced only for as long as the mighty can substitute force for concessions regarding the rights of their subjects. The balance in such cases is always a delicate one, however, as the pages of history books show.

To the extent that men become modern, along the lines staked out in chapter 2, the balance is especially precarious. The impulses of the democrat are not easily controlled either by other modern men with abundant guile or by tyrants who would simply repress them. And, in the American case, the democratic demiurge was well developed many decades before the industrialization process made factory hands of the yeomanry. If the noisiest and bloodiest battle over authority in the U.S. was that between the Union and the secessionist states, there have been protracted battles, bloody and otherwise, ever since, between those who manage and those employed in organizations.

The first misgivings about corporate leaders-cum-rulers that concerns us here were rooted, early in the "age of big business," in populist resentments over the arrogance of the swash-buckling Captains of Industry and the Robber Barons whose predatory pricing and other policies offended the helpless "little man." The worldwide depressions and the merger movements in the U.S. during the period 1873-1905[51] added enormously to growing doubts about the legitimacy of managers who unilaterally spun the system's "web of rules" without much fear of (or hindrance from) worker-citizens whose democratic rights stopped at the front door of employers' plants: The malperformance of managers as rational economic agents was all too evident to the victims of economic depressions, even as managers' cruelties were evident in their actions as local managers who could tyranize and exploit defenseless workers and workers' families.[52] Workers in an economic republic, heirs in some instances to the democratic demiurges of their forefathers in the New World and joined by immigrants, some of whom had read about capitalist chains in European tracts and mani-

---

51. Between 1897 and 1905, 5,300 firms, in line with Marxist forecasts, came under the suzerainty of 318 corporations. Other merger waves struck in the periods 1924-1930, 1951-1961, 1966-1968, and, as we have seen, again in 1977.

52. For an overview of the period beginning before World War II, cast in literary terms, see John DosPassos, *U.S.A.* (New York: Harcourt Brace Jovanovich, 1939).

festos, predictably sought to challenge this authority.[53] The membership boom in early trade unions was partial evidence of the growing restiveness among the subjects of baronial business leaders.

Reinhard Bendix has coupled the rising consciousness among workers of the problematical quality of managers' legitimacy with the emergent recognition of the entrepreneurs, themselves, that their privileged position in society was in question. Where students of businessmen's ideologies have focused, as we saw in chapter 4, on businessmen's rhetoric concerning economic decision-making roles, Bendix focused, in an historical analysis, upon their rhetoric about their roles as managers of people.[54] According to Bendix, entrepreneurs sensed, as time passed, that the application of Darwin's analysis of the "fitness" of evolutionary survivors to be successful business leaders was rather more a self-serving than an accurate rendering of the facts. As Charles Perrow asks, in a summary of Bendix's work,

> How could entrepreneurs justify the privilege of voluntary action and association for themselves, while imposing upon all subordinates the duty of obedience and the obligation to serve their employers to the best of their ability?[55]

If "social Darwinism" offered an answer to this question for the immediate post-Civil War era, it was an answer that made little impression on the millions who joined unions in the period before the first World War.

In due course, owner-entrepreneurs, no less than more bureaucratic-professional managers, succeeded in going well beyond the comparatively modest demands for reform noted above that F. W. Taylor's model of training, measurement, and cooperative teaching of workers comprehended. Managers had, after all, already been exposed to writings of behavioral scientists who had helped change the image of the worker from "a person to whom hope and virtue had been preached [in accordance with the application of the Darwinian "fitness" model, to a] person whose aptitudes and attitudes had to be tested," the better to assign him to his job.[56]

---

53. Karl Marx was not exactly inaccessible either; at the time he wrote columns and guest editorials for the old *New York Herald Tribune*, a fact that sometimes surprises younger Americans inclined to believe that little of what is substantively radical reached American readers between the Declaration of Independence and famed "Port Huron Statement," drafted by Tom Hayden for the Students for Democratic Society (SDS) in 1962. See Charles Perrow, *The Radical Attack on Business* (New York: Harcourt Brace Jovanovich, 1972), pp. 10–19.

54. Reinhard Bendix, *Work and Authority in Industry: Ideologies of Management in the Cause of Industrialization* (New York: John Wiley, 1956), especially chapter 5, pp. 254–340.

55. Perrow, *Complex Organizations,* p. 63.

56. Bendix, *Work and Authority,* p. 308.

Gradually . . . these leaders became more consciously preoccupied with the complex tasks of management. . . . Employers and their spokesmen tended to discuss the worker in terms of his "real" wants rather than in terms of an ideal image. This is the ideological dilemma Mayo resolved. He reinterpreted the nature of man so that workers, salaried employees, and managers could once again be discussed in terms of the same basic human qualities. By this reinterpretation he succeeded in eliminating the praise of "virtue.". . . Henceforth, managers as well as workers were to be the subject of scientific analysis, for Mayo based his image of both upon a series of scientific studies.[57]

The assessments of Elton Mayo and his colleagues and disciples in the human relations tradition thus opened up a critical chapter in the history of industrial sociology, a chapter to which numerous modern social scientists are still making contributions. This movement embodied an approach to the problem of managerial legitimacy that was and still is anchored in the putative social and psychological needs of workers: Managers could be exposed to social science findings, like those about worker satisfactions and trained to apply the lessons derived therefrom. The result, it was believed, would redound to managers' legitimacy. Where Taylor and his work simplification disciples in scientific management circles viewed workers as income-maximizing individuals, the emphasis that grew out of the Hawthorne investigations, by Mayo and his colleagues, was upon work settings as *social systems* of which workers and managers were the industrial member-citizens. Mayo was strongly influenced by Freudian views of personality (with their emphasis on unconscious processes); by the work of Emile Durkheim on the role of *anomie* (a sense of rootlessness resulting from the sense of social isolation) in suicides; by the theoretical work of Pareto (upon societies as equilibrating Newtonian, which is to say physical systems) and upon the role, in social systems, of peoples' "nonlogical sentiments"; by "functionalist" anthropologists (who sought to assign critically important social system-maintaining functions to tribal rituals and taboos); and by the ethos of the Harvard Business School.[58]

Mayo, a lay psychoanalyst in Australia before coming to Harvard, had also apparently learned from psychoanalytically oriented anthropologists, on their ways to and from studies of aborigines, for whom Freud's model of the child-rearing process had offered important clues to the culture-learning process and to the nature of both universals and variations in cross-cultural comparisons. Mayo's interests in Durkheim's and Pareto's works, with their emphasis upon the highly problematical quality of the nature of social relationships grew out of

---

57. Ibid, pp. 308-9.

58. For a critical discussion of human relationists by authors who belong to the Industrial Relations School, discussed below, see: Clark Kerr and Lloyd H. Fisher, "Plant Sociology: The Elite and the Aborigines," in Mira Komarovsky (ed.), *Common Frontiers of the Social Sciences* (New York: Free Press, 1957), pp. 281-309.

associations at Harvard. Also, at Harvard Mayo became well steeped in a tradition (now well developed as a correlate of the professionalization or bureaucratization of corporate control) that managers were not "born to manage" but could be trained for management careers.

Mayo wove a twentieth-century intellectual equivalent of a medieval tapestry out of these strands. He rejected, out of hand, economists' notions about the play in society of individual self-interest, which Mayo termed "the rabble hypothesis." Workers, for Mayo and his colleagues, were men and women whose social bonds had been shattered by individualistic systems of values born of nineteenth-century liberalism, of industrialization, of urbanization, in short of modernization.

For Mayo, workers were the victims, resulting from these disruptive changes, of *anomie*, even as they were hostages to their unconscious needs and "nonlogical" sentiments. Their unconscious needs, after psychoanalytic teachings, were to resist paternal authority; their nonlogical sentiments, in accord with which supervisory authority was "confused," in workers' minds, with parental authority, were far more amenable to manipulation by psychologically sensitive leaders than by the blandishments of calculating efficiency experts. The manager, Mayo argued, could apply social science knowledge about the impact of groups on individuals in ways that would solve the "social" and the "human problems of industrial civilization."

The advantages to managers of a work force that enjoyed a sense of social-psychological well-being were seen to lie in the opportunities for increased productivity that would emerge out of improved employee morale, morale that could, in turn, be enhanced by the simple expedient of capitalizing on workers' highly developed capacities for formation into "informal groups."

This important identity of morale with productivity, meantime, Mayo felt had been established in numerous investigations, including those at the Western Electric plant, in which productivity was observed to be perversely related to a variety of manipulable variables in workers' environments but directly and positively related to the enhanced feelings of belongingness.[59] These feelings, in turn, Mayo and his colleagues saw to be engendered among workers through their encounters with the social scientists who seemed to give full faith and credit to the sentiments of worker-respondents at Hawthorne. The finding, called the Hawthorne effect, was as much a social science landmark as the attack by Mayo on economists' views seemed devastating.[60]

---

59. Elton Mayo's major argument appeared, some years after the Hawthorne studies, as we have noted, in *The Human Problems of an Industrial Civilization* (Boston: Harvard University, Graduate School of Business Administration, 1946); *The Social Problems of an Industrial Civilization* (Cambridge, Mass.: Harvard University Press, 1945). See also T. N. Whitehead, *Leadership in a Free Society* (Cambridge, Mass.: Harvard University Press, 1936).

60. Recent reassessments of the original "Hawthorne" data have led two investigators to attribute far more weight, along economists' lines, to the role of economic

The earliest, full-blown statement of the new synthesis, by Chester Barnard of the New Jersey Bell Telephone Co., appeared almost simultaneously with the Hawthorne study. In this volume, Barnard anticipated Mayo's two post-World War II volumes, cited above, by codifying the new organizational and social theory to which the Harvard scholars pointed. Like Mayo later, Barnard emphasized the "social needs" of workers, the relationship of these needs to worker performance, and the prospects for managers to increase the latter by satisfying the former. Workers would form groups, status systems, systems of norms governing worker behavior, invent shortcuts, and set work standards anyway, he argued, in what quickly became a classic. By recognizing these patterns and applying social science knowledge it would be possible to turn the proclivities of workers to better purposes than the subversive ones served by these groups when workers are left to their own social devices: Effective leadership could mend workers' "nonlogical," i.e., unnecessarily subversive ways.[61] Like Mayo, Barnard saw the possibility of displacing conflict, based upon workers' understandable resentments of psychologically unsophisticated authority figures, by harmony. Unions, meantime, were the result of management failures as leaders, not of essential conflicts between workers and capitalists, or between workers and capitalists' representatives in the ranks of professional corporate managers.

In a refinement of our classification of approaches to work, Perrow points out that Barnard's "enormously influential and remarkable book contained within it the seeds of three distinct trends of organizational theory that were to dominate the field for the next three decades. One was the institutional school as represented by Philip Selznick . . . another was the decision-making school as represented by Herbert Simon . . . the third was the human relations school."[62] They have, as Perrow's assessment shows, however, a great deal in common with each other in their emphases: (1) upon the managerial use of social science knowledge; (2) upon the influence of groups on individuals; (3) upon the linkage of workers' morale to worker productivity; (4) upon the prospects of minimizing conflict and maximizing cooperation and understanding by arrangements, technical and otherwise, that promote social interactions and participation; (5) upon leadership styles that are on the democratic side of a

---

incentives in the productivity of the "girls" in the telephone assembly room. These investigators have noted that low-producing women were fired during the investigation, and replaced by high producers, a fact that critics see to be subversive of the more classic analysis, based as it was on group dynamics and the "effects" of the researchers. See "What Happened at Hawthorne?" *Science,* 183 (March 8, 1974), 922-32. See also Alex Carey, "The Hawthorne Studies: A Radical Criticism," *American Sociological Review,* 32 (June 1967), 403-16.

61. See Chester Barnard, *The Functions of the Executive* (Cambridge, Mass.: Harvard University Press, 1938).

62. Perrow, *Complex Organizations,* p. 75. Perrow treats each of these three schools very lucidly in his fifth, fourth, and third chapters, respectively.

continuum from benign on one end to autocratically coercive on the other; and finally (6) upon a therapeutic, psychological orientation toward interpersonal relations rather than a coldly hierarchical and custodial view. The data in support of the related positions of the schools deriving from the work of the human relations approach in the 1930s, together with newer versions of the approach, meanwhile, are precisely like those we have reviewed in this chapter's earlier sections.

We may say, by way of transition, that most of the schools that may be loosely characterized as derivatives of the approach for which Mayo and Barnard staked out the philosophical, ideological, and empirical lines have not been much troubled by the problem of managers' legitimacy, one of the central problems in society and in organizations to which Max Weber had addressed himself. One correlate of the equanimity with which human relationists have viewed the authority matter is the optimistic—some think naive or manipulative—view that the most devoted practitioners of this approach take toward conflict.

INDUSTRIAL RELATIONS

As we have seen, the human relations school has stressed the opportunities managers have to understand and influence the attitudes and behavior of workers by systematic considerations and manipulation of what we have termed proximal or organizational features of employees' environments. In the competing approach, there is less concern with leadership and with the nonlogical sentiments of workers, and more with the beliefs of leaders and the occupational and social circumstances of employees.

Indeed, many proponents of the industrial relations approach view much of the content (including the research designs and data interpretation) of human relations research, inadvertently or otherwise, to be the segments of a script whose lines are more serviceable to modern professional managers in search of justifications for their essentially unilateral exercise of authority than to a scientific appreciation of work in industrial societies. By employing the techniques, assumptions, and findings of the social scientist and appearing to subscribe to the therapeutic and putatively democratic premises of their application, it has been argued, managers have found a substitute in human relations doctrines for property rights in their claims to their authority over persons and to the disposition of other "factor inputs." In the absence of the prospects for constructing the "heavenly city" on earth, for reconstituting all the elements of the medieval synthesis, for restoring inegalitarian property rights in a democracy, critics have argued, managers could adopt the human relations approach and appear to "humanize" the work place.

This formulation is not very distant from that of Bendix and others whose work may be identified with that of the adherents to the industrial relations approach. These investigators are, comparatively speaking, unimpressed by the possibilities of harmonious relations between workers and enlightened bureaucratic managers trained to change wrongheaded and frustrated workers, or to cure psychological "complexes," or to reduce the need for troublesome psychological defense mechanisms by providing for deep-seated emotional needs, appointing benevolent supervisors, and selecting psychologically compatible peers in the recruitment process.

If an implicitly romantic view of manorial life in the premodern world has inspired some human relations advocates to thoughts of twentieth-century adaptations, then it is thoughts of the barricades from which eighteenth- and nineteenth-century attacks were launched against the old aristocratic order that have colored the thinking of many industrial relationists. Most industrial relationists, on the other hand, do not deny that psychological problems can have their genesis in workplace experiences; they tend, however, to be skeptical of prescriptions that evade or simply beg questions of power, of structural arrangements, and of political economy in favor of diagnoses rooted in the psychology and social psychology of motives and perceptions.

Industrial relationists thus view workers as members, loosely speaking, of both economic *and* political classes and, more precisely, of occupational and skill groups, of communities, of ethnic groups, and of families, as well as of the work groups and organizational departments favored in the research undertaken by human relationists. The nonwork memberships, in their view, have significant effects on workers' attitudes toward work, toward managers, to the sanction systems in accordance with which they are governed, and to the supervisors and managers responsible for their working conditions. They tend, furthermore, to view unions as expressions of democratic dissent against the hazards to workers' dignities and rights, and of *noblesse oblige*, rather than as the more or less unfortunate byproducts of the intraorganizational actions of unsophisticated managers. Finally, industrial relationists are much less optimistic about the net contributions to be made by reform programs targeted on intraorganizational arrangements. They are skeptical, in particular, about efforts aimed at enlarging and enriching jobs, thereby to make them more interesting, and at increasing worker participation. Social science findings of the types that industrial relationists find instructive are those bearing (1) on business conditions, occupations, skill levels, and income; (2) on discipline; (3) on upper level managers' practices and priorities; and (4) on industrial conflict. Readers may be referred to the discussion of strike data, in chapter 5, in connection with the last of these interests; the other four interests will concern us in the next several subsections of this chapter.

The Worker in Society

Industrial relationists are struck, first off, by the strong statistical associations between variations in workers' actions—strikes, turnover, and collective bargaining demands, especially—and variations in business conditions.

We have already noted in chapter 5 that there is an association, for example, between unions' wage demands and unemployment rates, an association suggesting that workers pursue interests in strategic ways as economic circumstances permit.

Next, workers apparently have generalized discontent about jobs sufficient to lead many of them who are not averse to risks to seek job changes. These discontents are somewhat more prevalent among younger workers who seek to move to better jobs in the period before they incur family obligations. Workers tend to "remain young" longer, in recent times, moreover, as the ages of first marriage and of first birth have increased. Both young and old have higher "quit" rates when economic circumstances are favorable, however.[63] These facts do not suggest that worker discontent is a variable phenomenon intermittently in need of human relations interventions. Rather discontentments over wages and working conditions are more like constants, the manifest expressions of which are alternately constrained or facilitated as workers take readings of the realistic prospects for controlling their circumstances. This is not to say that discontents are rife. We merely say that there is at *least* as much discontent in the work force over all and over time as is manifest in periods that actually afford workers opportunities to act upon them. Thus in very low unemployment periods there may be discontents, unacknowledged in surveys, among workers who in less promising times simply do not seek job changes or press their unions to demand higher wages.

Next, industrial relationists are struck by the degree to which employed persons compare their circumstances invidiously with those of person in more favored occupations rather than with those of persons in similar jobs. Thus calculations from a Michigan survey reveal that whereas 28 percent of workers feel that they are paid less than others in similar *jobs*, 39 percent felt that their earnings were *unfairly low* compared with those of incumbents of other *occupations*.[64] Within the overall pattern, college graduates and workers in low-income families who express dissatisfactions with their *jobs* are more likely than older and less educated workers to view *both* their *jobs* and their *occupations* as inequitably rewarded. Younger workers who are dissatisfied with their jobs are unique, meanwhile, in focusing more on job than on occupational returns.[65]

An analysis of data from the 1969 Working Conditions Survey, finally, indicates that the individual earnings of respondents tell us a good deal less about the work satisfaction of this national probability sample than their per-

---

63. Robert J. Flanagan, George Strauss, and Lloyd Ulman, "Worker Discontent and Work Place Behavior," *Industrial Relations* 13 (May 1974), 101–23.

64. Calculated from the Center for Political Studies, *1972 American National Election Survey Inter-University Consortium for Political Research*, Ann Arbor, Michigan.

65. From Berg et al., *Managers and Work Reform*, ch. 5. See also Burkhard Strumpel, "Inflation, Discontent and Distributive Justice," *Economic Outlook, USA* (Summer 1974).

ceptions or impressions of how "adequate" their families' income are to pay their bills and how sufficient these family incomes are to provide them with living conditions that are "comfortable."[66] These findings are entirely in line, meanwhile, with conclusions drawn from earlier studies of labor market behavior in which the relative deprivations, rather than the absolute values of the specific benefits and returns accorded by particular employers to employed Americans, are emphasized.[67]

Industrial relationists would point out that these findings point to forces affecting worker attitudes that lie well beyond those over which local employers have control. Managers may collectively influence tastes and aspirations over long time periods through advertising and, in similar ways, influence the patterns according to which the rewards to different occupations are distributed. They could not, however, readily reorder tastes, preferences, and reference group standards in the short run. Nor could they undo the effects of social definitions of equity on workers by manipulating intraorganizational arrangements.[68]

Discipline

Human relationists have stressed the importance to worker responses of supervisory practices, an emphasis that industrial relationists would not gainsay. The latter are disposed, however, to add that lower level supervisors' ways reflect those of *higher* level managers who are responsible, ultimately, for the selection and training of supervisors. They would also add that higher level managers give little evidence, after 40 years of human relations blandishments in collegiate and graduate business schools, and in literally countless business publications, of being less concerned with managers' prerogatives, seen as rights, than in days gone by.

Evidence in the matter does suggest that human relationists may oversimplify in their implicit imputations to managers of a newer look in their conceptions of their roles as "bosses." Although it is impossible to measure accurately or to interpret meticulously the trends in arbitration cases, there are

66. Berg et al., *Managers and Work Reform,* ch. 5. This weighing, by respondents, of *family* income in conjunction with their own *job* satisfactions may relate to the equanimity with which married males view their wives' employment. See Angus Campbell et al., *The Quality of American Life* (New York: Russell Sage, 1976), pp. 431-32.

67. See, especially, Lester Thurow, "Toward a Definition of Economic Justice," *Public Interest* 31 (Spring 1973), 69ff; and *Generating Inequality: Mechanisms of Distribution in the U.S. Economy* (New York: Basic Books, 1975).

68. For a recent statement of the radical Marxist critique of all of human relations and the industrial relations approaches for the lack of emphasis on workers' class, as compared to occupational and reference group comparisons, see D. Gvishiani, *Organization and Management: A Sociological Analysis of Western Theories* (Moscow, USSR: Progress Publishers, 1972), translated by Robert Daglish and Leonid Kolesnikov.

hints that discipline cases have increased in the period 1952-1972, and that managers are increasingly concerned with their claims to traditional rights to serve their own unilaterally-conceived definitions of their organizations' needs.[69]

While human relationists have attended to discipline questions they tend not to see managers in their larger organizational roles or as incumbents of roles to which legal interests attach. These interests, meanwhile, are regularly adjudicated in accordance with legal rather than with psychological or social psychological principles, in the usual sense of the terms, as Blumberg has shown in a study of requirements for loyalty and obedience among workers, discussed in chapter 4.[70]

Managers and Priorities

"Loyalty" issues are generally raised and joined in studies focused upon employees, their "quit" rates, their absenteeism, their subscription to rules and regulations, their willingness to perform duties above and beyond normal requirements during emergencies, and, sometimes, their attitudes toward means.

Rarely is the term loyalty used in reference to the behavior in organizations of managers. In accordance with a two-valued version of logical principles, an employer-manager who declares bankruptcy, relocates a plant, merges with another employer to whom manpower decisions often fall, or who lays off employees, is probably acting as an alert business leader should. If his decisions misfire, later, or otherwise affect his employees in problematical ways, it is because the leader has miscalculated in the enactments of his or her impersonal economic roles as rational calculator, entrepreneur, risk taker, and decision maker. Questions about his or her *sentiments*, like those raised in the investigations of work groups at the Hawthorne works, rarely arise. And if valuable business leaders resign from their posts to take attractive positions elsewhere, it is the organization that has failed to retain a person whose social mobility is credited to the wider system's efficiency and openness, not the leader's disloyalty that is remarkable.

A more complex view of managers and employees would recognize that the latter members of organizations may act fairly rationally to secure themselves against the consequence of judgments and decisions of the former, and that the actions of the two groups may be viewed as special cases of the same

---

69. For a general discussion, see Philip Selznick, *Law, Society and Industrial Justice* (New York: Russell Sage, 1969). For earlier and later empirical efforts to study industrial discipline, see Eli Ginzberg and Ivar Berg, *Democratic Values and Rights of Managers* (New York: Columbia University Press, 1964); Howard Vollmer, *Employee Rights and the Employment Relations* (Berkeley: University of California Press, 1960); and Berg et al., *Managers and Work Reform*, chs. 10 and 12.

70. For a full discussion, see Phillip I. Blumberg, "Corporate Responsibility and the Employee's Duty of Loyalty and Obedience: A Preliminary Inquiry," in Dow Votaw and S. Prakash Sethi, *The Corporate Dilemma: Traditional Values versus Contemporary Problems* (Englewood Cliffs, N.J.: Prentice-Hall, 1973), pp. 82-114.

behavioral modes, the same aspirations, and the same underlying logics, and sometimes, even, the same types of nonlogical behavior.

Thus Piore reports, from a study of 150 managers in 18 manufacturing plants and 11 corporate headquarters, that in their otherwise thoughtful search for innovative production techniques, they made judgments that "appear[ed] to be largely independent of labor market forces . . . [these procedures] *appeared*, nonetheless, to be consistent with the assumptions of cost minimization."[71] Diamond and Bedrosian report in an identical vein from a study of manpower practices regarding 10 entry level jobs in each of 5 white-collar and 4 blue-collar occupations and in a service occupation in the St. Louis and the New York Standard Metropolitan Statistical Areas (SMSAs). Though hiring standards were specific in these settings, they were unrelated across the two SMSA's, the 14 industries, and the 20 companies to employees job performance! There were only slight differences in performance attributable to workers' educational achievements in only 3 of 20 categories,[72] a finding that squares with those in a study of employment screening practices in the American economy generally.[73] In studies paralleling those by Diamond and Bedrosian, in all Minnesota firms employing 500 or more workers, Henneman found almost no manpower forcasting or planning in connection with decisions and plans regarding production, space, production facilities, acquisitions, expansions, or product pricing.[74] Managers do not emerge, in such data, as being more economically rational than the "nonlogical" workers in human relations studies.

Next, consider that 87 percent of the employers in a National Conference Board study reported that they give blue-collar workers from one to five days notice in regard to layoffs ordered for economic and entrepreneurial, i.e., involuntary, reasons.[75] In 1974, furthermore, nearly 10,000 firms failed; these firms employed nearly three quarters of a million persons.[76] Overall, Dun and

---

71. Michael Piore, "The Impact of Labor Market upon the Design and Selection of Productive Techniques within the Manufacturing Plant," *Quarterly Journal of Economics* 82 (November 1968), 602-20. Emphasis added.

72. Daniel E. Diamond and Hrach Bedrosian, *Hiring Standards and Job Performance*, Manpower Research Monograph, No. 18 (Washington, D.C.: Government Printing Office, 1970).

73. Ivar Berg, *Education and Jobs: The Great Training Robbery* (New York: Praeger, 1970), chs. 4-7, 9.

74. H. G. Henneman, Jr., and George Seltzer, *Employee Manpower Planning and Forecasting*, Manpower Research Monograph, No. 19 (Wahington, D.C.: Government Printing Office, 1970). See also the studies by Sayles and Chandler of subcontracting decisions, reported in chapter 4.

75. *Personnel Practices in Factory and Office: Manufacturing*, Studies in Personnel Policies, 194 (New York: National Industrial Conference Board, 1964), p. 139.

76. Dun and Bradstreet, *The Failure Record, 1974,* Employment estimates inferred from median establishment size, U.S. Bureau of the Census, *County Business Patterns,* 1972 (Washington, D.C.: Government Printing Office, 1973), Table 1C, p. 29.

Bradstreet report, 41 percent of these failures were attributable to managers' incompetence (49 percent in manufacturing) and another 36 percent to managers' unbalanced experience or to their lack of experience in their lines of business.[77] In 1972, finally, nearly 400,000 Americans were employed in 1,360 firms that were acquired by or merged with other firms.[78] Such statistics, once again, do not assure one that but for employers' lack of human relations skills employees can be made happy.

Other indicators bear upon the question of whether higher level business leaders have much ultimate interest in reformers' earnest efforts to apply combinations of older and newer human relations tactics and strategies. Thus Walton, a ranking leader of the newest effort to improve work, reports that some of the most famous of recent experiments have failed because consultants "drop out"; because employers drop out of experiments and "regress" to traditional management ways when confronted with changes in their economic environment; because managers are not able to maintain prerequisite conditions;[79] because managers have been unwilling to reduce their "investments" in close supervision; and because turnover in management ranks left consultants and workers effectively holding the bag.[80]

In one celebrated case, in which Walton himself applied modern-day Harvard Business School human relations techniques as a consultant, that of the celebrated Gainsburger plant in Topeka, Kansas, managers have soured on the experiments and have torpedoed them; managers, it is reported as this is written, are "stonewalling plant democracy."[81] A list of seven circumstances Walton finds favorable to successful work enlargement, work enrichments, and worker participation schemes reveals how unlikely are work reforms of the types currently advertised to become "operative":

1. small towns;
2. small work forces;
3. new plants where employees have no "deeply ingrained expectations about work and management;

---

77. Ibid, pp. 12-13.

78. U.S. Federal Trade Commission, Statistical Report on Mergers and Acquisitions, no. 6-15-16 (Washington, D.C.: Government Printing Office, 1973), Table 3, p. 2; and U.S. Bureau of the Census, *County Business Patterns*, 1972, U.S. Summary (Washington, D.C.: Government Printing Office, 1973), Table 1C, p. 29.

79. Richard E. Walton, "Innovative Restructuring of Work," in Jerome M. Rosow (ed.), *The Worker and the Job: Coping with Change* (Englewood Cliffs, N.J.: Prentice-Hall, 1974), pp. 145-76. Typically some of the ends, for example, to reduce employee turnover to 10 percent or less are among the prerequisites for experimental successes.

80. Ibid, pp. 167-68.

81. *Business Week*, March 28, 1977, pp. 78-82.

4. geographic separation of the experimental unit from other parts of the firm's facilities;[82]
5. the use of outside consultants;
6. long lead times;
7. no unions or where union-management relations are positive.

Walton adds elsewhere that while worker participation is an important end and means in work reform, there are low upper limits on the amount of constitutionalism-democracy that can be applied as component parts of work reform programs.[83]

In a detailed history of a carefully planned experiment, at Centertown Laboratories in the South, Glaser and his fellow consultants report that efforts were abandoned, after employees had cooperated fully, by the new managers when the plant was purchased by a German pharmaceutical company.[84]

The point is not that reforms are ill advised or that reform failures are absolutely foredoomed. Rather, it is the case that managers represent about the same mixture of logical and other sentiments, of wisdom and generosity, of economic and "noneconomic" instincts, of organizational loyalty and self-serving impulses, as other groups in society, but that our evaluation schemes involve us in the inevitable application of differentiated–two-valued–logics. Few, for example, would malign managers—15 percent of the 135,000 "truly policy level executives" in 1976—who changed companies.[85] Nor can anyone take much legal issue with top level managers who relocate operations to points closer to their homes or favored sports haunts. Thus a researcher at the National Industrial Conference Board reports that more than half of 13 major corporations that moved from New York City from 1968 to 1972 made location decisions

---

82. Reformers emphasize the prospects that reforms will increase productivity as well as worker satisfactions; they rarely explain what an employer will do with the uneven output that would result in the interrelated operations of firms able to prove the fourth of the tactics.

83. Richard E. Walton, "Criteria for Quality of Working LIfe," in Louis E. Davis and Albert Chernes (eds.), *The Quality of Working Life, Vol. 1, Problems, Prospects and the State of the Art* (New York: Free Press, 1975), p. 100.

84. Edward M. Glaser, Carrol E. Izzard, and Mary Faith Chenery, *Collaboration Between Management and Employees in Job Structuring: Draft-Final Report to Man-Power Administration* (Washington, D.C.: U.S. Department of Labor, 1975), mimeo. An evaluation of the experimenters' efforts and their report looking beyond the sale of the plant finds fault with the reformers' failures to follow up on all its details but exonerates the basic reformers' model. See Veronica F. Nieva, Dennis N. T. Perkins, and Edward E. Lawlor III, "Review of Centertown Reforms" (Ann Arbor: Institute for Survey Research, 1977), mimeo.

85. Arch Patton, "Ideas and Trends: The Boom in Executive Self-Interest," *Business Week* (May 24, 1976), p. 16. These numbers are increasing at a rate of 20 percent annually according to Patton's studies at McKinsey Co., a management consulting firm.

that were "influenced" by the chief executive officers' places of residence.[86] And Whyte reports that of 38 moves by major corporation, "31 moved to a place close to the top man's home. Average distance: about eight miles by road."[87] The logics by which business decisions in this area as in other areas, noted in this and in earlier chapters, simply does not accord with textbook images of top level leaders in which microeconomic models and the crossing of marginal cost with marginal revenue curves are wholly determinate.

CONCLUSION

An examination of findings bearing upon the attitudes and the behavior of workers and managers from investigations focusing on employment settings leaves one persuaded that reform efforts are likely to be less dispositively influential than enthusiasts have been prepared to argue. On one side, reforms aimed at the modification of tasks, with the intent of making them more interesting, often run afoul of employers' mixed interests in productivity *and* in the coordination and stabilization of production. Work enlargement and work enrichment schemes, embodying the best of human relations lessons and favoring workers in the most tedious jobs, can also run afoul of better situated workers' interests in preserving skill, wage, salary, and preserving status differentials.

On another side, it appears to be the case that employees respond to questions about their work and behave regularly in ways suggestive of marked influences stemming from nonworksite conditions. These conditions have to do with macroscopic business-cyclical developments, with widergoing income allocation determinates, and with forces shaping the invidious comparisons American workers make as members of social and occupational strata with whom they identify as reference groups.

Finally, even as we typically employ different logics in examinations of unions and corporations, as we saw in chapters 4 and 5, so we use different perspectives in looking at the ways and means of employees and managers. In both cases, the differences in the assumptions and premises informing the assessments lead one readily to overlook similarities in the "hows and whys" of the two sets of roles, usually in favor of managers' economic rationality. The results of such assessments are a good deal less useful guides to either scientific understanding or to private or public policy prescriptions than assessments anchored in less tortured logics would be.

---

86. "When Business Moves Where the Boss Lives," *Business Week* (September 30, 1972), p. 69.

87. William H. Whyte, *New York Magazine* (September 20, 1976), pp. 90-91.

CHAPTER 7
PASTS, PROLOGUES, AND PROSPECTS

INTRODUCTION

If the vast and differentiated bodies of materials considered in this work have lent themselves only to highly distilled statements suggestive of a few arresting issues, a conclusive summary is quite out of the question. However, it is possible to "key" on a few of the themes, to borrow a term from the athletic scene. Such an enterprise is most consistently undertaken if we use the macro-, mezzo-, and microscopic rubrics that provided us with an ordering device complementing our alpine metaphor.

In the sections that follow our aim is to identify a few of the issues that will preoccupy industrial sociologists in the future, issues whose contours are already discernable but investigations about which specifics are only beginning to get underway.

MACROSCOPIC ISSUES: INTERNATIONAL AND NATIONAL DEVELOPMENTS

Institutional developments over the next decade of a political-economic nature will be higher on the agenda of industrial sociologists than they have in times gone by during which emphases were placed, instead, on organizational phenomena. Thus, for example, the problematics of energy and food—their availability and their costs—will have consequences for the structures and functions of international, national, sectoral, and local markets. The effects of food and energy price increases upon the real value of incomes, for the living standards of social strata already differentiated along income lines, and thus for the demands made on policy makers across the public and private spectra of agencies engaged in the production of goods and services, meanwhile, are only beginning to attract social scientists' attentions. The fact that nations' experiences on these fronts are international in character, thus highlighting their mutual interdependencies, may or may not lead to collaboration, especially among fully and less "developed" nations: The resolution of that question in favor of cooperation will likely contribute to convergences in the characters of industrial nations' institutions that will go beyond those currently encouraged by the behavior of present-day multinational corporations, trade blocks, and military alliances. If international collaboration occurs only on a fragmented "nationalistic" basis, or fails to materialize much beyond present-day levels, on the other hand, convergences will be less likely and international homogenization slowed. To the extent that nations go their separate ways it is unlikely that there will be a division of the world's labor along new international lines. While neo-Marxists, so-called, have been especially attentive to issues growing out of the dependency of some nations upon others, as noted in the earliest chapters, much remains to be observed, counted, sorted, and evaluated about the impacts of true international collaboration in production and distribution on their incomes, the "webs of rules," the organizations, occupations, and the workways of employers and employees in particular nations.

Next we may note the possibility that new entrants into industrial nations' labor forces will find growing job opportunities resulting from declining birth rates, on one side, and the inducements to employ more people as an offset to high energy-consuming and therefore more expensive capital equipment, on the other. Such prospects do not necessarily imply an increase in more rewarding, "better" jobs, in the upper ranges of nations' occupational ladders, however; and one can only engage in highly speculative ways, at present, on the implications of such developments for trade unionism, and for inflation rates, wage demands, and so on.

The last observation calls to mind another national-level question that will increasingly concern students of industrial sociology: How will the demand of unemployed people for reductions in wastefully high unemployment rates be traded-off against the demands of employed workers and investors that their earnings and saving be protected against inflation? There is, of course, considerable room for argument about the precise costs to employers and society of hiring the members of society who, because of "deficient" child-rearing, educational, and training exposures, make for their "deficient" productivity; such deficiencies presumably contribute to inflation when the demand for labor increases sufficiently to cause employers to go to the bottom, so called, of the manpower barrel. But there is no doubt that the fact of already high levels of unemployment in the U.S. has contributed little to the reduction of inflation rates, as each group in society seeks to protect itself from what are perceived to be the other fellow's inflationary demands for higher wages, or price increases, or inflation-pegged social security payments, or tax-supported transfer payments, or subsidies, or import restrictions.

While the questions can be asked, in abstract terms, at what we called the macro- or mezzoscopic levels, our efforts to insulate ourselves from the corrosive effects of inflation ultimately impinge directly upon the relations among individuals and groups in communities, in corporations, in unions, in offices, and in shops. Managers will seek to rewrite the work rules we have discussed in efforts to obtain cost-reducing production methods for higher wages; workers, meanwhile, seek to protect work rules as part of the returns on their investments of loyalty and training in their jobs and skills. National developments, like inflation, thus do not only have slowly-developing "trickle down" effects but rather immediately reverberating consequences for daily life in a nation's work places.

Consider, in this context, that policies governing the salaries and wages of public servants hammered out in federal, state, and municipal budget-making and bargaining processes are often seen in isolation from developments in the private sector. As we saw earlier, however, the largest proportion of "public servants" are in occupations—mechanics, clerks, translators, sweepers, bookkeepers, pharmacists, security guards, cooks, stenographers, statisticians, and the rest—in which "private servants" also find themselves. The fact is that members of equivalent worker groups in the two sectors are perfectly capable of comparing their circumstances invidiously. Private employers, some private sector union leaders, and large numbers of tax-paying private sector employees, themselves, have thus been progressively more attentive to a growing gap between these labor forces' rewards, a gap that has recently favored those in the lower, the middle, and the upper middle levels of the *public* services.[1] The "coercive comparisons" that follow are not infrequently translated into organized efforts to defeat public school bonds, proposals to increase local property taxes, to unseat elected local officials, and into angry divisions among local labor leaders in the public and private sectors. In the absence of these embittering divisions there might in fact have developed a more unified labor movement in America. Unions' political efforts, regarding such plant-level issues as safety, or regarding such community-level issues as strikes and picketing, thus suffer divisive consequences that may be added to those noted in the discussion of unions in chapter 5. Readers are invited to consider the consequences for the viability of our pluralistic system of the forces leading to fractionation in the public apparatuses, the private corporate apparatuses, and the union apparatuses that are themselves viewed by many observers to be among the key "countervailing" forces in the economic republic. We may be confident that researchers will be obliged to observe these developments with an eye to the evolving character of our democratic industrial society.

1. It should be pointed out that professional and *top* level public servants often earn less than their peers in private industry.

MEZZOSCOPIC ISSUES:
LABOR FORCE DEVELOPMENTS

We may anticipate, from the foregoing references to occupational developments, that a clearer picture of labor market developments will more likely emerge from investigations of labor market trends than from studies in individual work settings, furthermore. Among the currently most notable developments on this score are those associated with the mounting labor force participation rates, and the changing employment experiences of women in the economy. The impacts of shifts favoring women will predictably draw the attentions of industrial sociologists as well as those who study the American family, sex roles, and child-rearing patterns.

Next we may note the growing concern over the American version of western Europe's "guest workers," especially the large but uncounted and presently uncountable numbers of Mexican nationals. The issues involved have not yet been much attended by social scientists,[2] though the differing interests of employers, farm unionists' leaders, community groups, and public policy makers have been given wide publicity in Sunday supplements and in television documentaries.

Next are emergent issues, joined by employers, government regulators, trade union leaders, public as well as vested interest groups, and individual grievants, on all sides, concerning sex and race discrimination. The delegation by the U.S. Department of Labor of many equal opportunity enforcement functions to existing regulatory agencies already involved with specific industries—common carriers, educational institutions, communications—has already contributed additional orders of complexity to a network of regulations that provide a mixed variety of forms and venues for the adjudication of rights. Although members of Congress, state legislators, judges and enforcement agents are the obvious principals in equal opportunity and employment-linked civil rights cases, there are few Americans who do not experience at first hand the tugs and pulls that are embodied in a large segment of the web of rules that is still spinning. Among the benefits of equal opportunity regulations to social scientists, their personal preferences in these matters aside, will be a large number of data banks that employers are obliged to maintain on the yearly experiences of employees. Public accesses to these records will provide rich information on the organizational mobility patterns, the rewards and the demographic traits of most employed Americans. Equal opportunity requirements may lead to changes in the segment of the web of rules that is still spinning. Equal opportunity requirements, especially requirements that employment goals for the future hiring of "protected groups"—women and some monorities—be set, may also lead to the development of planning efforts of corporations in the

---

2. A notable exception: William A. Rushing, *Class, Culture and Alienation: A Study of Farmers and Farm Workers* (Lexington, Mass.: D.C. Heath, 1972).

manpower area as in the other areas of business decision making. As we saw in chapter 4, managers have rarely conducted such rational planning efforts in the past under the force of market pressures perhaps because fairly high orders of market imperfections in the economy reduce the market's capacities to ensure the more fully rational and humane uses of human resources.

Third, there are a number of researchable issues concerning the differential experiences of similarly situated but differentially able or differentially educated employees in the economy (studies were conducted in 1970, 1974, and 1978).[3] The evidence to date shows, as we noted in earlier chapters, that underutilized workers are inclined to be more or less critical of their working conditions, overall, in proportion to which they enjoy marginal increments of economic returns over those accorded to their less educated peers in roughly similar jobs. One possibility is that large shifts will occur in social norms that simply *favor* an essentially artificial upgrading in jobs requirements, and that this shift will contribute significantly to a passivity toward, or a reasonably accommodated acceptance of what we have termed underutilization. The other possibility is, of course, that dissatisfactions among underutilized workers will become more marked under the force of the increased *pro forma* use of education as a "screening" device. The developments that do occur, either way, will most assuredly have direct consequences for the interests of workers, unions, and managers in work reforms depending, as we have said, on the play of other forces shaping workers' reactions to their jobs.

Finally, we may note that social scientists and policy makers will be increasingly attentive, especially at the community and plant levels, to the effects of regulatory activities that impinge, in greater or lesser degree, on profit levels, manpower requirements, and location decisions. To the extent that environmental, equal opportunity, or tariff regulations, for example, cause managers and workers to work in closer league, the results will raise questions about the adequacy of the reciprocal limitations of democratic and industrial-economic logics, one upon the other.

Whatever the specific outcomes, it is certain that public and private policies, like those involving the so-called military-industrial complex discussed in chapter 4, will slowly blur the lines that separate many erstwhile interests among groups that were more visibly in contention in other days. In their uses of public authority, modern industrial citizens thus already appear to be relearning and applying the lessons in the uses of social technology, involving the public systems in particular, that were the essential ones, as we saw, in the preindustrial period of guilds. The new social synthesis—involving wage and price guidelines, public subsidies, complex regulatory networks, and many more of the

---

3. Ivar Berg, *Education and Jobs: The Great Training Robbery* (New York: Praeger, 1970), chs. 5, 6; Robert P. Quinn, Graham L. Staines, and Margaret R. McCullough, *Job Satisfaction: Is There a Trend? Manpower Research Monograph No. 30* (Washington, D.C.: Government Printing Office, 1974); and Ivar Berg, Marcia Freedman, and Michael Freeman, *Managers and Work Reform: A Limited Engagement* (New York: Free Press, 1978), chs. 5, 6.

institutionalized linkage mechanisms we have alluded to throughout our journey—will differ more in degree than in kind from many features of the so-called medieval synthesis. These linkages will be most readily apprehendable at the middle or mezzoscopic levels of analysis. Several of the extant devices may be noted: (1) "Big Mac," the public-private agency currently working with bankers, New York City political leaders, New York City trade unions, federal executive agencies, and Congressional committees to shore up an economy directly involving 18 million citizens. Among the issues joined in New York by the efforts of "big Mac" to solve New York City's problems are work rules in the building trades, union pension funds, corporate location decisions, and public employee job rights and incomes. (2) The New York Port Authority, with its rent-earning airports, its toll-collecting bridges, and its rent-earning trade centers vitally affects the economy of the northeast corridor and, because of its high income, is increasingly viewed as a source of funds for improvements in New York's public transportation system whose well-being directly affects job holders' accesses and their employers' prospects. (3) Comsat, the public corporate agency involved with satellite communications, vitally affects the capacities and the operational modes of television, radio, and telephone companies in the nation, companies whose doings are also affected by the Federal Communications Commission, the Anti-trust division of the Department of Justice, and the Securities and Exchange Commission. (4) Brookhaven Laboratories, a public apparatus in which many of the nation's leading scientists, from a variety of separated organizations, share accesses to high-powered scientific instruments. (5) The Educational Testing Service and the College Entrance Examination Board whose scientific experts develop screening devices used on a national basis in the selection of candidates for public licenses to practice automobile repair skills, for admission to exclusive private nursery schools, and, only more familiarly, for admission to a large number of public and private institutions of higher learning.

Although these illustrative linkages are by no means the select linch pins that help hold together an integrated American economy, they are symptomatic of the growing interdependencies of an industrial system that lead industrial man to augment vaguer "webs of rules" with institutional mechanisms and with more sharply delineated social technologies. More such mechanisms will likely emerge as industrial man continues to experience new integrative problems flowing from the otherwise intractably disintegrated processes of differentiation. There is, in short, thus, a constant need in industrial society to develop new social technologies or to dust off old ones and adapt them to new conditions. The results of macro- and mezzoscopic changes impinge directly on the daily realities of occupational and organizational life, which is to say, on organizational structures, skill requirements, work routines, and task assignments. The extra-organizational genesis of these results cannot be overlooked by industrial sociologists, as they essentially were in the post-World War II era.

MICROSCOPIC ISSUES

Enough has been said in chapters 5 and 6 to suggest that we are likely to continue to observe intraorganizational problems of the types there described. The facts that work dissatisfactions as measured in worker surveys have remained relatively constant and low among different population groups since World War II, that they are taken more seriously by employers during periods of "tight" than "loose" labor markets, and that they are unaccompanied by much explicit demand among workers themselves for reform leave us skeptical of the prospects for human relations-inspired proposals for improvements in the quality of working life. Data on workers' behavior, meanwhile, points to (1) the capacities of workers, when economic conditions are favorable, to redress a number of what must sensibly be regarded as urgent grievances by seeking better jobs; and (2) their additional dependency upon legal arrangements that protect due process, free speech, and rights of association. The decline of unions in the private sector, under prevailing conditions, suggests that grievances are either modest in character or that they are adequately resolved to employees' *essential* satisfactions, at least, in less organized ways than those specifically identified with collective bargaining.

CONCLUSION

The foregoing may serve as a kind of end note to a diary-like statement of our descent from our metaphorical peak. The following points will serve to recall our themes.

1. Industrialization takes place as part of wider processes. The "logics of industrialization," as the Interuniversity Consortium calls them, both impact upon and are impacted upon by these parallel, historical, and cultural processes. Industrialism's "logics" therefore are not at all unambiguous ones: Indeed, as some divine them, they are sometimes rather more syllogistic than logical in the formal sense. We avoided the pitfalls of simplified causal reasoning, meanwhile, by urging that one strive to identify modalities and variations around central tendencies rather than that one seek to infer the "iron laws" of industrial societies.
2. Next, we suggest that machine technology, as a "variable" in social scientific discourse, be treated most gingerly in efforts to discern primary forces. The factory system with its grinding gears, spinning wheels, and whirring motors must be taken into account, but it is man's organization of other men—the social technology—that deserves the lion's share of analytical attention in efforts to understand industrial developments.
3. We have also emphasized the need to consider changes in property forms. On one side, the facts of ownership are not systematically related to the most imposing of the patterns in industrial systems that beg for

explanation. On another side, new conceptions of ownership point to the need for new conceptualizations of rights, the better to comprehend the force, the meaning, of evolving forms of proprietary claims.

4. Finally, we have stressed the shift from manufacturing to nonmanufacturing activities in the "advanced" industrial societies, and, especially, the growth of the public sector. Though we may be well into a new "postindustrial" age, as some prominent social scientists have it, the implication of the transitions underway are far from clear.

INDEX

AUTHOR INDEX

Aaron, Henry J., 39n
Adams, Walter, 84n, 99n, 114
Adelman, Irma, 45, 54
Art, Robert J., 93n
Ashenfelter, Orley, 141

Bachrach, P., 97
Bailyn, Bernard, 15n
Bain, Joe S., 114
Baran, Paul A., 118n
Baratz, M. S., 97
Barber, Bernard, 14n, 52n
Barnard, Chester, 173, 174
Barnet, Richard J., 26n
Bartell, H. Robert, Jr., 144n
Bauer, Raymond A., 130n, 159
Baumol, William, 107, 108
Becker, Gary, 54n
Bedrosian, Hrach, 113, 179
Bellah, Robert, 18
Bendix, Reinhard, 16n, 42n, 63n, 110n, 114, 115n, 170
Bentham, Jeremy, 10
Berg, Ivar, 43n, 54n, 55n, 88n, 90n, 95, 96n, 112n, 138n, 140, 142, 148n, 153n, 159n, 163n, 165n, 176n, 177n, 178n, 179n, 187n
Berger, Peter L., 21, 22, 23
Berle, Adolph A., 3, 104, 105
Bibb, Robert, 67, 68
Blades, Dean, 94, 95n
Blair, James M., 92n

Blauner, Robert, 167, 168
Blitz, Rudolf C., 141
Blumberg, Phillip I., 94, 95n, 178n
Blumer, Herbert, 68n
Blumrosen, A. E., 94, 95n
Bok, Derek C., 124, 128n, 138, 147
Bonilla, Frank, 130n
Bowles, Samuel, 55n, 82n
Boyle, Stanley E., 103n
Brady, Robert A., 26n, 88n
Braibanti, R., 10n
Brembeck, C. S., 53n
Britt, David, 141, 142
Bunting, David, 100n, 101n
Burck, Charles C., 107, 110
Burns, Arthur, 116, 117, 118
Burns, James MacGregor, 29n

Campbell, Angus, 177n
Carey, Alex, 173n
Carter, Jimmy, 118
Caves, Richard, 99n
Chamberlain, Neil W., 89, 130n, 131, 132, 134n
Chandler, Alfred D., 42n
Chandler, Margaret K., 113
Chenery, Mary Faith, 181n
Chernes, Albert, 181n
Clayton, James L., 92n
Coleman, J. S., 54, 149n
Commons, John R., 46n
Compton, Rosemary, 167, 168n

191

INDEX

Coser, Lewis A., 19n
Cox, Archibald, 85n
Crenson, M. A., 97

Daglish, Robert, 177n
Dahl, Robert A., 95
Darvall, F. O., 43n
Davis, Louis E., 181n
Dean, Phyllis, 10
deGaulle, Charles, 15
Denison, Edward F., 49, 54n
Dexter, Lewis Anthony, 130n
Diamond, Daniel E., 113, 179
Dickson, William J., 137n
Dirlam, Joel B., 113n
Dofny, Jacques, 68n
Domhoff, G. William, 96n
Dore, Ronald P., 15n, 27n, 30, 31
DosPassos, John, 169n
Dowd, Douglas F., 89n
Drucker, Peter F., 105n
Drupp, Sherman, 42n
Dubin, Robert, 139n, 158
Dunlop, John T., 58, 59n, 62, 77n, 82, 83n, 84, 124, 125, 128n, 138, 147
Durkheim, Emile, 45, 50, 73, 86, 171

Eckstein, Otto, 104
Eichner, Alfred S., 99n
Eisenhower, Dwight D., 92, 116
Eisenstadt, S. N., 9, 19
Engels, Friedrich, 98, 153
Engler, Robert, 92n
Epstein, Edwin M., 89

Faris, Robert E. L., 14n
Feiwel, George R., 35, 36n
Felkin, William, 43n
Fiedler, Fred, 159
Fisher, Lloyd H., 171n
Fitzgerald, A. Ernest, 93n
Flanagan, Robert J., 26n, 141, 160n, 176n
Florence, P. Sargant, 27n, 105n
Form, William A., 48n, 68n, 73, 74n, 75n
Form, William H., 67, 68, 76, 144n, 145n
Franklin, Raymond S., 24n
Freedman, Marcia K., 27n, 28n, 54n, 55n, 64n, 140n, 142, 153n, 159n, 187n
Freeman, Michael, 54n, 55n, 140n, 142, 153n, 159n, 187n
Freeman, Richard B., 55n
Freidson, Eliot, 68n
Friedland, William H., 18n
Friedman, Milton, 116
Fromm, Erich, 52n, 104
Fuchs, Victor R., 24n

Galbraith, John Kenneth, 84n
Galle, Omer R., 141, 142

Gintis, Herbert, 55n, 82n
Ginzberg, Eli, 77n, 80n, 95, 178n
Glaser, Edward M., 181n
Goldner, William, 141
Grossman, Gregory, 15n, 21n, 34n
Gusfield, J., 7n
Gvishiani, D., 177n

Hackman, J. Richard, 158
Hagen, Everett E., 51
Hammond, Nancy, 18n
Hancock, M. Donald, 50n
Hansen, Alvin, 141
Harbison, Frederick, 54n, 58n, 59n
Hartman, Paul T., 125n
Harvey, Edward B., 63n, 149
Haug, Marie R., 68n
Hayden, Tom, 170n
Healey, Derek T., 34n, 35n, 36n, 37n, 38n
Healy, James J., 137n, 138n, 139n
Heneman, H. G., Jr., 113, 179n
Henle, Peter, 150n
Henry, Kenneth, 90n
Herrnstadt, Irwin L., 71
Hiestand, Dale L., 80n
Hirschman, Albert, 54
Hitler, Adolf, 52
Hodge, R., 63n
Hoffa, James R., 148
Homans, George C., 157n, 158, 159n
Hook, Sidney, 88n
Horowtiz, Morris A., 71
Hoselitz, Bert F., 16n, 45n
Hoxie, Robert F., 142n
Hunt, J. G., 158
Hunter, Floyd, 96
Hurwitz, S. J., 10n
Hyman, Herbert, 63n, 82n

Ingham, Geoffrey K., 166, 167
Inkeles, Alex, 14n, 17, 18, 19, 52, 53, 54 63n
Izzard, Carrol E., 181n

Jacoby, Neil H., 89, 106
Jaynes, Philip W., 103n
Jencks, Christopher, 82n
Johnson, George E., 141
Johnson, Lyndon B., 117

Kaplan, Abraham D. H., 112–13
Katzell, Raymond K., 161
Kennedy, John F., 117
Kerr, Clark, 58n, 59n, 82, 84n, 133, 134, 135n, 140, 142n, 171n
Keynes, John Maynard, 132
Khalaf, Samir, 15n
Killingsworth, Charles, 138n
Kirsch, Glenn K., 90n

INDEX

Kissinger, Henry, 19
Kluckhohn, Clyde, 52n
Knight, Frank H., 45n
Kocher, James, 7n, 21n, 23n
Koenig, Thomas, 101n
Kolesnikov, Leonid, 177n
Komarovsky, Mira, 171n
Kornhauser, Arthur, 139n
Krupp, Sherman, 155n
Kuhn, James W., 29n, 123n, 130n, 131, 132, 134n, 138n, 142, 168
Kuznets, Simon, 49, 50

Ladd, Everett C., 89
Landes, David, 15n
Lane, Robert E., 119
Lanzilotti, Robert, 113n
Larner, Robert J., 105n
Larsen, Otto N., 19n
Lawlor, Edward E., III, 158, 181n
Lazarsfeld, Paul F., 111n
Lerner, Daniel, 54
Letchie, J. M., 34
Levitan, Sar, 130n
Levitt, Theodore, 141
Lewin, Kurt, 158
Lewis, Arthur, 7n
Liebenstein, Harvey, 54
Lieberman, Evsei G., 35
Lieberson, Stanley, 13n, 94
Lippit, Ronald, 158
Lipset, Seymour M., 54, 63n, 149n
Little, Ian, 37n
Livernash, Robert E., 137n, 138n, 139n
Low, Iris J., 92n
Lowi, Theodore J., 89

McAdams, Alan K., 130n
McCarthy, James D., 34n
McClelland, David C., 51
McCullough, Margaret R., 161, 162n, 164, 187n
Magdoff, Harry, 92, 93n
Mann, Floyd C., 158
March, James G., 41n
Markham, Jean, 104
Marx, Karl, 50, 73, 98, 104n, 153, 154, 167, 170n
Mathewson, Stanley B., 137n, 138n
Mayo, Elton, 126n, 171, 172
Means, Gardner C., 104
Medrin, Norman, 92n
Melman, Seymour, 92
Merton, Robert K., 111n
Miles, Raymond E., 159
Miller, Delbert C., 73, 74n, 75n, 76, 144n, 145n, 158
Mitchell, Daniel J. B., 125n
Molotch, Harvey, 96n

Montagna, Paul D., 64n, 66
Moore, Barrington J., 48n
Moore, Wilbert E., 10n, 14, 23, 24, 32n, 33, 41, 49n
Morris, Cynthia Taft, 45, 54
Morris, James, 20n
Morse, Chandler, 18n
Morse, Dean, 27n
Mueller, Eva, 71
Mueller, William F., 102, 103
Muller, Ronald E., 26n
Murray, Henry A., 52n
Myers, Charles K., 54n, 58n, 59n
Myrdal, Gunnar, 19n, 38n, 44n

Nadel, Mark V., 89
Nader, Ralph, 118n
Nagy, T., 35n
Neumann, Franz Leopold, 26n, 88n
Nieva, Veronica F., 181n
Nisbet, Robert, 8, 16, 17, 19
Nixon, Richard M., 116
Nurkse, R., 7n

Oberschall, Anthony, 8n
Orlans, Harold, 65n

Pareto, V., 171
Parsons, Talcott, 7n, 14n, 45, 55n, 83
Patton, Arch, 181n
Perkins, Dennis N. T., 181n
Perlman, Selig, 126n
Perrow, Charles, 42n, 89n, 170, 173
Persner, L. W., 54n
Peter the Great, 46
Peterson, Richard A., 52n
Piore, Michael, 179
Polanyi, Karl, 9, 11n
Pool, Ithiel de Sola, 130n
Porter, Lyman W., 158, 166
Potter, David M., 52n
Pryor, Frederick, 34n, 47n

Quinn, Robert P., 160n, 161, 162n, 163, 164, 187n

Reed, John Shelton, 82n
Rees, Albert, 141
Reich, Charles, 40n, 120n
Reubens, Beatrice G., 80n
Riesman, C. K., 63n
Ritchie, J. B., 158, 159
Roethlisberger, Fritz J., 137n
Rogers, David, 43n, 44n, 90n
Rosow, Jerome M., 180n
Ross, Arthur, 125, 139n
Rossi, P., 63n
Rostow, Walt W., 10n
Roy, Donald, 138n

Rushing, William A., 186n
Ruttenberg, Stanley H., 92n

St. Simon, Henri, 153, 156
Sampson, Anthony, 92n
Samuelson, Paul, 68
Sayles, Leonard R., 112n, 113, 149, 157n, 158, 168
Scherer, F. M., 99n, 104n
Schneider, Eugene V., 11
Schultz, Theodore W., 49, 54n
Schumpeter, Joseph A., 118n
Scitousky, Tibor, 37n
Scott, Maurice, 37n
Seashore, Stanley, 159, 160n, 161n, 162n
Seltzer, George, 113, 179n
Selznick, Philip, 95, 111n, 173, 178n
Sethi, S. Prakash, 178n
Shapero, Albert, 112n
Shils, Edward A., 111n
Shwayri, Emilo, 15n
Siegel, Abraham, 82, 84n, 142n
Siegel, P., 63n
Simon, Herbert, 69n, 173
Sjoberg, Gideon, 50n
Slichter, Sumner H., 137n, 138n, 139n
Sloan, Alfred P., 42n, 44n
Smelser, Neil J., 7n, 14n, 15n, 18n, 45, 47 48n, 55n, 121n
Smith, Adam, 20n, 131
Smith, David H., 18n, 19
Snyder, David, 139n
Sonquist, John A., 101n
Speier, Hans, 111n
Spencer, Metta, 7n, 65n
Spengler, J., 10n
Staines, Graham L., 161, 162n, 164, 187n
Stano, Miron, 108
Steiner, Peter O., 103n
Stern, Robert N., 141
Stinchombe, Arthur, 41, 42, 43
Stone, Christopher D., 47n, 95
Strauss, George, 141, 149, 157n, 158, 160n, 176n

Strumpel, Burkhard, 176n
Summer, Charles, 85n
Sutton, Francis X., 118
Sweezy, Paul, 88n, 92, 93n, 118n

Tannenbaum, Frank, 126n
Taylor, F. W., 156, 170
Themis, Malcolm T., 43n
Thompson, T. J., 53n
Thurow, L., 67n, 136n, 177n
Tobin, James, 39n
Trow, Lester, 149n
Tumin, Melvin, 63n

Ulman, Lloyd, 141, 160n, 176n

Veblen, Thorstein, 73, 104n
Vernon, Raymond, 26n, 89n, 91n
Vogel, Ezra F., 15n
Vollmer, Howard, 178n
Votaw, Dow, 178n

Walton, Richard E., 180, 181n
Weber, Arnold A., 26n
Weber, Max, 18, 37, 45, 46, 50, 51, 73, 87, 104n, 110, 111, 156, 174
Wedderburn, Dorothy, 167, 168n
Weidenbaum, Murray, 89n
White, Orion, Jr., 50n
White, Robert K., 158
Whitehead, T. N., 172n
Whyte, William H., 182
Wildsmith, J. R., 107
Williams, Robin, 119n
Wright, Charles, 82n

Yankelovich, Daniel, 161
Yukl, Gary, 158

Zald, Mayer N., 34n, 62, 88n, 96n, 162n
Zeitlin, Maurice, 89n, 106, 155n
Zimet, Melvin, 90n

SUBJECT INDEX

Abortion, 46
Acquisitions, 102-6
Advertising Council, 90
Allende government, overthrow of, 91
Amalgamated Clothing Workers, 143
American Federation of Labor (AFL), 127, 128
Antitrust law, 102-103
Automation, 69

Beliefs and structures, 51-55
Bell Telephone Co., New Jersey, 173
Blue laws, 46
Bookkeeping, double-entry, 10
Brookhaven Laboratories, 188
Bureaucratization, 109
Business Council, 90
Business Roundtable, 90

Capital, 154
Capital formation, 12, 33-41
   market and planning approaches to, 33-37
   sectoral tradeoffs, 37-38
Census Bureau, U.S., 42
Central Intelligence Agency, 91
Change, frequent, as hallmark of industrial societies, 62
Collective bargaining, 28-29
College Entrance Examination Board, 188
Communications Workers, 142
Computerization, 69
Conglomeration in enterprise, 101-106
Congress of Industrial Organizations (CIO), 128
Continental system, 43
Corporate influence on local community, 95-97
Corporate managers and economy, 98-106
Corporate ownership and control, 98-116
Corporate power
   and industrial rights, 94-95
   political and economic, 88-106
Corporation, and local community, 95-97
Cottage industry system. *See* Putting-out system
Council of Foreign Relations, 90
Cutter Laboratories, 181
Czechoslovakia, roles of market forces in, 35

Determinism, technological, 12
Directorates, interlocking 100-101
Dun and Bradstreet, 179-80

Economic Development, Committee for, 90

Economic planning, 34
Economic power, concentration of, 99-100
Economic take-off, 10
Economies of scale, 103
Education, economic value of, 49
Educational Testing Service, 188
Electrical Workers, International Brotherhood of, 90
Employment opportunity requirements, equal, 95
Expenditures, credit-based, 39

Federal Communications Commission, 188
Federal government, influence of corporations on, 88-91
Federal Mediation and Conciliation Service, 150
Foreign policy, influence of corporations on, 91
Fortune, 110
Free market system, 35

General Electric, 143
General Motors, 143
Government employment and payrolls, 78
Gross national product, 49-50
Guild system, 11-12

Haves and have nots, gap between, 33
Hawthorne effect, 172
Hawthorne works, 178
Health and education, growth of services in, 77
Housing and credit, 38
Huddersfield, road to, 20, 33
Human capital formation, 48-56
Human relations, 155-74
   critiques of, 169-74
   technology, size, satisfaction, and productivity, 160-69
   workers and work groups, 157-60
Human relations school, 156-57, 171

Import substitution, 37-38
Indicative planning, system of, 15
Industrial base of community, 73
Industrial common law, 85
Industrialism, three views of, 2-3
Industrialism and modernity, 6-9
Industrialization
   and industrial revolution, 9-14
   modernization, and social integration, 14-16
   prerequisites for, 33
   steps to, 45

196 INDEX

Industrial man, modern, 16–20
Industrial relations, 154–55, 174–82
   and conflict, 139–43
   discipline, 177–78
   managers and priorities, 178–82
   worker in society, 175–77
Industrial systems, varieties in, 20–30
International Telephone and Telegraph, 91
Iowa Plan, 44
Issues
   macroscopic, 183–85
   mezzoscopic, 186–88
   microscopic, 189

Japan, employment practices in, 26–27
Jobs that create jobs, 75
Justice, Department of, 188

Kinship groups, extended, 47

Labor, Department of, 129
Labor force, profile of, 61
Labor Statistics, U.S. Bureau of, 142
Landrum-Griffin Act, 90, 128
Luddites, 19, 43, 136

Management, labor and family relations, models of, 145
Managerialism, 98
Managers, 106–19
   careers, backgrounds and beliefs, 108–16
   and ideology, 116–19
Meritocratic career progression, 19
   Japanese, 28
Military Industrial Complex, 92–95
Modern, the, defined, 18
Modernization
   basic facets of, 17
   process of, 6, 8
Monopoly power, 116
Montgomery Ward Company, 143
Multinational corporations, 26

National Conference Board, 179
National Industrial Conference Board, 181
National Industrial Recovery Act, 90
National Labor Relations Act, 90
National Labor Relations Board (NLRB), 150
National Science Foundation, 161
New York Port Authority, 188
New York Standard Metropolitan Statistical Areas, 179

Occupational structures, 62–64
Occupation as percentage of industry group, 60
Occupations, industry and community, 73–77

Occupations and group memberships, 65–68
OPEC, 91

Paraindustrial population groups, 81
Pension Reform Act of 1975, 72
Post-industrial revolution, 70
Preindustrial system, 11
Profit, 35
Protestant ethic, 50
Puritanism, 50
Putting-out system, 40, 42, 44

Quality of Working Life Surveys, 1973, 161, 164

Robber barons, 118, 169

Securities and Exchange Commission, 111, 188
Service workers required by population, 74
Seven Sisters, the, 91
Skill hierarchies and labor stratification, 64–65
Social groupings, non-kinship, 47
Social technology, 41–48
   institutional perspective, 44–46
   and legal institutions, 46–48
   and physical technology, 48
   temporal perspective, 41–44
State and local government employment, 79
Supplemental Unemployment Benefits (SUB), 143

Taft Hartley Act, 90, 128
Teamsters, 90, 143, 148
Technological change, 68–72
Technology, automation and economic progress, National Commission on, 70
Temporary National Economic Committee, 88
Tension management, 23–24
Trade, 12

Unions, 120–51
   communities and members, 143–46
   and the economy, 130–39
   five general types by price stability, 133
   impact on wage levels, 135
   membership control of, 147–50
   and the public, 124–125
   and the social system, 127–30
   and society, 122–24
   and theorists, 125–27
United Auto Workers Union, 90
United Kingdom, Japan, and United States, similarities between, 25–26
United Mine Workers, 143
United Steel Workers Union, 90

Verrazano Bridge construction, 148

Wagner Act, 128
Web of rules, 26, 58, 82-86, 120, 122, 135, 151, 184, 186
Western Electric, 156, 172
Worker loyalty, 178
Worker quit rates, 178
Workers, parttime, 27
Work ethic, 51
Work force, 58-68
   private sector, 80

public sector, 80
service sector, 13, 59, 77-82
   industry, government, and employment, 77
   services and goods producers, 77-82
Working Conditions Surveys, 1969, 161, 164, 176
Work rules, 72, 85

Zaibatzu, 26n
Zero-sum situations, 138